Advance Pra
The Executive Guide to F

"Great facilitation produces real commitment to solving p̤. ̤̤̤̤̤̤̤̤̤̤̤̤̤̤̤̤g y̤ṳ ̤̤g̤̤̤̤̤̤̤̤.
That's why we put special emphasis on the Drivers Model as we train our next generation of leaders.
This book is like having an executive MBA program in facilitating strategy at your disposal. Michael
Wilkinson is a master facilitator and a world-class teacher."

—Mark O'Connell, Director, Advanced Leadership Program, United Way Movement

"As the leading CEO membership organization in the world, we know firsthand that when it comes to
meeting tough challenges or realizing high aspirations for your business, a solid strategic framework is
an invaluable asset. The Drivers Model will get you where you want to go!"

—Ruby L. Randall, President and Chief Operating Officer, Vistage International, Inc.

"After our U.S. operation used Michael and his team to guide them through strategy using the Drivers
Model, we were so impressed that we have had him facilitate strategy with our Canadian division and our
foreign name plate subsidiary. Comprehensive planning and focused execution has made a difference."

—Richard G. Roy, President and CEO, Uni-Select Inc.

"The Drivers Model drove us to clarity: a strong strategic plan that identified clear priorities, defined
critical factors for success, recognized obstacles to avoid, and better yet, resulted in complete buy-in
and engagement from the participants who crafted the plan. This process helped us to survive the
downturn and set our stage to thrive in the years ahead."

—Jim Hamilton, PE, President, Southern Civil Engineers, Inc

"Michael Wilkinson provides a refreshing and systematic way of approaching the critical and painful
task of defining our strategies. His latest book zeroes in on an oft-overlooked aspect of strategy
development—the leader's role. It is mandatory reading for my strategy team."

—Steve Bushkuhl, Downstream Chief of Staff, Saudi Aramco

"The Drivers Model is a great business tool for nonprofits to develop strategic direction for their
organizations. I have used the Drivers Model for over fifteen years both as a leader of an association and
chief executive of a non-profit. Simply put, it works."

—Wayne McMillan, President and Chief Executive Officer, Bobby Dodd Institute

"One of the compelling aspects of this book is that it lays out simple definitions of terms and links them
together in a well-defined process. There are too many ways that people define concepts like mission,
goals, strategy, initiatives, etc. So having a definitive way to think about them (instead of having to
debate, for example, what is the difference between a mission and a vision) helps teams focus on the real
purpose of a strategy exercise, which is making decisions."

—Chris Johnson, SVP Strategy & Innovation, Fiserv Biller Solutions

"I've used the Drivers Model in my role as the chief human resources officer for two organizations.
Whether you're in an established Fortune 500 company, an entrepreneurial startup, an organization
experiencing a major turn-around or a high growth business, this executive guide provides a road map
for developing an effective strategic plan while building the alignment and commitment needed for
successful execution."

—Sylvia Taylor, Executive Vice President, The Weather Channel, LLC

"Following our recent merger, we used the Drivers Model to bring executives from both organizations together to develop a common vision and a set of operating strategies for joint execution. If you are looking for a simple but comprehensive approach to strategy, read this book!"

—Max C. Dull, Vice President & General Manager, Beck/Arnley Worldparts, Inc.

"*The Executive Guide to Facilitating Strategy* is an exceptional tool for developing and leading the strategy process for an organization. We rely heavily on volunteers for guidance and understanding in order to fulfill member needs. Because we have limited time and financial resources, the continuity and focus provided by a thorough strategic plan are critical to our success. This book provides a solid delivery of tools which are essential for executives as they lead volunteers through the strategic development process."

—Teresa S. Witham, Executive Director, National Association Elevator Contractors

"The strategic planning and execution strategies in this book led our senior leadership team and business unit presidents all the way from a well-conceived shared vision through the details of priority setting and accountable execution. The book is an executive roadmap to wherever your organization aspires to go and how to get there together."

—George Doyle, President, Lexicon Relocation; Director, The Suddath Company

"*The Executive Guide to Facilitating Strategy* hits a home run. Using the Drivers Model, our United Way was able to align the entire organization around focused community impact goals and quantifiable results. Michael Wilkinson nails it. *The Executive Guide to Facilitating Strategy* is a must read."

—Allen H. Elijah, President & CEO, The United Way of the Greater Dayton Area

"Most organizations need better direction and a strategic plan that encompasses the very best ideas from the team. For, when you involve your team members in setting the direction, priorities and goals, they become intrinsically committed to achieving success. Michael Wilkinson's book gives you the framework, tools and techniques needed to develop and monitor a workable and achievable strategic plan. Our firm has been achieving its goals for years by using the Drivers Model. Naturally, I hope my competition never reads this book."

—J. Larry Tyler, Chairman and CEO, Tyler & Company

"I have been a devotee of the Drivers Model for nearly two decades and have consistently witnessed its principles hold true and its process work masterfully. Whether you are addressing public education, conducting community planning, or strategizing private philanthropy, the Drivers Model is smart, highly engaging and motivating."

—Lesley Grady, Senior Vice President, Community Foundation for Greater Atlanta

"Too often, executives approach planning without a shared understanding of the planning process or of the distinction between critical terms—vision and mission, goals and objectives, strategies and actions, guiding principles and values. The result is confusion, wasted time and weak outputs. *The Executive Guide to Facilitating Strategy* resolves these negative outcomes by laying out a straightforward planning process along with clearly defined terms. Given the pace of change that organizations face today, this guide to planning is invaluable!"

—Jim Rankin, Director, Organization Alignment, Hydro One, Inc

"We found the substance and approach contained within this book so invaluable that we made them the core of a five-day national residential program in which teams use the model to develop solutions to critical issues facing the business. This, in turn, has resulted in some of our business units consistently using the model as the preferred approach in business planning at an operational level."

—Joan Wilkinson, Senior Business Partner–Integration, MLC & NAB Wealth—
The National Australia Bank Group

Michael Wilkinson
CEO, Leadership Strategies—The Secrets of Facilitation

THE EXECUTIVE GUIDE TO
Facilitating
Strategy

Featuring the Drivers Model

Published by Leadership Strategies Publishing
A division of Leadership Strategies—The Facilitation Company

56 Perimeter Center East, Suite 103
Atlanta, Georgia 30346
800-824-2850

www.leadstrat.com

Substantial discounts on bulk quantities are available to corporations, governments, non-profits, and other organizations. For details and discount information, contact Leadership Strategies at 800-824-2850.

Publisher's Cataloging-In-Publication Data
(Prepared by The Donohue Group, Inc.)

Wilkinson, Michael, 1957-
   The executive guide to facilitating strategy : featuring the Drivers Model /
Michael Wilkinson. -- 1st ed.

   p. ; cm.

   Includes bibliographical references and index.
   ISBN: 978-0-9722458-1-4

   1. Strategic planning. 2. Group facilitation. 3. Communication in
management. I. Title. II. Title: Facilitating strategy

HD30.28 .W545 2011
658.4/56

Manufactured in the United States of America

First Edition

HB Printing

10 9 8 7 6 5 4 3 2 1

*Dedicated to the hundreds of executives
over a twenty year span who trusted me
and my organization to use the Drivers
Model to help them facilitate strategy.*

Kathy

Focused Strategy —
Full Buy-in ~
Flawless Execution.
That's what this
book is all about —

Michael

Michael Wilkinson
CEO, Leadership Strategies - The Secrets of Facilitation

The Executive Guide to
FACILITATING
STRATEGY

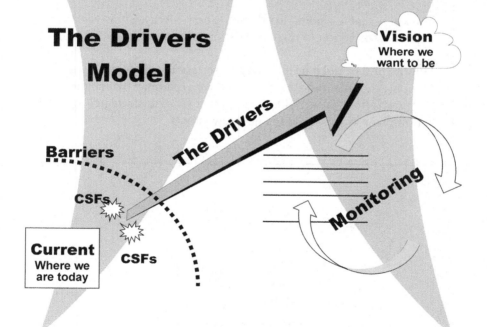

The Drivers Model

Vision Where we want to be

The Drivers

Barriers

CSFs

Current Where we are today

CSFs

Monitoring

Featuring the Drivers Model

Imagine...

You are the executive director of an association of meeting planners.

- Your membership size has been stagnant at five hundred for each of the previous three years.

- Attendance at meetings is in decline.

- Getting volunteers to take on leadership positions has become a chore.

- Due to declining resources, you have had to pull from reserves to fund operations. Even involvement in community activities is down.

You know that it is going to take some new energy, a new vision, and a new direction to revitalize the organization.

How helpful would it be if, through a series of facilitated strategy sessions, your planning team could create a roadmap that defined the new vision, measurable targets, and specific strategies and action plans as shown on the next few pages?

Take a look
at the plan on
the next page!

Meeting Planners Association

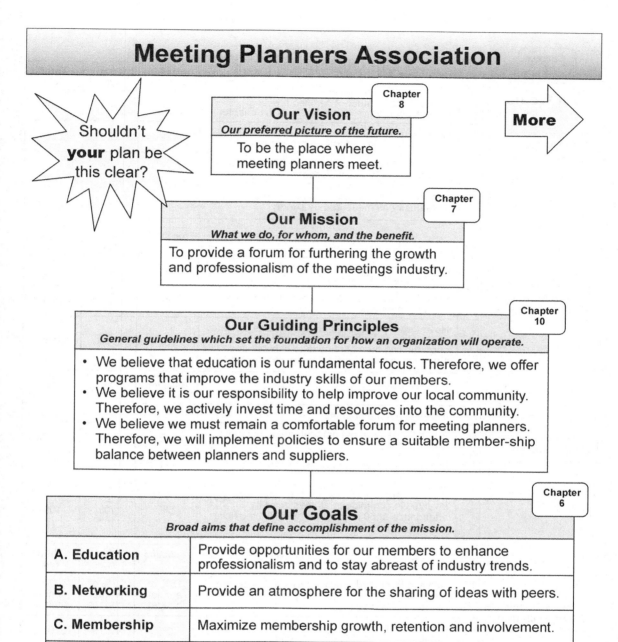

Shouldn't _your_ plan be this clear?

More

Our Vision
Our preferred picture of the future.

To be the place where meeting planners meet.

Chapter 8

Our Mission
What we do, for whom, and the benefit.

To provide a forum for furthering the growth and professionalism of the meetings industry.

Chapter 7

Our Guiding Principles
General guidelines which set the foundation for how an organization will operate.

Chapter 10

- We believe that education is our fundamental focus. Therefore, we offer programs that improve the industry skills of our members.
- We believe it is our responsibility to help improve our local community. Therefore, we actively invest time and resources into the community.
- We believe we must remain a comfortable forum for meeting planners. Therefore, we will implement policies to ensure a suitable member-ship balance between planners and suppliers.

Our Goals
Broad aims that define accomplishment of the mission.

Chapter 6

A. Education	Provide opportunities for our members to enhance professionalism and to stay abreast of industry trends.
B. Networking	Provide an atmosphere for the sharing of ideas with peers.
C. Membership	Maximize membership growth, retention and involvement.
D. Organization	Maintain sufficient financial and organizational resources to support programs.
E. Community	Provide funds and services to support the local community and provide a vehicle for organization recognition.

Strategic Plan 20XX-20XX

Our Goals

Chapter 9

Our Objectives

A. Education

			Baseline	First Year	Third Year
1	Increase the number of certified meeting professionals who are members of the chapter.		43	55	90
2	Achieve target total number of attendees in full-day and multi-day education programs.		192	220	300
3	Have target percentage of respondents indicate satisfaction or high satisfaction with the opportunities the association offers members to enhance professionalism and stay abreast of the industry as measured by survey.		NA	60%	80%

B. Networking

			Baseline	First Year	Third Year
1	Achieve target average number of attendees in quarterly networking events.		76	90	120
2	Achieve target average number of attendees in monthly meetings.		175	200	250
3	Have target percentage of respondents indicate satisfaction or high satisfaction with the opportunities members have to network and share ideas with peers as measured by survey.		NA	60%	80%

C. Membership

			Baseline	First Year	Third Year
1	Increase net membership.		500	550	650
2	Annually retain target percentage of members from prior year.		61%	65%	75%
3	Increase average attendance at monthly meetings.		175	200	250
4	Achieve target percentage of members actively involved in committees as measured by attendance at 50 percent or more of the official committee meetings/functions.		5%	7%	10%

D. Organization

			Baseline	First Year	Third Year
1	Achieve target financial reserves as measured by lowest daily bank balance during the last quarter of each year.		15% of annual budget	22% of annual budget	40% of annual budget
2	Maintain staff and contractor fees within target range as a percent of annual budget.		9%	8-10%	8-10%
3	Have an average number of qualified candidates running per open office annually.		1.3	1.5	2.0

E. Community

			Baseline	First Year	Third Year
1	Achieve target funds raised for charities.		$105K	$115K	$140K
2	Achieve target number of members who participate in at least one community activity.		72	90	120

NA – Not available

Our CSFs & Barriers *(Critical Success Factors)* — Chapter 11	**Our Strategies** — Chapter 12 ▷ More

<table>
<tr><td>Barriers | CSFs</td><td>
• Wide understanding of the benefits of a CMP.
• High perceived value of education programs.

• Lack of understanding of the professional development needs of our members.
</td><td>
A1 Hold annual member needs assessment to identify professional development needs and program topics.
A2 Convene quarterly study groups with mentors to prepare for CMP.
A3 Hold four single or multi-day education programs per quarter with topics aligned to address the results of the needs assessment.
A4 Implement awareness strategy with member testimonials to increase awareness of the benefits of programs and certification.
</td></tr>

<tr><td>Barriers | CSFs</td><td>
• High perceived value of association's networking events and monthly meetings.
• Frequency of events at a rate aligned with member needs.

• Lack of awareness by all committee chairs on how to maximize networking in our events.
</td><td>
B1 Implement awareness strategy with member testimonials to increase attendance at networking events.
B2 Hold quarterly networking events, adjusted to take into account information gained from annual member needs assessment, to provide networking opportunities.
B3 Provide recommendations to education and membership committees on how to maximize member networking at events.
</td></tr>

<tr><td>Barriers | CSFs</td><td>
• Dynamic presenters with timely, substantive topics to increase meeting attendance.
• High awareness by meeting planners of the association and its benefits to attract members.

• Inadequate process for getting new members involved results in burnout of a few and low retention.
</td><td>
C1 Use assessment surveys and industry referrals to select quality speakers and topics.
C2 Hold monthly membership meetings to provide education and networking opportunities.
C3 Revise new member registration process to ask desired committee.
C4 Hold quarterly committee fairs after meetings to increase involvement.
C5 Implement PR program to report activities to the local media to increase awareness of the association.
</td></tr>

<tr><td>Barriers | CSFs</td><td>
• Commitment from board to building reserves and exercising financial prudence.
• Large number of members desiring to serve as officers.

• Lack of understanding by officers of budgeting processes.
</td><td>
D1 Create and implement reserve reporting as part of the monthly budget report to raise awareness of the state of reserves.
D2 Provide mandatory half-day budget training for all new officers.
D3 Implement leadership development committee to develop and implement a program to recruit and formally develop members for leadership positions.
</td></tr>

<tr><td>Barriers | CSFs</td><td>
• High perceived value of association's community outreach events.

• Low awareness by our members of the charitable need and impact we can have.
</td><td>
E1 Implement awareness strategy with member testimonials to increase attendance at community outreach events.
E2 Hold quarterly community outreach events to provide association members with an opportunity to serve the community while networking with others in the industry.
</td></tr>
</table>

Our Positioning Statement
How we will win: the direction and focus for the organization

We believe that budget cuts and staff reductions have resulted in an environment in which planners will invest their time and money only if they can see an immediate, tangible return. Therefore we must focus our programs on maximizing ROI and invest in marketing that promotes the benefit of our association to our target audience.

Who		Our Priority Strategies	Deliverables
Assessment chair	A1	Hold annual member needs assessment to identify professional development needs and program topics.	• Needs assessment report. • Recommendations.
Certification chair	A2	Convene quarterly study groups with mentors to prepare for CMP.	• Study group sessions. • Assigned mentors.
Education VP	A3	Hold four single or multi-day education programs per quarter with topics aligned to address the results of the needs assessment.	• Education programs. • Attendance and satisfaction report ("Sat." report).
Marketing VP	A4 B1 E1	Implement awareness strategy with member testimonials to increase awareness of the benefits of programs, certification, networking events, and community events.	• Awareness plan executed. • Member testimonials.
Networking chair	B2	Hold quarterly networking events, adjusted to take into account information gained from annual member needs assessment, to provide networking opportunities.	• Networking events. • Attendance and Sat. report.
Meeting chair	C1 C2	Hold monthly membership meetings to provide education and networking opportunities based on the use of assessment survey and industry referrals to select quality speakers and topics.	• Recommended topics. • Monthly meetings. • Attendance and Sat. report.
Marketing VP	C5	Implement PR program to report activities to the local media to increase awareness of the association.	• PR strategy and report.
Nominations chair	D3	Implement leadership development committee to develop and implement a program to recruit and formally develop members for leadership positions.	• Leadership development plan. • Executed program. • List of qualified candidates.
Community chair	E2	Hold quarterly community outreach events to provide association members with an opportunity to serve the community while networking with others in the industry.	• Quarterly events. • Attendance and Sat. report.

When	Our Monitoring Plan
Monthly	**Are we doing what we said we were going to do?** Strategy leaders will update status of action plans to ensure we are doing what we said we were going to do. The plan coordinator will distribute a report of performance to all members of the planning team.
Quarterly	**Are we getting the results we want to get?** The planning team will meet to review status of strategies and progress on objectives. The planning team will decide which current strategies to stop or continue and what new strategies to start. The planning team will adjust objectives as warranted based on issues and priorities.
Annually	**What adjustments do we need to make to our targets and our priorities?** The planning team will meet to review progress for the year, identify new barriers and critical success factors, change objectives and re-establish priorities and action plans.

Our Strategy Partner

Leadership Strategies
www.leadstrat.com

Strategy:	C5. Implement PR program to report activities to the local media.

Objectives Supported:	Membership: 1. Increase net membership.
	Membership: 2. Increase average attendance at monthly meetings.
Owner:	Marketing VP
Deliverables:	PR strategy and report

Due Date:	Feb. 1 / Year 2	Person-Days:	27	Total Costs:	$2500

Action Step	Who	Due	Person-Days	Costs
1. Assemble new PR team.	Exec committee	Feb. 1	1	
2. Develop PR objectives.	PR team	Feb. 15	3	
3. Develop promotion program.	PR team	Mar. 1	3	
4. Hold board presentation to present PR strategy and gain approval.	PR team, Board	Mar. 15	1	
5. Implement PR strategy.	PR team	May 1 and ongoing	15	$2500
6. Assess promotion effectiveness.	PR team	Jan. 15 / Year 2	2	
7. Produce PR report of results.	PR team	Feb. 1 / Year 2	2	

Table of Contents

Acknowledgements

Thank God for Ann Hermann-Nehdi, CEO of Hermann International, the whole-brain thinking organization that brings the world the HBDI family of products. When she read the first draft of this book, she politely and very graciously explained to me how I had completely missed the mark, that no executive would be interested in a detailed guide for facilitating a strategy session. But they would be interested in a guide that clearly explained strategy, supplied a high-level roadmap, and showed the pitfalls to avoid.

In essence, she hated the draft. And thank God she did.

She recommended dividing the material into two different books—one specifically for executives and then a detailed guide for facilitators. The Executive Guide is the result, and The Facilitator's Guide will shortly follow. Thank you, Ann. I can always rely on you to be both a truth-sayer and a wonderful friend.

Along with Ann, I also want to say thank you to seven others whose frank and insightful comments made this a better book. To Jim Rankin, from Toronto's Hydro One, thank you for bringing both an executive's and a facilitator's views to your comments. Thanks to Simon Wilson, from our UK partner, Wilson-Sherriff. Thanks to Dawn Sutherland, your strategic marketing perspective provided unique insights and made a difference. Thanks to Kris Casariego, the head of marketing at Leadership Strategies. And thanks to three reviewers who also serve on our Core Facilitation Team, Richard Smith, Leigh Ann Rodgers, and September Spore.

Thank you, Sarah Cypher, the CEO at Threepenny Editor, for your patience and support, and for putting together a tremendous team, including Kristin Summers, to marshal this book through the publishing process.

Thanks to all the associates at Leadership Strategies who make coming to work fun. To our Facilitation Team, for consistently delivering high-quality client service, to our Marketing Team for the superb job you do in managing and promoting our brand, to our Sales Team for both establishing and managing superb client relationships, and to our Operations Team for making all the behind-the-scene things happen successfully over and over again for every client. I simply say thank you.

Finally, to the four women who let me share in their lives, Sherry, Danielle, Gabrielle, and Mom, thanks for your love and for allowing me to create this book to benefit others.

Michael Wilkinson
Sharing the Power of Facilitation with the World™

"The last one was just too painful. We spent most of the time arguing over definitions. What's a goal? What's an objective? What's the difference between mission and vision? What a waste."

"Sure, planning is important. But we're too busy fighting fires to take time out for anything that is not critical."

"We spent several months putting together a detailed strategic plan. When we finished, I put my copy on that bookshelf over there. That was two years ago. How many times do you think I've touched it since? I don't even remember what's in it."

Sound familiar? This book was written to address issues similar to these. Far too often, people experience strategic planning as a wasted activity—painful, unproductive, and irrelevant to the issues at hand. And once planning is done, people often find that the product created is seldom, if ever, looked at again.

What you will find in this book

- Key steps you can use to gain full buy-in to undertake planning.

- How to determine who should be involved in your planning effort and at what level.

- What information should be gathered so everyone starts from a common foundation.

- The two critical items participants must gain from a review of the current situation.

- The proven technique for helping groups develop and adopt a mission statement—in most cases, in under ninety minutes.

- How to get your organization to discover its broad goals.

- How to guide your group through setting objectives that are not only specific and measurable, but also critical to driving the success of your organization.

- How to move your organization's values from being listed on a plaque on the wall to serving as a vehicle that your people use every day.

- How to make sure your team's choice of strategy overcomes your most important barriers and creates the critical conditions for long-term success.

- How to prevent your planning effort from resulting in a document that merely sits on a shelf, rather than being a living plan that your team regularly monitors, adjusts, and uses for effective decision-making throughout the year.

- And more…

Introduction

This book is about the Drivers Model and the secrets I and my team at Leadership Strategies have discovered in using it with hundreds of organizations—including governments, non-profits, associations, and corporations that cover a wide spectrum of industries, including software and hardware companies, insurance, utilities, financial services, retail, health care, education, electrical contractors, and so on.

Yet the Drivers Model has also been applied to department planning, program planning, project planning, and individual coaching. On an individual basis, the Drivers Model has been used for career planning, life planning, planning a family reunion, and even for helping a teenager plan for moving out of the house!

What This Book Will Do for You

In writing *The Executive Guide to Facilitating Strategy*, my goal has been to provide you, the primary executive, a tool you can use to take a strategic approach to developing a plan for your corporation, government agency, non-profit organization, business unit, department, or team. This book provides you with a proven framework that you can use immediately to move your organization through the process of building and implementing a plan, whether the plan is a strategic plan for the entire organization, a department plan for the area you lead, a committee plan for your volunteer work, or just about any other planning you may need to do.

However, along with providing the Drivers Model, which gives you what the team must do, I will also focus on your role in making it happen. As the author of *The Secrets of Facilitation* and Managing Director of Leadership Strategies, the largest provider of professional facilitators in the US, I am providing you in this book our best practices from working with leaders on hundreds of planning efforts. While some leaders have been overbearing and great at shutting down their team, other leaders have taken such a passive role in strategy development that the rest of their team felt the activity wasn't worth their full effort. In this book, I will make clear the most important role for you to play through each phase of the planning process.

In *The Executive Guide to Facilitating Strategy*, you'll gain the benefit of our many strategy experiences and our expertise in group facilitation. You'll discover the common team pitfalls and how to avoid them. You'll get the insider's view of how to lead your team through mission creation, setting measurable targets, deciding priorities, and so on. You'll learn the proven techniques our facilitators have used for over two decades.

How This Book Delivers

Following the next chapter, which gives an introduction to the Drivers Model, the book is divided into the following stages of the Drivers Model process, shown in the diagram below.

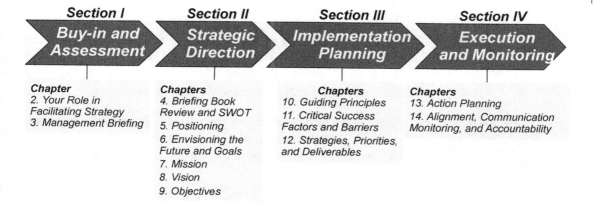

Section I	Section II	Section III	Section IV
Buy-in and Assessment	Strategic Direction	Implementation Planning	Execution and Monitoring

Chapter
2. Your Role in Facilitating Strategy
3. Management Briefing

Chapters
4. Briefing Book Review and SWOT
5. Positioning
6. Envisioning the Future and Goals
7. Mission
8. Vision
9. Objectives

Chapters
10. Guiding Principles
11. Critical Success Factors and Barriers
12. Strategies, Priorities, and Deliverables

Chapters
13. Action Planning
14. Alignment, Communication Monitoring, and Accountability

Each chapter is packed with tools and information that you can use right away to guide your team through developing your strategy.

What is in each chapter?

- A summary, so you can quickly scan the contents.

- An overview highlighting the key strategy secrets.

- A step-by-step process for guiding your team in developing the strategy component covered in that chapter.

- Samples of the output created, which show you what other organizations have done and can provide you with ideas for your own strategy.

- A quality checklist to confirm that your team has produced quality work.

- A specific description of your role in leading your team members, as they develop that chapter's strategy component.

If you're similar to the leaders I've worked with in the past, you'll likely find the output samples and the quality checklists a true bonus.

Let's take a deeper look at the contents in each of the four sections and the rest of the book.

Introduction

Section I

Buy-in and Assessment

- Following Chapter 1's detailed description of the Drivers Model, Chapter 2 gives you an overview of the role you'll play as the leader in each strategy activity. The chapter makes specific recommendations for how to get your ideas on the table without overpowering the group.

- In Chapter 3, you'll learn the secrets to reaching agreement in order to begin a planning process. You'll discover how the management briefing can be a crucial tool for gaining your leadership team's commitment to both planning and to using the Drivers Model as their preferred planning process.

Section II

Strategic Direction

- We split the plan development process into two primary workshops: strategic direction setting and implementation planning. Chapters 4–9 provide the key steps for each component of the strategic direction workshop.

- In these chapters, you'll see how your team will extract key learnings from assessing the current situation, developing a mission statement, discovering your goals, and creating objectives that are SMART—specific, measurable, achievable, relevant, and time-bound.

Section III

Implementation Planning

- While the direction is set in the first workshop, the second workshop focuses on how to implement that direction. In Chapters 10–12, you'll find proven techniques for identifying barriers and critical success factors, and for creating strategies that overcome the barriers and create the critical conditions your team needs in order to achieve the strategic direction.

- You'll also learn how to lead your group through prioritizing and developing the alignment plan, the monitoring plan, and the plan for accountability.

Section IV

Execution and Monitoring

- This section covers the steps to get your plan implemented and the ongoing monitoring processes that will prevent the plan from becoming something that sits on a bookshelf, rather than a vehicle for driving your organization's success.

- Chapter 13 shows you how to lead a staff review and the development and approval of action plans.

- Chapter 14 takes you through the alignment and monitoring processes, including monthly check-ins, quarterly reviews, and annual update sessions.

Special Topic: Choosing a Facilitator	• This special topic provides guidance on knowing when to bring in an outside facilitator, key questions to ask that will help you choose an appropriate resource, and steps to take to prepare the facilitator to work with you and your team.
Appendix	The appendix section contains the following:

- Appendix I: Summary of the twenty-seven secrets covered in the book.

- Appendix II: Glossary of the strategic planning terms.

- Appendix III: Strategy resources, including instructions for accessing web-based templates, articles, training, and a password to access an exclusive resource area.

The Drivers Model and Other Types of Planning

Before completing this introduction, I should make a brief point about the applicability of The Drivers Model. *The Executive Guide to Facilitating Strategy* shows how the Drivers Model is used in developing a strategic plan for organizations of different sizes. However, the Drivers Model also applies to many different types of planning, including department planning, program planning, project planning, team planning, career planning, and so on. You'll see that any time there is a gap between where you are and where you want to be, the Drivers Model can provide you with the tools you need to bridge the gap.

• • •

The word facilitation comes from the Latin word *facil*, which means to make easy. My hope is that this book will indeed make your next planning effort truly easy.

Michael Wilkinson

- The Questions
- The Drivers Model: A Tool for Masterful Planning
- The Strategy Document
- Monitoring
- The Deliverables of the Drivers Model
- Executing the Drivers Model: How Much Time?
- How is the Drivers Model Different?
- What's Next

I believe this is the most important chapter in the book.
Please don't skip it.

As a professional facilitator, I have led literally hundreds of planning sessions. Over this time period, there have been only three sessions that I wish I could go back and do over. In one of them, I allowed the chief executive to skip the briefing on the Drivers Model and receive an abbreviated briefing later. Big mistake. Since he never fully understood the planning process, he consistently pushed back on process decisions made by his team and changed content to make it align better with what he was already familiar with, rather than use what his team had adopted. It was frustrating to many. Yet, I was at the root cause of the frustration because I didn't insist that the chief executive be in the room when the team reviewed and made decisions on the planning model.

Don't do that to your team. In this chapter, my intention is to provide you with a complete overview of the Drivers Model, so that you're fully equipped with the foundational understanding to guide your team going forward. For this reason, it is the longest chapter and also the most important.

The Questions

As you take on strategy development, a critical step is to ensure that you and your team have a common understanding of the language of strategy and a solid process to carry you through strategy development. It is important to put the language and process in place early to avoid the confusion, debates, and wasted time that come from lacking an agreed-upon approach and set of definitions.

The Drivers Model is the tool I have been using for over two decades to provide a robust, yet simple, method for taking an organization through strategic planning, project planning, program planning, and numerous other planning activities. The Drivers Model is fully scalable and applies to Fortune 500 companies, non-profit organizations, government agencies, entire enterprises, single business units, field offices, individual departments, and any work team.

When I first introduce the Drivers Model to a team, I find that I can gain maximum buy-in to the process by starting with simple, everyday examples to highlight the fundamental concepts. Accordingly, in this section, I will start my description of the Drivers Model, using an example you may relate to: seeking to buy a house with my wife. Later in the chapter, I will focus on what the Drivers Model's output looks like in written form.

Question 1: Where are we today?

The Drivers Model focuses on four core strategic questions starting with, "Where are we today?" So, with the house-buying example, my wife and I would start by looking at the strengths and weaknesses of the home in which we were living, as shown in the table that follows.

Strengths	Weaknesses
• It's in a nice neighborhood. • It's rented, so we can more easily make a change. • It's got a big attic.	• The floorboards are warped. • The paint is peeling from the plaster. • Leaky roof. • Not enough room.

Question 2: Where do we want to be?

After understanding where you are, the next step is to understand where you want to be. In this step, you create your vision of the future. So, where do my family and I want to be?

Our Vision

- My wife grew up in a family of seven with one bathroom. You can imagine the first words out of her mouth: "At least three bathrooms."

- Then it was my turn. "I want my house to have my private office," with the operative word being "private." It doesn't have to double as a guest bedroom, and it doesn't have to be a place where the kids play when it's raining outside. It's my private office.

- What did the kids want? A huge playroom over the garage.

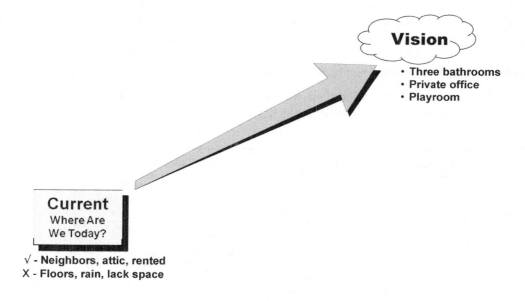

Vision
- **Three bathrooms**
- **Private office**
- **Playroom**

Current
Where Are
We Today?

√ - **Neighbors, attic, rented**
X - **Floors, rain, lack space**

Question 3: How do we get there?

Once you have created your vision, you're ready to turn to defining your drivers—the actions you'll undertake to drive your success. Your drivers have to do two important things. First, the reason you are where you are is because there are certain barriers standing between you and your vision. Your drivers must break through those barriers.

For us, the barriers were pretty steep. We felt the home we were seeking was going to cost about $300,000. As first-time homebuyers, we qualified for a special loan at 5 percent down, or $15,000. Yet, we had never saved more than $5000 in our lives. So, that $15,000 was a major barrier standing in the way of us achieving our vision. We could dream about the house we wanted, we could search through the newspaper for it, we could even find it and go knock on the door. However, until we overcame the $15,000 barrier, the house would most likely never be ours.

A second barrier for us was related to our debt-to-equity ratio. For someone to loan us the rest of the money, we had to have pretty good credit. And let's just say that our credit card debt was high and getting higher—definitely another barrier.

Along with overcoming barriers, the drivers must also address the critical success factors (CSFs). The Drivers Model defines CSFs as key conditions that must be created to achieve the vision. I like to think of CSFs as the fuel that propels the Drivers rocket to the vision. With CSFs, if you overcome the barriers and create the key conditions, you achieve your vision. For my wife and me, a key condition was finding a house that someone wanted to sell, that had the features we desired, in a neighborhood where we wanted to live, at a price we could afford—all at the same time. In essence, if we had overcome the two barriers (the down payment and the high credit card balances), but hadn't created the critical condition (finding a suitable home), we would not have been successful.

With the barriers and CSFs identified, we are now ready to focus on the drivers. What are the things we are going to do to overcome the barriers and create the critical conditions?

Our Barrier / CSF	Our Drivers
$15K down payment	• Implement a savings plan to target $300 in savings per month (e.g., minimize eating out, limit unnecessary expenditures).
	• Take on weekend jobs to save an additional $300 per month.
High credit card balances	• Cut up credit cards. Pay down debt monthly.
Finding a suitable house	• Hire a realtor and target viewing eight homes per month.

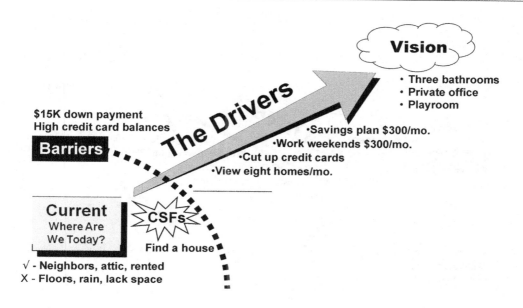

Question 4: How will we monitor our progress?

There was one more driver we had to put in place that was more important than any of the others. That driver is the monitoring driver. The purpose of the monitoring driver is to track the progress of all the other drivers. So, going back to our plan for the new home, we did our monitoring on the first Sunday of every month, at 6 p.m. At that time, all activities in our household would stop and we would ask ourselves a series of questions.

- First, how much money did we save this month? We saved $350. Great!

- How much did we get from the extra jobs? Another $300. Wonderful!

- How's the credit card debt doing? It's down 10 percent. Fantastic!

- How many homes did we look at? Five. Why only five? What was the problem? The real estate agent wasn't available and sometimes wouldn't return our calls. As you can imagine, we needed to find a new agent. We had a plan, and she was getting in the way!

Monitoring is critical to ensure that you stay on track. Monitoring also allows you to make adjustments along the way as you learn new information, encounter new barriers, or identify other CSFs. But perhaps most importantly, monitoring keeps you motivated. Typically, it takes considerable effort to move from where you are today to where you want to be. The monitoring process helps keep your vision in front of you and can give you the continual motivation needed to implement your drivers.

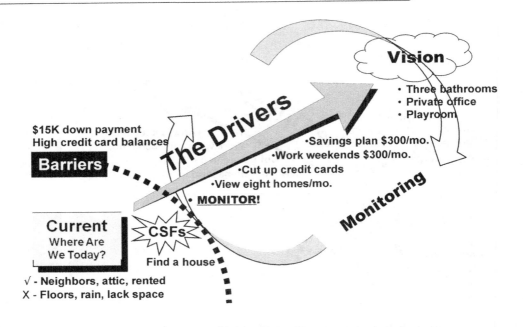

The Drivers Model: A Tool for Masterful Planning

The Drivers Model process covers seven key principles for masterfully planning any activity. The seven principles are summarized in the table that follows. Let's break down each one.

Seven principles of masterful planning	
	1. Be clear on purpose.
	2. Start with an accurate assessment of today.
	3. Create a shared vision of success.
	4. Identify your critical successful factors and barriers.
	5. Define the drivers: your strategies and priorities.
	6. Monitor and report results.
	7. Have rewards and consequences to build accountability.

1	**Be clear on purpose.**

With any activity, start with purpose: Why are we doing this? With the house example, our purpose was to find a house that was more suitable to our needs. Purpose always answers the question, "Why?"

2	**Start with an accurate assessment of where you are today.**

You should always start with an accurate assessment of where you are today. Why is that important? Because you may think that you have overcome certain barriers when you really haven't.

Perhaps an example will illustrate the importance of starting with an accurate picture of today. Let's say you wanted to drive across the US from Atlanta, in the Southeast, to Los Angeles, on the West Coast. You would have to drive west to get there. But what if your perception was that you were in Atlanta, but in reality, you were already on the West Coast except way up in Seattle? What happens when you drive west? You might end up a little wet, which probably was not part of your vision. So, you may create a compelling vision of where you want to be. However, if you don't clearly define where you are today, you may end up thinking you're outside certain barriers. As a result, you can end up doing the wrong things and not getting the result you want. Therefore, the second principle is that you must start with an accurate assessment of where you are today.

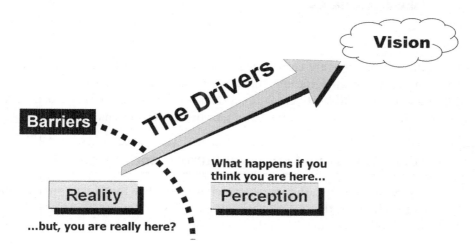

| 3 | **Create a shared vision.** |

Once you have an accurate picture of today, you then create a shared vision—not just a vision, but a shared vision. You can probably imagine what would have happened if my wife and I had different visions of the type of home we wanted. (Yes, that's right—we would end up getting the house my wife wanted!) But can you imagine the conflict and struggle along the way? Because we would want different things and pull in different directions, many of the decisions we needed to make along the way would have resulted in major fights over whose vision would prevail. By creating a shared vision up front, we have the "fight" only once. Once the vision was created, we would be able to make decisions together in line with achieving that vision.

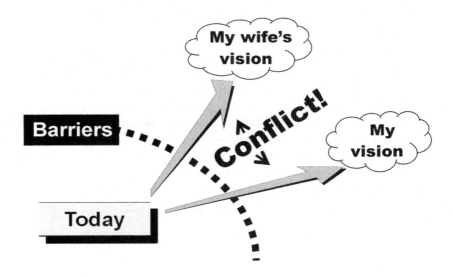

In many organizations, there are entire departments that have different visions of where the organization needs to be. Imagine the chaos when each department goes off in a different direction. And sometimes, those different directions are mutually exclusive—if one is successful, the other has to fail. What a waste—all resulting from the lack of a shared vision

| 4 | **Identify your critical success factors and barriers.** |

With that shared vision defined, the fourth principle is that you then focus on identifying the major barriers to achieving that vision. Ask yourself, "Why haven't we achieved our vision already? What's standing in our way? What's keeping us where we are today?"

Then, you must isolate your CSFs. What's critical to getting you where you want to be? What are the key conditions that, if you create them, will drive achievement of the vision?

| **5** | **Define your drivers.** |

After identifying your barriers and CSFs, the fifth principle is to define your drivers. What are the key strategies that are going to get you to your vision? Remember that the strategies must address each of the barriers and CSFs.

| **6** | **Monitor.** |

With principle six, you monitor your progress to stay on track and motivated to achieve your vision.

| **7** | **Have rewards and consequences to build accountability.** |

Finally, be sure to have rewards and consequences to build accountability. Even with a monitoring process, if there is no formal accountability, people quickly learn that their attention to the drivers is not required.

The Strategy Document

Now that we have looked at the Drivers Model conceptually, let's focus on the primary document that results from the Drivers Model process. The diagram on the next page shows the Drivers Model in layout format, which we call the *strategy document*.

In this sample layout, we again use a simple example. The graphic provides an extract of a strategic plan for a meeting planning organization—an association of people who plan and coordinate business meetings. The members of the association are meeting planners as well as people who supply to the meetings industry (e.g., hotel owners, audio visual companies, and transportation companies). Let's walk through each component of this strategy document to focus on how the pieces of the Drivers Model fit together.

Mission

	Definition	**Example**
Mission	A statement of the overall purpose of an organization that describes what you do, for whom you do it, and the benefit.	*To provide a forum for furthering the growth and professionalism of the meetings industry.*

Extract of a Sample Strategic Plan Document

Meeting Planners Association
(Extract)

VISION
To be the place where meeting planners meet.

MISSION
To provide a forum for furthering the growth and professionalism of the meetings industry.

GUIDING PRINCIPLES
We believe that education is our fundamental focus. Therefore, we offer programs that improve the industry skills of our members.

We believe it is our responsibility to help improve our local community. Therefore, we actively invest time and resources into the community.

We believe we must remain a comfortable forum for meeting planners. Therefore, we will implement policies to ensure a suitable member-ship balance between planners and suppliers.

GOALS

Education
Provide opportunities for our members to enhance professionalism and to stay abreast of industry trends.

Membership
Maximize membership growth, retention, and involvement.

Networking
Provide an atmosphere for the sharing of ideas with peers.

Organization
Maintain sufficient financial & organizational resources to support programs.

Community Outreach
Provide funds and services to support the local community and provide a vehicle for organization recognition.

CRITICAL SUCCESS FACTORS
- Dynamic presenters with timely, substantive topics to increase meeting attendance.
- High awareness by meeting planners of the association and its benefits to attract members.

STRATEGIES
- Utilize surveys and referrals to select quality speakers and topics.
- Revise new member registration process to ask desired committee.
- Hold quarterly committee fairs.
- Implement PR program to report activities to the local media.

OBJECTIVES (Three Years)
- Increase net membership from 500 to 650.
- Annually retain 75% of members
- Increase average attendance from 175 to 250 per meeting.
- Achieve 10% committee involvement.

BARRIERS
- Inadequate process for getting new members involved results in burnout of a few and low retention.
- High membership turnover hinders consistent growth.

ACTION PLAN
- Assemble new PR committee (Exec., Feb. 1)
- Develop PR goals and promotion (PR, Mar. 1)
- Present to board (Chair, Apr. 15)
- Implement promotion (PR, May. 1)
- Assess effectiveness (PR, Oct. 1)
- Present results to board (Chair, Dec. 15)

POSITIONING STATEMENT
We believe that budget cuts and staff reductions have resulted in an environment in which planners will invest their time and money only if they can see an immediate, tangible return. Therefore, we must focus our programs on maximizing return-on-investment to planners and implement marketing campaigns that promote the association's benefit to our target audience.

18

With the Drivers Model, a mission statement answers three simple questions: (1) What do you do? (2) For whom do you do it? (3) What is the benefit? The mission statement from the meeting planners association illustrates an excellent example of how a mission statement can answer these three questions succinctly.

- What do you do? *Provide a forum.*

- For whom? *The meetings industry.*

- What's the benefit? *Furthering growth and professionalism.*

So, what is their mission statement? *To provide a forum for furthering the growth and professionalism of the meetings industry.* It's simple, succinct, meaningful, and memorable.

Vision

Now, let's contrast the difference between a mission statement and a vision statement.

	Definition	Example
Vision	A picture of the "preferred future"—it's a statement that describes how the future will look if the organization fulfills its mission.	*To be the place where meeting planners meet.*

While a mission explains the overall purpose of the organization—what you do, for whom you do it, and the benefit—a vision statement gives the picture of the preferred future. A vision statement answers the question, "If the organization fulfills its mission, what will the future look like?"

Going back to our meeting planners association, meeting planners find places for other people to meet. For this association, if they fulfill their mission by *providing a forum for furthering the growth and professionalism of the meetings industry,* they indeed will be the place where meeting planners meet.

The Centers for Disease Control, a US government health agency, provides another excellent example of the distinction between mission and vision. Prior to a recent change, the CDC's mission statement read: *To promote health and quality of life by preventing and controlling disease, injury, and disability.* So, if the CDC is successful at fulfilling that mission what will the future look like? *Healthy people in a healthy world*—the previous CDC vision statement.

Guiding Principles

	Definition	Example
Guiding principles	General guidelines that set the foundation for how an organization will operate.	*We believe we must remain a comfortable forum for meeting planners. Therefore, we will implement policies to ensure a suitable membership balance between planners and suppliers.*

Introduction

Guiding principles are general guidelines that set the foundation for how an organization will operate. With the Drivers Model, guiding principles are different from values. *Webster's Dictionary* defines a value as "a principle, standard, or quality considered worthwhile or desirable." In organizations, values can play an important role in defining an organization's character and its culture. Values also can provide the basic foundation on which an organization is built.

When organizations define their values, it isn't unusual to hear statements similar to the following:

- We focus on the customer.
- We respect the individual.
- Integrity is non-negotiable.
- Our people are our most critical resource.

While values such as these are important, organizations using the Drivers Model gain greater benefit by transforming their values into guiding principles. Guiding principles define the value and describe the behaviors that the organization believes support that value. To ensure that you focus on both the value and the behavior, the Drivers Model uses the following format for guiding principles: "We believe... (value). Therefore, we will ... (behaviors)."

The example from the meeting planners association illustrates the value/behavior relationship well. *We believe we must remain a comfortable forum for meeting planners. Therefore, we will implement policies to ensure a suitable membership balance between planners and suppliers.* Recall that the members of this association are, not only the people who plan meetings, but also all the suppliers to that industry, such as resorts, limousine companies, and audio-visual companies. The suppliers have meeting planners as their customers—wouldn't you want to attend events where all your customers gathered? However, the association was concerned that they could easily become overrun by suppliers. So, from this guiding principle, they implemented policies to prevent that from happening. For example, one of their policies was that in order for a supplier to join, a planner had to join as well.

Positioning Statements

	Definition	Example
Positioning statements	Broad determinations about the organization's direction and focus.	*We believe that budget cuts and staff reductions have resulted in an environment in which planners will invest their time and money only if they can see an immediate, tangible return. Therefore, we must focus our membership programs on maximizing ROI and invest in marketing that promotes the benefit of our association to our target audience.*

Positioning statements set the broad direction for the organization. Positioning statements are a response to the organization's current situation and identify how the organization will win; that is, how the organization must position itself to successfully respond to the current conditions. Positioning statements have a specific format: "We believe… (the current conditions). Therefore, we must… (the response strategy)." The response strategy of a position statement typically is reflected later in the strategy portion of the strategic plan.

Goals

	Definition	Example
Goals	Broad, long-term aims that define fulfillment of the mission.	*Maximize membership growth, retention, and involvement.*

The Drivers Model defines goals as broad, long-term aims that define fulfillment of the mission. If you were to turn back to the full strategy document, you would see that the meeting planning organization realized that, to fulfill its mission, it had to be successful in five areas: education, organization, membership, community outreach, and networking.

Look at the wording of the membership goal: *Maximize membership growth, retention, and involvement.* Of course, many membership-based organizations would have this as a goal. So, goals are very broad statements. But what's key is that these statements define the five areas where this organization must succeed in order to fulfill its mission.

With the Drivers Model, goals are long-term and change infrequently. As an example, when is the meeting planners association going to want to stop maximizing membership growth, or providing educational opportunities, or promoting meeting management as a viable career? Probably never. So, goals are intended to be written in terms that are broad and long-term. For this reason, goals don't start with verbs like build, establish, or develop. These are finite verbs. Once you have *built, established, or developed* something, the goal has been accomplished.

With the Drivers Model, goals are long-term aims; therefore, goals should start with "infinite verbs," verbs that imply "never-ending" such as *provide, promote, maximize,* and *maintain.*

What follow each goal are the measures of success, which the Drivers Model refers to as *objectives.*

Objectives

	Definition	Example
Objectives	Specific, quantifiable, realistic targets that measure the accomplishment of a goal over a specified period.	*Increase average attendance from 125 to 250 per meeting by the third year.*

While goals are broad aims, objectives are specific, measurable targets that define accomplishment of the goal. Going back to the sample, one of the goals for the meeting planners' association is to *maximize membership growth, retention, and involvement.* The organization identified four key targets that measured accomplishment of the goal over a three-year period. How did they determine the objectives? They accomplished this by focusing on the wording of the goal as follows.

Introduction

Membership goal	Maximize membership growth, retention, and involvement.

By breaking down the wording of the goal, the team was able to determine what the key measures should be.

Breaking down the wording of the goal to identify key measures	• *Maximize membership <u>growth</u>*. At the end of the year, what would tell us that we maximized membership growth? (Key measure: number of members.) • *Maximize <u>retention</u>*. At the end of the year, what would tell us that we maximized retention? (Key measure: number of members retained from the prior year.) • *Maximize <u>involvement</u>*. At the end of the year, what would tell us that we maximized involvement? (Key measures: number of members attending meetings, number of members involved in committees.)

Based on these key measures, the following objectives resulted:

Membership objectives	• Increase net membership from 500 to 650. • Annually retain 75 percent of members from prior year. • Increase average attendance from 175 to 250 per meeting. • Achieve 10 percent committee involvement.

Note that in the sample layout, we only show the membership objectives due to space limitations. You can imagine that each of their five goals have objectives tied to them.

The point is that each objective is specifically selected because it measures accomplishment of the goal, based on the way the goal is worded. This means, of course, you have to be very careful about how you word your goals. Otherwise, you could be measuring the wrong objectives!

The Difference Between Goals and Objectives

So, what's the difference between goals and objectives? While goals are broad, objectives are specific and measurable targets to be reached. You need both. Why? Well, suppose you just had goals (broad aims) and no objectives (specific, measurable targets that defined accomplishment of the goal). At the end of the year, how would you know whether or not you've been successful? Suppose the meeting planners organization just had the goal of maximizing membership growth, but no specific targets? At the end of the first year, they would ask themselves, "Did we maximize membership growth?" They could respond yes, but how would they know? Without defined measurable targets, the best they could respond is, "Well, it sure feels like we maximized membership growth. We did a lot of work and we did get some new members. So yes, we maximized membership growth." Yet, without defined targets, you really don't know.

Now, if objectives are so important, then why not just have objectives? You don't really need goals, do you? Well, of course you do. Think of it this way. What if one year the meeting planners set objectives to increase net membership to 650, achieve average attendance of 250, and so on? Then, the following year, they set objectives to have a satellite chapter in a neighboring city, and then the following year to have at least three events with other related associations. And so on. The problem with just having objectives is that you're setting targets, but to what end? What are the targets for? What are you trying to achieve? Are your targets covering everything that is important to you?

This is the purpose of goals. The goals tell you what is important to you. **Your goals tell you the areas in which you need to have objectives.** It is important to recognize that the objectives only tell you where you want to be with each of the goals by a given point in time.

By the way, it doesn't matter what you call these components. The Drivers Model calls them goals and objectives; you might reverse the names and call them objectives and goals, or key performance areas and key performance indicators, or strategic intent and strategic outcomes. It doesn't matter what you call them. The key is that you need both: something broad that defines your aims, and something specific and measurable that sets targets for a specific time period.

Results vs. Activity

There is one other key point to understand about objectives: Objectives measure results, not activity. Look back again at the objectives this organization has for membership. Notice that there isn't an objective that says, "Hold two membership drives." What would be wrong with this objective? To assess the objective, let's take it through the SMART acronym, which often is used to ensure that an objective is suitable.

Does this objective pass the traditional SMART test?	*Hold two membership drives.*
	• Is it <u>s</u>pecific? Yes, it refers to membership drives.
	• Is it <u>m</u>easurable? Yes, we want to hold two of them.
	• Is it <u>a</u>chievable? Presumably we can hold two membership drives in three years.
	• Is it <u>r</u>ealistic? Again, presumably we can hold two membership drives in three years.
	• Is it <u>t</u>ime-bound? Yes, it is a three-year objective.

The objective appears to pass the SMART test, so what is wrong with the objective? There is a big problem with the objective and a problem the Drivers Model prevents by using a different definition for the "R" in SMART. As stated above, "R" stands for "realistic," which in many ways overlaps with the "A," which stands for "achievable." In the Drivers Model, the "R" stands for "relevant." The question then becomes, "Is the objective a relevant measure of the goal?"

To answer this question, we have to go back to the wording of the goal.

- *Maximize membership growth.* Does the objective measure membership growth? No.
- *Maximize retention.* Does the objective measure retention? No.
- *Maximize involvement.* Does the objective measure involvement? No.

In essence, the objective doesn't measure the goal at all. In fact, the objective is measuring activity instead of results. *Holding two membership drives* is an activity to increase membership growth, not a relevant measure of whether you have achieved membership growth.

This problem of measuring activity instead of results is all too common in corporations, governments, and non-profits. And what's worse, let's say we had our two membership drives, but didn't get any new members. At the end of the year, we would congratulate ourselves for achieving the objective, but we wouldn't have achieved the goal of maximizing membership growth. That's the danger of having objectives that measure activity, instead of focusing on results. If we don't measure results, we can get so caught up in the activity that we lose sight of the real goal. So, we must be careful when we create objectives to avoid measuring activity (such as holding membership drives), but focus on the true desired outcome (increasing members).

Keep in mind that activity measures aren't necessarily bad. They just don't make good objectives. Many activity measures become strategies or might serve well as leading indicators. As an example, a key strategy for increasing new members might be to have every member invite potential members to a free event hosted by the association. An activity measure might be the number of potential members attending the free event. This isn't an objective for membership growth because it doesn't serve as a measure of that variable. But, instead of serving as an objective, it very well could serve as a leading indicator of membership growth because the number of new members each year could be highly correlated with the number of potential members attending free events.

Strategic Direction Setting vs. Implementation Planning

The objectives represent the completion of strategic direction setting, which you can consider the first half of the strategy development effort. Once an organization has identified its objectives, it has also defined where it is going and the measures that signal success.

The second half of strategy development is called *implementation planning*. During implementation planning, the entire focus is on how the organization will achieve the objectives. However, you may be tempted to jump straight to strategies to answer the question, "What do we do to accomplish the objectives?" The Drivers Model encourages you to slow down and focus on two important areas that will help ensure you identify the most important strategies.

Strategic Direction vs. Implementation Plan

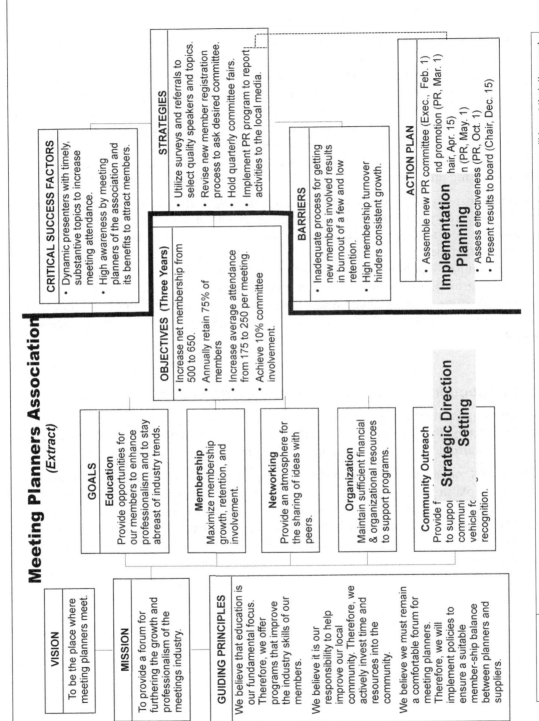

Meeting Planners Association
(Extract)

VISION
To be the place where meeting planners meet.

MISSION
To provide a forum for furthering the growth and professionalism of the meetings industry.

GUIDING PRINCIPLES
We believe that education is our fundamental focus. Therefore, we offer programs that improve the industry skills of our members.

We believe it is our responsibility to help improve our local community. Therefore, we actively invest time and resources into the community.

We believe we must remain a comfortable forum for meeting planners. Therefore, we will implement policies to ensure a suitable member-ship balance between planners and suppliers.

GOALS

Education
Provide opportunities for our members to enhance professionalism and to stay abreast of industry trends.

Membership
Maximize membership growth, retention, and involvement.

Networking
Provide an atmosphere for the sharing of ideas with peers.

Organization
Maintain sufficient financial & organizational resources to support programs.

Community Outreach
Provide f
to suppoi
communi
vehicle fc
recognition.

Strategic Direction Setting

CRITICAL SUCCESS FACTORS
- Dynamic presenters with timely, substantive topics to increase meeting attendance.
- High awareness by meeting planners of the association and its benefits to attract members.

OBJECTIVES (Three Years)
- Increase net membership from 500 to 650.
- Annually retain 75% of members
- Increase average attendance from 175 to 250 per meeting.
- Achieve 10% committee involvement.

STRATEGIES
- Utilize surveys and referrals to select quality speakers and topics.
- Revise new member registration process to ask desired committee.
- Hold quarterly committee fairs.
- Implement PR program to report activities to the local media.

BARRIERS
- Inadequate process for getting new members involved results in burnout of a few and low retention.
- High membership turnover hinders consistent growth.

ACTION PLAN
- Assemble new PR committee (Exec., Feb. 1)
- nd promotion (PR, Mar. 1)
- hair, Apr. 15)
- n (PR, May. 1)
- Assess effectiveness (PR, Oct. 1)
- Present results to board (Chair, Dec. 15)

Implementation Planning

Critical Success Factors and Barriers

	Definition	Example
Critical success factors	Key conditions that must be created to achieve one or more objectives.	*High awareness by meeting planners of the association and its benefits to attract members.*
Barriers	Existing or potential challenges that hinder the achievement of one or more objectives.	*Inadequate process for getting new members involved results in burnout of a few and low retention.*

I believe that CSFs are among the most important concepts in planning because they encourage you to identify and focus on what factors you absolutely need in order to be successful. Once you have created your objectives, you can then identify your CSFs by asking, "What key conditions, if we create them, will drive achievement of our objectives?"

With the meeting planners, one of their objectives was to *increase net membership from 500 to 650*. What is the CSF for increasing membership? What is the key condition that, if they create it, will drive achievement of the objective? *High awareness by meeting planners of the association and its benefits to attract members.*

Another objective is to increase meeting attendance from 175 to 250. What's the key condition? *Dynamic presenters with timely, substantive topics to increase meeting attendance.*

Now, let's look at barriers. Barriers are existing or potential challenges that hinder the achievement of one or more objectives. They're the roadblocks that keep you where you are today, and prevent you from getting to where you want to be. To identify your barriers, you ask the question, "What is standing in the way of our achieving these objectives? Why aren't we there already?"

When the meeting planners looked at their membership data for the prior two years, they realized that 70 percent of their turnover was made up of people who had been members for a year or less. In essence, people were joining the organization, looking around, and then leaving. The people who got involved with the organization tended to stay. Therefore, they determined that one of their major barriers was that they had *an inadequate process for getting new members involved, resulting in burnout of a few and low retention.*

Strategies

	Definition	Example
Strategies	Broad activities required to achieve an objective, create a critical condition, or overcome a barrier.	*Use assessment surveys and industry referrals to select quality speakers and topics.*

Introduction

Once you have identified your CSFs and barriers, you're now ready to determine your *strategies*. Strategies are your drivers, the things you actually do to achieve your objectives, create a critical condition, or overcome a barrier. Going back to the meeting planners example, note how each strategy is designed to address a CSF, a barrier, an objective, or some combination of the three.

Strategy	Affects which Objective, CSF, or Barrier
1. Use assessment surveys and industry referrals to select quality speakers and topics.	Obj: Increase average attendance from 175 to 250 per meeting. CSF: Dynamic presenters with timely, substantive topics to increase meeting attendance.
2. Revise new member registration process to ask for member's committee preference.	Obj: Achieve 10 percent committee involvement. Obj: Annually retain 75 percent of members from prior year. Bar: Inadequate process for getting new members involved results in burnout of a few and low retention. Bar: High membership turnover hinders consistent growth.
3. Hold quarterly committee fairs after meetings.	Obj: Achieve 10 percent committee involvement. Obj: Annually retain 75 percent of members from prior year. Bar: Inadequate process for getting new members involved results in burnout of a few and low retention. Bar: High membership turnover hinders consistent growth.
4. Implement PR program to report activities to the local media.	Obj: Increase net membership from 500 to 650. CSF: High awareness by meeting planners of the association and its benefits to attract members.

Given that nearly all organizations have scarce resources, why would any organization invest in a strategy that wasn't creating a critical condition for success or overcoming a major barrier standing in their way? Why would an organization do that? And why, as I have found, do they do it all the time?

Of course, one reason is because they have no choice. For example, government organizations have congressional mandates that they must accomplish, even if the mandate is not related to their objectives, barriers, or CSFs. In the same way, a CEO may insist on implementing a strategy that others in the company recognize isn't key to achieving the strategic objectives of the organization.

However, the primary reason I've found that organizations invest in strategies that don't address their CSFs and barriers is that they've never determined what their CSFs and barriers are. In essence, they're doing things (strategies), but are they doing the most important things? Maybe or maybe not. We don't know because they haven't determined their CSFs and barriers.

Therefore, one of the keys to effective planning is to identify what is critical to achieving your objectives and to isolate the barriers that are standing in your way. Only then, can you make sure you invest in only the most important strategies. Do you see how important CSF and barrier analysis can be?

Prioritizing and Action Planning

In the meeting planners example, there are five goals and four strategies for the goal area called "membership." If each goal had four strategies, then this plan would generate twenty strategies. Can you do twenty strategies all at once? Of course not. So, that's why you prioritize. You go through an activity of prioritizing the most important strategies to start on first. Then, you write *action plans* for each of those priority strategies.

	Definition
Action plans	Specific steps to be taken to implement a strategy. Includes what will be done, by whom and by when, and the resources required.

An action plan provides the details for how a priority strategy will be implemented. The action plan describes what will be done, by whom and by when. The action plan also estimates both the people resources and the out-of-pocket dollars required.

Sample Action Plan

Strategy: Implement PR plan to report activities to the local media	
Objective(s) Supported	Increase net membership from 500 to 650.
Owner	PR chair
Deliverables	PR plan with objectives and annual performance against objectives. Implemented promotion plan. Presentation to board on plan and results.
Due Date: December 31 **Total Costs:** $1000 **Person Days:** 27	

Introduction

	Action Step	Who	Due	Cost	Person-days
1.	Assemble new PR committee. (Target: 5 people)	Exec. director	Feb 1		1
2.	Develop PR objectives.	PR comm.	Mar. 1		3
3.	Develop promotion program.	PR comm.	Mar. 15		3
4.	Hold board presentation.	Chair, board	Apr. 15		0.5
5.	Begin promotion implementation.	PR comm.	May 1	$1000	15
6.	Provide interim report of progress.	Chair, board	Aug. 15		1
7.	Assess promotion effectiveness.	PR comm.	Nov. 1		3
8.	Present results to board.	Chair, board	Dec. 15		0.5

Action plans also allow you to monitor the activity to ensure that the priorities are being accomplished. With the Drivers Model, you should have no more than three months between action steps to ensure ongoing progress.

Drivers Model Components: Definition and Example

The table below summarizes the definition of each component.

Vision	A picture of the "preferred future"—it's a statement that describes how the future will look if the organization fulfills its mission. *To be the place where meeting planners meet.*
Mission	A statement of the overall purpose of an organization that describes what you do, for whom you do it, and the benefit. *To provide a forum for furthering the growth and professionalism of the meetings industry.*
Guiding principles	General guidelines that set the foundation for how an organization will operate. *We believe we must remain a comfortable forum for meeting planners. Therefore, we will implement policies to ensure a suitable membership balance between planners and suppliers.*
Goals	Broad, long-term aims that define fulfillment of the mission. *Maximize membership growth, retention, and involvement.*
Objectives	Specific, quantifiable, realistic targets that measure the accomplishment of a goal over a specified period of time. *Increase average attendance from 125 to 250 per meeting.*

Positioning statements	Positioning statements are broad determinations about the organization's direction and focus.
	We believe increases in the quality of manufacturing in third-world countries will result in an acceleration in the downward pressure on retail prices for lighting products. Therefore, we must seek offshore opportunities for sourcing products, and in the longer term, establish our own international manufacturing capability.
Critical success factors	Key conditions that must be created to achieve one or more objectives.
	High awareness by meeting planners of the association and its benefits to attract members.
Barriers	Existing or potential challenges that hinder the achievement of one or more objectives.
	Inadequate process for getting new members involved results in burnout of a few and low retention.
Strategies	Broad activities required to achieve an objective, create a critical condition, or overcome a barrier.
	Use assessment surveys and industry referrals to select quality speakers and topics.
Action plans	Specific steps to be taken to implement a strategy. Includes what will be done, by whom and by when, and the resources required.
	Assemble new PR committee. (Exec., Feb. 1) *Develop PR objectives. (PR, Mar. 1)* *Develop promotion. (PR, Mar. 15)*

Monitoring

We have talked about all the components of the plan. Let's now look at the monitoring process.

Top-down Planning, Bottom-up Implementation

With the Drivers Model, you plan from the top-down. But you implement from the bottom-up. What do I mean by this?

First, with the planning effort, you take a top-down approach.

Top-down planning
- You first define your goals.
- Then, you define the objectives to achieve the goals.
- You then identify the CSFs and barriers related to the objectives.
- Next, you define the strategies to create the critical conditions, overcome the barriers, and achieve the objectives.
- Finally, you define action plans to achieve each priority strategy.

While this is top-down planning, when you implement, you implement from the bottom-up.

Bottom-up implementation	• If you achieve the action plans, you achieve your strategies. • If you achieve strategies, you create the critical conditions and overcome the barriers. • If you create the critical conditions and overcome the barriers, you achieve your objectives. • If you achieve your objectives, you achieve your goals for the time period. • If you achieve your goals, you fulfill your mission. • If you fulfill your mission, you move toward your vision.

What Do You Grade?

So, how do you know if you're achieving what you set out to achieve? This is where monitoring comes in. Periodically, as I will explain in more detail later, you should take a full stop and grade your progress. In doing so, of course, you should review all of the plan's nine components: vision, mission, guiding principles, goals, objectives, CSFs, barriers, strategies, and action plans. However, I recommend that you assess your performance by grading progress in only one element. Which one?

• Is it vision, mission, guiding principles, or goals? No. These are too broad.

• Perhaps, CSFs or barriers? No, you can't really grade those.

• So now, we're down to deciding whether to grade objectives or the strategies/action plans. Which do you grade?

The answer may be obvious to you. Let's say you go through and you're at the one-year point, or the two-year point, or even the three-year point of a three-year plan, and you've achieved every one of your strategies and action plans, but you haven't achieved your objectives. Are you going to be happy? Probably not.

On the other hand, let's say after a year, two years, or three years, you've achieved every one of your objectives, every single one, but you haven't done all your strategies and actions. Are you going to be happy? Absolutely. You're going to be ecstatic because you achieved your objectives and you didn't have to do all that work!

The key to the grading progress is to focus on the objectives—they're your measurable targets. These are the results you're trying to achieve. If you're grading your performance based on strategies or action plans, all you're asking is, "Did we do what we said we were going to do?" If you determine that you've done what you said, you might give yourself an "A" even though you may not have gotten the results you desire. As you can imagine, this happens frequently, especially when organizations haven't defined their objectives or when their objectives focus on activities and not results.

If you're measuring and grading your objectives, you're asking if you're getting the results that you expected to achieve. This is another reason to have specific, measurable targets. If you don't have objectives, you'll likely measure your progress based on activities, not results.

The Drivers Model Monitoring Process

As you'll see in Chapter 14, the Drivers Model uses a bottom-up approach, which includes a three-part monitoring progress.

Three-part monitoring process

- **Monthly:** With the Drivers Model, your team will track strategies and action plans monthly by asking the question, "Are we doing what we said we were going to do?" You'll make adjustments along the way to action plans as needed.

- **Quarterly:** Every three months, your team will review progress on objectives and ask, "Are we getting the results we expected to get?" During the quarterly sessions, your team will adjust objectives as warranted, based on issues and priorities and will decide which current strategies to stop or continue, and which new strategies to start.

- **Annually:** The planning team will meet to review progress for the year, identify new barriers and CSFs, change objectives, and reestablish priorities and action plans.

The Deliverables of the Drivers Model

Now that you have seen the components of the Drivers Model and the monitoring process, let's now look at the Drivers Model deliverables. The diagram that follows illustrates the five major deliverables from the Drivers Model when used for strategic planning.

Briefing book

Documents the current situation by providing information and assessments from multiple views.

- Customer/stakeholder views
- Employee views
- Upper management views
- Industry trends
- Competitor analysis
- Organization analysis

Please note that the briefing book components in the diagram use corporate terminology in referring to customers and competitors. For government organizations and some non-profits, it may be more appropriate to use the term "stakeholders" instead of "customers," and "partners" instead of "competitors." For simplicity, I'll use the customer and competitor terminology and from time to time, make reference to the differences for non-corporate organizations.

Strategy document

Serves as the primary strategy document; typically fits on an 11x17 page folded in half and contains the core components of the strategic plan. The four pages at the front of this book give an example of a strategy document for the meeting planner's organization.

- Vision and mission
- Goals
- Objectives
- Positioning statements
- Guiding principles
- CSFs
- Barriers
- Strategies

The Deliverables of the Drivers Model

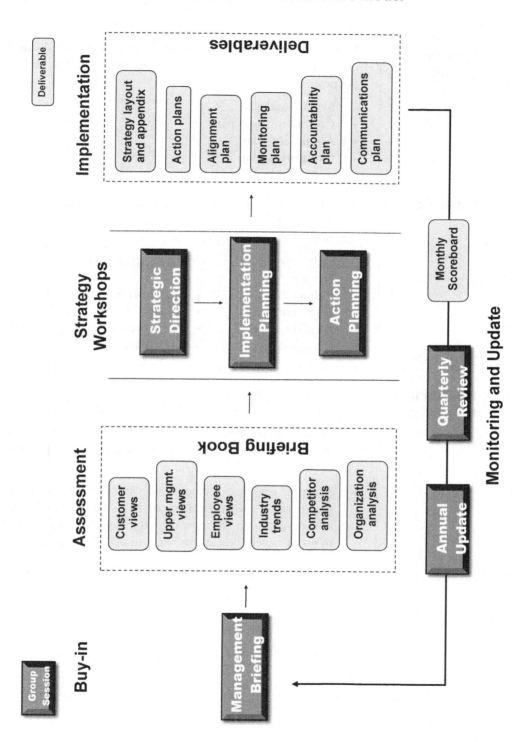

Appendix document	Provides detailed analysis and other plans developed during the planning process that are not included in the strategy document.

- SWOT analysis
- Communication plan
- Alignment plan
- Monitoring plan

Action plans	Provides a separate plan for each priority strategy with a step-by-step list of activities and responsibilities needed to accomplish each priority strategy.

For each action plan
- Owner
- Deliverables
- Total costs
- Total resources
- Due date

For each action step
- Action
- Responsibility
- Costs
- Resources
- Due date

Monitoring reports	

- Monthly scoreboard: Presents a color-coded view (green, yellow, red) of the status of each priority strategy.

- Quarterly review: Provides a review of progress and adjustments to objectives, strategies, and priorities as needed.

- Annual update: Includes an assessment of annual performance, identification of new barriers and CSFs, and revisions to the overall plan, including adjustments to goals, objectives, strategies, and priorities as needed.

Executing the Drivers Model: How Much Time?

The Drivers Model is scalable to nearly any organization size. In its full form, the Drivers Model includes five facilitated workshops to develop the components of the plan, and four facilitated monitoring sessions per year to track progress. However, an organization might adjust the sessions to better align with its needs. The table below shows sample durations for three types of organizations.

Facilitated Workshops	Larger Organizations	Midsize Organizations	Smaller Organizations
Management briefing	2 hours	2 hours	2 hours
Strategic direction setting	2 days	1.5 day	1 day
Implementation planning	2 days	1.5 day	1 day
Action planning and staff briefing	1 day	1 day	(not done)
Action plan review	1 day	(not done)	(not done)
Monthly monitoring	*Not facilitated; done by phone or online*		(not done)
Quarterly monitoring (three quarters)	3 hours per quarter	3 hours per quarter	(not done)
Annual update	1 day	1 day	1 day
Total workshop time	8+ days	6+ days	3+ days

How Is the Drivers Model Different?

From time to time, I'm asked to explain how the Drivers Model differs from other planning models. I divide this question into two parts: First, what is different about the way the Drivers Model is structured? And second, what is different about the way the Drivers Model is executed? Let's look first at the structure.

Introduction

What's different about the Drivers Model structure	Elegantly simple	Many executives see planning, and specifically strategic planning, as a highly challenging and complex activity. The Drivers Model provides an approach that is elegantly simple, yet robust and comprehensive enough to serve both a multi-billion-dollar corporation and a half-million-dollar non-profit.
	Strategy document	In a single, 11x17 page folded in half, you have all the core elements of your strategic plan. For management teams and employees, the strategy document serves as an easily accessible and understandable roadmap of the strategic direction. Some organizations even find it helpful to create an edited, "external" version of the strategy document to give to suppliers and customers.
	Clear definitions	The Drivers Model provides a more complete analysis of strengths, weaknesses, opportunities, and threats by identifying both the attribute and impact of each element. This deeper analysis helps ensure a common understanding of the current conditions facing the organization.
	SWOT format	The Drivers Model provides a more complete analysis of strengths, weaknesses, opportunities, and threats by identifying both the attribute and impact of each element. This deeper analysis helps ensure a common understanding of the current conditions facing the organization.
	Mission–vision distinction	The clear distinction between mission *(what you do, for whom, and the benefit)* and vision *(the preferred picture of the future)* helps you to be both definitive and aspirational at the same time.
	Goals–objectives relationship	The relationship defined between goals *(broad aims that define fulfillment of the mission)* and objectives *(specific, measurable targets that define accomplishment of the goal)* ensures that your objectives focus on measuring results rather than measuring activities.
	CSFs and barriers	How do you make sure your strategies are the most important activities for your organization's focus? The Drivers Model answers the call by having you identify the critical conditions for success and the major barriers standing in your way. So, each of your strategies should create a critical condition, overcome a barrier, or both.
	Monitoring processes	Many plans fail in execution, due to a lack of focus and commitment. The three-level monitoring model encourages both the focus and commitment needed to deliver on the plan's promise.

While the model's structure is one difference, the other difference is in how the Drivers Model is facilitated and executed. The facilitation processes are designed to deepen understanding of the current situation, focus the conversation on the most essential elements, and build buy-in and commitment to execution along the way. This book contains over twenty-five secrets related to executing the Drivers Model. The secrets are highlighted throughout the book. However, I've summarized several key ones below.

What's different about the Drivers Model execution	The management briefing	You can gain buy-in to the planning activity by holding one or more management briefings. Use the management briefing to have the planning team identify the most critical issues facing the organization. Then, show how the planning process will help the team address those issues.
	Briefing book review	Early on in many planning processes, teams spend considerable time compiling a briefing book that assesses the current situation. But how do you ensure that key information from the briefing book is carried through the planning process? With the Drivers Model, planning team members identify key observations from the briefing book review, and document potential strategies for addressing them. The potential strategies serve as the bridge between the past and the future, and are considered during strategy development that occurs later in the Drivers Model process.
	Informed majority process	Teams often waste time debating the exact words to use to describe, for example, a goal or a positioning statement. The Drivers Model includes a structured process called "informed majority" to minimize time wasted in wordsmithing.
	The power of verbs	The Drivers Model defines specific differences among the verbs used for each planning component.

- Goals start with infinite verbs (*e.g., maximize, provide, maintain*).

- Objectives begin with quantity verbs (*e.g., increase, decrease, reduce*).

- Strategies use finite verbs (*e.g., establish, develop, implement*).

These distinctions provide a level of consistency that helps produce a quality plan.

Introduction

What's different about the Drivers Model execution

(cont.)

Establishing the mission
The structured process to help organizations define their mission often results in a mission statement developed in under an hour. The three key questions, "What do we do? For whom? What is the benefit?" bring focus and clarity to mission development.

Identifying goals
The Drivers Model includes a powerful visualization process that helps teams visualize future success. From the visualization, teams are able to quickly identify their goals and build robust goal statements.

Defining objectives
The Drivers Model eases this notoriously difficult process through a simple, five-step process that results in specific, measurable targets for each goal.

Developing strategies
While brainstorming potential strategies is an important part of any planning process, the Drivers Model follows the brainstorming with a rigorous review of CSFs and barriers to ensure that the plan addresses major impediments and creates the critical conditions for success.

Setting priorities
Developing strategies is important, but few organizations can simultaneously undertake all the activities of a typical plan at once. It is essential to set priorities. The Drivers Model priority-setting process includes a period of controlled lobbying to build strong consensus and commitment. The lobbying process gives each person the floor for a brief period to lobby the entire group in support of one or more strategies. The lobby process helps build consensus around particular solutions, as participants repeatedly hear support for a small number of strategies. In addition, once the prioritization is complete and it is time to assign responsibilities, people volunteer more readily to lead items for which they lobbied.

Success strategies and quality checks
Each component of the Drivers Model includes a list of success strategies that outline best practices for developing that component. The Drivers Model also includes component-specific sets of quality checks to confirm that your team has done a good job.

I believe these structure and execution differences help make the Drivers Model a superb approach to planning for organizations of all sizes and types.

What's Next?

In this chapter, I've presented an overview of the Drivers Model. With this overview as a foundation, the chapters that follow detail how to execute the Drivers Model and your role in leading strategy development.

- Chapter 2. Your Role in Facilitating Strategy
- Chapter 3. Gaining Buy-in: The Management Briefing

Section I	Section II	Section III	Section IV
Buy-in and Assessment	**Strategic Direction**	**Implementation Planning**	**Execution and Monitoring**
Chapter	**Chapters**	**Chapters**	**Chapters**
2. Your Role in Facilitating Strategy	4. Briefing Book Review and SWOT	10. Guiding Principles	13. Action Planning
3. Management Briefing	5. Positioning	11. Critical Success Factors and Barriers	14. Alignment, Communication Monitoring, and Accountability
	6. Envisioning the Future and Goals	12. Strategies, Priorities, and Deliverables	
	7. Mission		
	8. Vision		
	9. Objectives		

Your Role in Facilitating Strategy 2

- Why Do You Need a Plan?
- How is Facilitating Different from Leading?
- Seven Key Activities
- Is Your Team Ready to Plan?
- A Final Note

Over the past two decades, I've worked with over 100 leaders in strategic planning initiatives. I believe I've seen a full range of executives, from those who seemed to live and breathe strategy every waking moment, to the executive who told me at the initial meeting, "I don't see how a strategic plan would change one iota of what we do this year." So, before jumping into your role in facilitating strategy, let's answer the bigger question.

Why Do You Need a Plan?

Developing strategy takes time and resources. It requires the time and commitment of some of the most highly paid and highly experienced people in your organization. So, if your team isn't willing to invest what is needed, I recommend that you don't do it. Poor planning is often worse than no planning at all.

So, why do you need a strategy? Why take time for planning? There are many reasons. But the Drivers Model focuses on five in particular.

To set direction and priorities

First and foremost, you need a strategy because it sets the direction and establishes priorities for your organization.

It defines your organization's view of success and prioritizes the activities that will make this view your reality. The strategy will help your people know what they should be working on, and what they should be working on first.

Without a clearly defined and articulated strategy, you may very well find that your priority initiatives—the ones that will drive the highest success—are being given secondary treatment.

To get everyone on the same page

If you find that you have departments working to achieve different aims, or going in different directions, you need a strategy.

Once you define your strategic direction, you can get operations, sales, marketing, administration, manufacturing, and all other departments moving together to achieve the organization's goals.

To simplify decision-making

If your leadership team has trouble saying no to new ideas or potential initiatives, you need a strategy. Why? Because your strategy will have already prioritized the activities necessary for success. Priorities make it easier to say no to distracting initiatives.

To drive alignment

Many organizations have hard-working people putting their best efforts into areas that have little to no effect on strategic success. They're essentially majoring in the minors—because their activities aren't aligned with the priorities.

Your strategy serves as the vehicle for answering the question, "How can we better align all our resources to maximize our strategic success?"

To communicate the message

Many leaders walk around with a virtual strategy locked in their heads—they know where their organization needs to be and the key activities that will get it there. Unfortunately, the strategy isn't down on paper and hasn't been communicated thoroughly. As a result, few people are acting on it.

When your staff, suppliers, and even customers know where you're going, you allow even greater opportunities for people to help you maximize your success in getting there.

Once you recognize the need to plan, you now have the role of becoming the catalyst: for facilitating the buy-in and commitment of your leadership team and the rest of your organization. I've found that very few executives truly understand how to maximize their role in facilitating strategy. This chapter is focused on you, the leader of the organization, and on the vital role you play in facilitating strategy throughout your organization. Let's get started.

How Is Facilitating Different from Leading?

A major difference between leading and facilitating is that a leader often tells; a facilitator always asks. In my book, *The Secrets of Facilitation*, I described how I learned what I call the fundamental secret of facilitation.

Learning The Fundamental Secret of Facilitation

I began understanding the secret during my career with the management consulting division of what was then one of the Big-8 accounting and consulting firms. In the eight years I spent in that consulting practice, we had a standard way of addressing a client problem. We might be called in to review a particular department or activity. We would arrive with our army of bright people, interview those whom we believed were the key stakeholders, develop a set of recommendations based on our interviews and experience, and create what might be called the "100 Percent Solution." We would go away and come back a year later and perhaps, if we were lucky, 15 percent of the recommendations would be implemented.

In my final years with that organization, the practice in which I worked began taking a different approach. We would come in with a smaller group of consultants and work shoulder to shoulder with client personnel. Together we would convene group interviews (facilitated sessions) that typically included 8–20 people. In the facilitated sessions, the participants would create the recommendations, not the consultants. In most cases, they would only come up with what we might consider the 60 percent or 70 percent solution. So, we would float ideas based on our experience. Some they would accept, others they would reject as "not beneficial" or "not implementable" in their environment. When all was done, they might have created what we would consider the "85 Percent Solution." Yet, a year later, when we came back, amazingly 80–90 percent of the solution would be implemented!

Why wasn't more of the "100 Percent Solution" implemented? Why would the "85 Percent Solution" gained through facilitation achieve far greater success? Therein lie the secret and the power behind it.

Secret #1   **If they create it, they understand it and accept it.**

You can achieve more effective results when solutions are created, understood, and accepted by the people affected.

As an expert consultant, we were "telling" our clients what they needed to do. As a result, there was very little buy-in by our clients and their people. When we began "asking" the questions that resulted in clients creating their own answers, the difference was staggering.

In *Transforming the Mature Information Technology Organization*, Dr. Robert Zawacki from the University of Colorado put the secret this way:

$$ED = RD \times CD$$

Effective Decisions = The Right Decision x Commitment to the Decision

Dr. Zawacki's point is that the multiplication sign in the formula means that even the best decision can be rendered completely ineffective if commitment to the decision is lacking.

What does this mean to you?	If you, the leader of the organization, know the right strategy to take, but your team has zero commitment to it, the effectiveness of your strategy will be zero.
	If you dictate the strategy and they aren't committed to it, it will be as if you're pressing on the accelerator, while they're stomping on the brake—a lot of energy expended and a lot of smoke in the air, but with little to show for it.

I've seen this happen in real time. The leader of a unit within a government agency decided to undertake a strategic planning effort. Though the work of this unit was accomplished primarily through its three operating divisions, this leader chose to develop the plan with just the members of her direct office. The leader intentionally excluded the division heads and their deputies from the table because she believed that they wouldn't have the big picture, would be too parochial in their thinking, and would waste the group's time by advocating for what was in their individual best interests, rather than that of the entire unit.

The plan was indeed developed quickly. However, when the time came to implement it, the pushback began. Each division felt the plan lacked substance, didn't address the real issues facing them, and was more of a distraction than an aid. As a result, the general response by the divisions was to give as little energy as possible to the plan, but just enough to still be perceived as supporting it. As you can perhaps guess, the implementation was ineffective.

Building Commitment

A natural tendency for leaders is to figure out the strategic plan first and then attempt to build commitment to what they've determined is the right direction. I call this the old way of planning. In the facilitative way, you invite the people affected by the decision to help develop it. This builds commitment into the process of developing the right decision, as shown in the diagram that follows.

The Old Way	**The Facilitative Way**
Figure out the right decision and then try to build commitment to it.	Invite the people affected by the decision to help develop it.

 X
Right Decision X Commitment to the Decision
Right Decision X Commitment to the Decision

How do you build commitment?	You build commitment by inviting those affected by the decision to help create it. If they create it, they understand it, and they accept it.

The purpose of this book is to guide you through the process of building a strategic plan with your team, while using facilitation principles to build their buy-in and commitment all the way through implementation. How do you do it? Let's get into your role.

Seven Key Activities

As the strategy leader, you have seven activities that will help you build a strong strategy with your team's full buy-in and commitment. I recommend you pay close attention to these seven.

The leader's role in facilitating strategy	• Gain your team's commitment and buy-in to the process.
	• Ensure all voices are heard.
	• Ensure key information is brought into the room.
	• Get your ideas on the table without overpowering the group.
	• Ensure that the plan components meet the quality checks.
	• Follow through and hold people accountable all the way through implementation.
	• Decide if an outside facilitator would be helpful.

Let's examine each of these activities and the recommended actions related to them.

Gain Your Team's Commitment and buy-in to the process

If your leadership team members are like most with whom I've worked, they're stretched for resources and have more on their plate than they can likely accomplish in the time available. Therefore, for many of them, the prospect of taking valuable time and resources to develop a plan that will add to their already overloaded plates is NOT a welcomed idea.

So, how do you gain their commitment to planning? How do you gain their buy-in to a planning process, such as The Drivers Model? In Chapter 3, I show you how by introducing what I consider to be my secret weapon for buy-in: the management briefing. With the management briefing, you'll have your team identify the most critical issues facing the organization. Then, they'll make adjustments to the planning process as needed to ensure that the process addresses those issues. The management briefing increases commitment to planning by providing your team with a roadmap, showing how their individual needs will be served during the strategic planning sessions.

Management briefing agenda	
	• Getting started.
	• Identify the key issues to be addressed by planning.
	• Overview the Drivers Model.
	• Modify the planning approach to ensure the approach addresses our issues.
	• Identify the information needed to plan effectively (briefing book).
	• Define logistics and next steps (the who, when, and where of the planning retreat).

Ensure All Voices Are Heard

The fundamental secret of facilitation indicates that you can increase buy-in and commitment by inviting those affected by the plan to help create it. However, everyone in your organization will be affected by the strategic plan. Does that mean everyone should be at the table creating the plan?

No, of course not. Nor is it necessary. Involvement doesn't necessitate being at the table. There are several ways to provide people with an opportunity for involvement, as shown in the table that follows.

How do you ensure all voices are heard?	• For some, merely being given a chance to offer input through a survey or a suggestion box is adequate.
	• For others, focus groups, one-on-one interviews, or other methods for gaining in-depth input may be more appropriate.
	• And for others, their responsibilities, influence, expertise, or perspectives are so important that it will make sense to have them seated around the table.

One of your important roles is to determine who should be at the table. Another is to put avenues in place to ensure all voices are given the opportunity to be heard. Providing the opportunity for input is essential to a facilitative approach and to gaining adequate buy-in for successful, organization-wide implementation.

Ensure Key Information Is Brought into the Room

You may have been in the room when a team made a decision, based on the best information available, only to discover in hindsight that not all the needed information was present—resulting in a poor decision. Sound familiar? Well, part of your role is to make sure that this doesn't happen.

My company's work in the area of consensus building has shown that one of the primary reasons people disagree is due to a lack of shared information. Many disagreements can be resolved, and even prevented, by making sure all parties have the same information.

With the Drivers Model, the briefing book serves the purpose of ensuring all your team members start with a common set of data. In Chapter 3, you'll learn what data to research, compile, and distribute in advance to each planning team member.

Typical briefing book contents	• Customer/stakeholder views.
	• Employee views.
	• Upper management views.
	• Industry trends.
	• Competitor analysis.
	• Current situation data (e.g., financial, product performance, prior plan).

As Chapter 4 describes, your team will review the briefing book contents during the first planning session and identify key observations and potential strategies that will help formulate the overall strategy.

Get Your Ideas on the Table Without Overpowering the Group

As indicated earlier, it's important that all voices be heard—yours included. Unfortunately, if you're like most leaders, your voice comes with considerable baggage. When the boss speaks, people listen. And they listen differently from when other people speak.

Sure, there will likely be some people in the room who treat your voice like every other voice in the room. Whether the idea comes from you or a first-year manager, these people will state their agreement or disagreement in the exact same way, regardless of the source. Unfortunately, this probably isn't the case for most people at the table. When you speak, most may be quick to respond when they agree, and very, very slow to respond when they disagree—so slow, in fact, that sometimes they may never get around to it.

Lacking a challenge, the leader's views can easily overpower the group. Even when someone dares to challenge with a question, some leaders, often without knowing it, respond with statements that belittle the questioner or not-so-subtly communicate that challenging the boss is unwelcome.

Consider the following strategies.

Strategies for getting your ideas on the table without overpowering the group	Explain how your role differs inside and outside the room. Let your team know the following:
	• Your leadership title was left outside the door when you walked in.
	• Inside the planning room, you're one member of the planning team and have one vote, just like everyone else.
	• The strategic plan being formulated inside the room is the recommendation of the team and will go to the leader for the final decision.

Strategies
(cont.)

- Outside the planning room, you put your leader title back on and will have the final say on the recommendation of the team. Should you, as the leader, decide to not accept a recommendation, you'll let them know why.

If you have a vision, goal, strategy, or other element that you know you want to have the team consider, be intentional about getting it on the table.

- In some cases, it will be more helpful to state your view up front and gain feedback. (See "My Story" later in this chapter.)

- In other cases, it will be more helpful to give the team a chance to develop their ideas first and to suggest your idea only if the group didn't come to it on its own.

How do you decide which approach is more appropriate?

- Generally, if your idea is focused on broad strategic direction (i.e., vision, mission, goals, and to some extent, objectives), consider putting them on the table first for reaction.

- If your idea is more narrow or focused on implementation (i.e., CSFs, barriers, strategies, or actions), it may be more appropriate to suggest your idea only if the group doesn't come up with it on their own.

Avoid being the first, second, or third person to respond.

- Many leaders find it difficult to sit back when a comment is made that is clearly off track or may take the discussion in what they believe is the wrong direction. As a result, they speak up and give their comments first, and predictably, the rest of the group typically follows the leader.

- When I facilitate strategy sessions, I make it a point before the first session to ask leaders specifically to not be the first, second, or third person to respond to comments. I ask them to allow their people to speak up first and to comment only after at least three others have given their views.

Strategies
(cont.)

Use open, rather than closed, language.

- When a person says, "It won't work," that response is what I call closed language. The words say you've already made up your mind. And unfortunately, if people have a different opinion, they'll have to disagree with the boss, which many are reluctant to do.

- A more open language statement would be, "I don't see how that would work and still make us money." The simple phrase, "I don't see how," implies that someone may be able to show you. The phrasing invites people to provide you with information.

- As a leader, you may very well find that using open language gives people permission to give you information that they might otherwise keep to themselves.

My Story: Sharing Ideas in My Own Organization

As the leader of my organization, I've had to use these same strategies myself. For example, in our 2007 strategic planning session, I knew that I wanted us to seek to double our size in three years. I prepared a presentation to the team of both why this was important and general bullets of what it might require from each department. I then asked the team to respond first by saying what they liked about what they heard, and then what concerned them about it and ideas for how to make it better.

I was surprised by what came out. Several team members felt the target was too modest and that we should be looking to triple our size in three years, not double. Others felt that to achieve the growth rate that I was suggesting meant we had to focus on getting our processes more standardized and effective. Others felt that we needed to focus more on just a few products, while others felt we needed to add more products.

What followed was a rich discussion that resulted in essentially full buy-in to the target and excitement around developing the plan to make the target a reality.

Ensure that the Plan Components Meet the Quality Checks

In the Drivers Model, each component is dependent upon the components that came before it. So, for example, if you do a poor job of defining your mission and vision, your goals and objectives will suffer. Likewise, if your goals and objectives are misaligned, your CSFs and barriers will also be off. And if your CSFs and barriers are inadequate, your strategies and action plans will fall short, too. Therefore, it's essential that you do a quality job at every step of the way through the planning process.

The Drivers Model is designed to help you do this. From vision and mission through strategies and action plans, the Drivers Model provides a specific quality check for each component of the strategic plan. These quality checks help ensure that your plan is comprehensive, robust, inspiring, and implementable. As the leader, it's your role to ensure that each component of the plan passes its quality check. On the second page of each chapter that follows, you'll find a quality checklist that will help you evaluate your team's work on that component of the plan. Below I have summarized one or two key elements from the quality checklist for each of the plans' components.

Management briefing	• Have the critical issues that the plan should address been identified? • Has a planning process for addressing the issues been accepted?
Briefing book review and SWOT	• Has the planning team reviewed the briefing book to identify key observations and potential strategies? • Does each strength, weakness, opportunity, and threat identify both the attribute and the impact?
Positioning statements	• Have positioning statements been created for the key external trends affecting future success? • Have each of the positioning statements been formatted to identify both the belief and the action taken by the belief, such as, "We believe… Therefore, we must…"?
Mission	• Does the mission statement broadly describe what you do, for whom you do it, and the benefit? • Does the mission statement indicate the industry or market that the organization serves?
Vision	• Does the vision represent the organization's preferred future? • Does the vision simply represent a logical extension of today or are out-of-the-box results represented?
Goals	• As a group, do the goals represent all key areas of strategic focus for the organization? • If the organization achieves these goals, and only these goals, will the organization most likely have fulfilled its mission?

Objectives
- Are the objectives SMART: specific, measurable, achievable, relevant, and time-bound?
- If all the objectives are achieved, and only these objectives, will the goal be accomplished for the time period?

Guiding principles
- Do the guiding principles identify all the key values for the organization?
- Are the principles worded in such a way as to indicate both the value and the expected behaviors (i.e., "We believe… Therefore, we will…")?

CSFs
- Have the most critical conditions that must be created and the major barriers affecting success been identified?
- Are the CSFs stated as nouns with conditions (e.g., "effective dealer network") and not as verbs (e.g., "develop")?

Barriers
- Are the barriers phrased in such a way as to encourage strategies for overcoming them?
- Do you have at least two and no more than seven barriers per goal?

Strategies
- Are the strategies phrased as activities to be accomplished and NOT results to be achieved?
- If the strategies are implemented, is it highly likely that the objectives will be achieved?

Action plans
- Have all the key deliverables been identified? If the deliverables are done, will the strategy be completed?
- Have all the important actions been identified? Is each action worded so that it's clear what needs to be accomplished? If all the actions are completed, will all the deliverables be created?

Follow Through and Hold People Accountable

If you've been involved in strategic planning processes, you know the game that occurs far too often: A lot of energy goes into a plan that just sits on the executive's shelf, only to be looked at when it's time to do strategic planning once again.

The Drivers Model strives to end this game. As you'll see in Chapter 14, you and your team will assemble a detailed process for aligning the organization and ensuring monthly check-ins, quarterly reviews, and an annual update to the strategic plan. This structured monitoring process is intended to help the plan move from paper to implementation.

A sample alignment and monitoring process follows:

One-time	The organization will identify and implement adjustments to your organization's structure, activities, roles, processes, systems, and rewards to drive achievement of the plan.
Monthly	Strategy leaders will update the status of action plans to ensure you are doing what you said you were going to do. The overall plan coordinator will distribute a performance report to all members of the planning team.
Quarterly	The planning team will meet to review the status of strategies and progress on objectives. The planning team will decide which current strategies to stop or continue and what new strategies to start. The planning team will adjust objectives as warranted, based on issues and priorities.
Annually	The planning team will meet to review progress for the year, identify new barriers and CSFs, change objectives, and reestablish priorities and action plans.
Rewards	Those teams that complete their deliverables by the end of the fiscal year will receive additional shares in the annual bonus pool.
Consequences	On a monthly basis, the team leaders of those teams not meeting their monthly activity target will roll the accountability die and be assigned the consequence indicated.

Chapter 14 provides additional information on alignment, monitoring, accountability, and potential rewards and consequences.

Decide Whether an Outside Facilitator Would Be Helpful

With an activity as critical as strategic planning, it's essential that the effort be facilitated by someone who is skilled in facilitation, but also has considerable experience guiding a team through strategy. Some organizations have internal resources with both the facilitation and the strategy expertise. But others choose to bring in professional facilitators with years of training, experience, and proven results.

When should you bring in an outside facilitator? It's your role as the leader to make this call. In our Special Topics chapter, I provide insights on this decision and recommend a process for choosing a facilitator if one is needed.

Is Your Team Ready to Plan?

Leaders must lead. Whether you lead a large corporation, a non-profit organization, a government agency, a department, a project, or a team, the leader is responsible for ensuring that the organization has a clear strategic direction and a plan for making that direction a reality.

Unfortunately, sometimes, leaders are ready for strategic planning, but their team isn't. What if *your* team isn't ready? What do you do? And perhaps more importantly, how do you know whether your team is ready to take on strategic planning?

Below is a list of questions that can help you determine if your team is ready to develop a strategic plan.

Questions to determine if your team is ready to plan

- Is there a widely held belief that the group needs a shared direction and agreed-upon priorities?
- Are the key issues to be addressed by the plan identified?
- Have the outcome and benefit of planning been clearly delineated?
- Have an approach and timeline for strategic planning been agreed to?
- Has the group agreed how this planning process needs to be different from past processes?
- Has the team determined who should be in the room when the plan is developed and how you'll gain buy-in from those not in the room?
- Are the people who need to be in the room willing to commit the time and resources required?
- Has the information that needs to be compiled in advance of planning been identified, including results from past planning efforts?

If your team isn't ready for planning, or if you're not sure whether they're ready, the first step, as you'll see in the next chapter, is the management briefing. I've found that the management briefing is a tremendous tool for preparing your team for planning. Specifically, the management briefing is designed to achieve the following objectives:

- Gain senior management's commitment to taking time to develop and execute the plan.

- Identify the critical issues to be addressed by the plan.

- Reach agreement on a clearly defined planning process that will address the issues.

- Develop a plan for gathering information about the current situation, including past plans, current initiatives, customer perceptions, employee opinions, industry trends, and the competitive landscape.

Chapter 3 gives you a roadmap for executing the management briefing and preparing your team for the strategy work ahead.

A Final Note

The seven activities described in this chapter provide an overview of your role in facilitating the Drivers Model process in your organization. Each chapter that follows includes a more detailed description of your role in that particular part of the plan.

You may be wondering if bringing in an outside facilitator impacts this role. Whether you serve as the facilitator for the strategy sessions or you bring in someone to take this role, you, as the leader, remain ultimately responsible for the activities described. However, as you'll see in the Special Topics section, if you use an outside facilitator, it's important that you and the facilitator are in agreement on how you'll execute these activities together.

Gaining Buy-in: The Management Briefing

3

- Overview
- How to Minimize Terminology Debates
- Gaining Buy-in to Plan
- Defining the Briefing Book Information
- Summary of the Benefits of the Management Briefing
- The Staff Briefing
- The Process
- The Quality Check
- Your Role in the Management Briefing

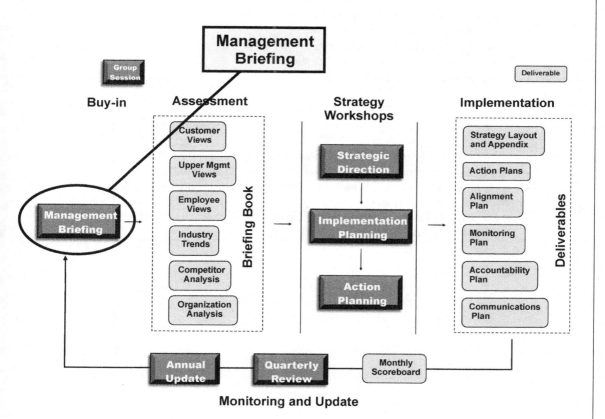

Summary: The Management Briefing

Definition	The management briefing is a meeting whose purpose is to identify critical issues, provide a briefing on the proposed planning approach (Drivers Model), and gain buy-in to proceed with and participate in planning.

Success Strategies

- Introduce the session.
- Use teams to identify key issues.
- Provide an overview of the Drivers Model and the deliverables.
- Link the critical issues to the Drivers Model.
- Identify what participants like about the process.
- Identify concerns with the process and possible strategies.
- Describe the briefing book and the assessment process.
- Build the briefing book action plan.
- Select the situation assessment team.
- Determine the logistics and the logistic team.
- Define immediate next steps.

Quality Check

- Have the critical issues that the plan should address been identified?
- Has a planning process for addressing the issues been accepted?
- Have potential problems with the planning process been identified and potential solutions been developed?
- Have all necessary steps to prepare for the plan been identified, and have responsibilities been assigned?

The Management Briefing

Overview

In my twenty years of facilitating planning processes, I've found that usually, many members of the planning team have little interest in going through a planning exercise. Why? Typically, because they believe they know exactly what's going to happen—the same thing that happened the last time, and the time before that.

Far too often, under the guise of "strategic planning," executive teams are put through what they see as an academic exercise that does little to address the real issues facing the organization. And then, after all the time and resources have been put into the planning exercise, a strategic planning book is created that sits on the shelf and isn't looked at again until the next academic exercise begins.

This less-than-enthusiastic response to planning has happened so often that I've come to expect it. Therefore, I believe it's essential to have processes in place that help you achieve high levels of buy-in right from the very beginning. This gets us to the next secret to facilitating strategy.

Secret #2	**Gain buy-in to planning by holding one or more management briefings.**
	Use the management briefing to have the planning team identify the most critical issues facing the organization. Then, show how the planning process will help the team address those issues.

You can think of the management briefing as your secret weapon for gaining buy-in. I believe it's the most important activity in the early stages of planning. A sample agenda for the management briefing follows:

Management Briefing Agenda

Purpose	To gain buy-in from the management team to execute the planning process.
Products	• Key issues facing the organization. • Planning approach. • Information needed for the briefing book. • Names for the planning team and situation assessment team. • Next steps.
Timing	90–120 minutes

Management Briefing Agenda *(cont.)*

Agenda	<ul><li>Getting started.</li><li>Identify the key issues to be addressed by planning.</li><li>Overview of the Drivers Model.</li><li>Modify the planning approach to ensure the approach addresses our issues.</li><li>Identify the information needed to plan effectively (the briefing book).</li><li>Define logistics and next steps (the who, when, and where of the planning retreat).</li></ul>

Note that it may be necessary to have more than one management briefing. It isn't unusual to first brief your direct reports and then hold a second briefing that includes your top reports plus the other members of the organization who will participate in the planning process.

How to Minimize Terminology Debates

Another common problem that can occur in planning processes is debates over planning terminology, such as these: "What is a goal? Shouldn't the vision be a short-term target that can be reached? What's the difference between strategies and tactics?" These debates are especially prevalent on management teams with members who have come from different organizations and have had planning experiences where they previously worked. How do you avoid these debates? This gets us to our next secret for facilitating strategy.

Secret #3 | **Avoid terminology debates by educating the team on the components of the Drivers Model.**

Avoid debates about terminology by using the Drivers Model and the strategy document during the management briefing to educate the participants on the plan's components.

During the briefing, you'll want to walk your team through the strategy document, while educating the team on items, such as the difference between mission and vision, goals and objectives, and strategies and action plans. You'll also make them aware of the importance of having objectives measure results and not activity, and the role of CSFs and barriers in focusing your strategies on the most important areas for success. By educating the management team on the Drivers Model and highlighting key points like the ones mentioned above, this demonstrates how all the pieces of the Drivers Model carefully fit together.

In my work on hundreds of planning initiatives, I very rarely encounter debates over terminology. People tend to readily adopt the Drivers Model terms and definitions once I've reviewed them. They often find the terminology simple to understand and easy to adopt. Sometimes, a team will change the terms to fit the terminology they've used in the past. For example, I had a team choose to use the term *performance indicators* for *objectives* and the term *initiatives* in place of *strategies*. Other teams have switched the meaning of goals and objectives by having objectives be the broad aims and goals serve as the measurable targets. But even in cases when the terms are changed, the planning members still want to use the Drivers Model definitions to apply to their terms. So, continuing the example, a *performance objective* would still be defined as a "specific, measurable target that defines fulfillment of the mission."

Gaining Buy-in to Plan

Describing the terminology of the Drivers Model will help avoid debates over terms, but that alone will not guarantee buy-in to the process. This next secret, however, will help considerably.

Secret #4	Increase buy-in to the Drivers Model by having the team link their issues to the process.

Recall that you start the management briefing by having your management team identify the critical issues affecting the organization. You then review the Drivers Model. At this point, you can now go back to the issues the management team has listed and ask team members to identify where in the Drivers Model their issues will be addressed. For example, some issues will be covered as goals, others as strategies, others as objectives or CSFs. Others will be handled through the monitoring process. I find that all or nearly all the issues are covered through the process. Having planning team members identify how their individual issues will be addressed helps solidify their buy-in and commitment to the planning process.

Defining the Briefing Book Information

After reviewing the planning process and gaining feedback from the team, you're ready to focus on the information that must be gathered in advance to make the planning process productive. The briefing book provides all planning team members with a common understanding of where the organization is today on a variety of fronts. The briefing book contains information on the following:

Briefing book contents

- Customer/stakeholder views.
- Employee views.
- Upper management views.
- Industry trends.
- Competitor analysis.
- Organization analysis (e.g., financial data, product analysis, market analysis, performance against prior plan).

Chapter 4 provides a more detailed description of the contents of the briefing book and the amount of time required to create it. During the management briefing, the planning team will define what information is already available and what information should be compiled in each of these areas. The planning team will also identify the members of the sub-team responsible for compiling the briefing book, distributing it prior to the first planning session, and presenting the results at the first planning session. Typically, the planning team will assign a different member of the team to present each of the briefing book's components.

Summary of the Benefits of the Management Briefing

To summarize, there are several benefits to doing a management briefing.

Benefits of a management briefing	Your team members will walk away with a common view of the issues to be addressed and will accomplish the following tasks.

- They'll have determined what modifications might be needed to the standard planning approach to ensure that their issues are fully addressed.

- They'll have agreed on a set of strategy definitions.

- They'll have begun identifying the information they need to gather to make the planning session highly productive.

- They'll have assigned responsibilities for ensuring that the key information is gathered and that the necessary steps are taken to prepare for the retreat.

- They typically will walk away with increased buy-in and commitment to the planning effort, and will follow through on actions.

The Staff Briefing

Once the decision is made to proceed with the planning process, you can hold a staff briefing to gain the staff's perspectives of the issues to be addressed, review the approach agreed to by the management team, identify the role the staff will play in the planning process, and let them know the next steps that will be taking place.

Secret #5   **Use a staff briefing to engage employees right from the beginning.**

During the staff briefing, be sure to highlight the various places in the process where staff involvement is critical, as shown below.

Staff involvement in the Drivers Model

- Staff briefing prior to the plan to identify issues and review the planning process.
- Employee survey to gain staff views on the current situation and future directions.
- Staff briefing following the draft of the plan to review it and offer comments.
- Staff involvement in action planning to outline the implementation of priority strategies.
- Quarterly reports during implementation to communicate progress.

The table that follows summarizes the agenda for the typical staff briefing.

Staff Briefing Agenda

Purpose	To provide an overview of the planning process and to highlight staff's role.
Products	Staff list of the issues facing the organization.
Timing	45–60 minutes.
Agenda	• Getting started. • Identify the key issues that planning will address. (Also, show additional issues identified by the management team.) • Review the planning approach (the Drivers Model). • Identify how the planning approach addresses staff issues. • Review how staff will be involved in the planning process. • Identify next steps.

The Process

I've summarized the nine steps of the management briefing process as follows:

Gaining Buy-in

1 Identify critical issues.

After opening the session, start the management briefing by asking the members of the planning team to identify the critical issues facing the organization.

2 Review Drivers Model.

Step the team through an interactive review of the Drivers Model in which you highlight the key components of the model, including mission, vision, goals, objectives, and strategies.

3 Link issues to the Drivers Model.

After the model review, have the planning team identify where in the planning process each of their issues will be addressed. This process of linking their issues to the Drivers Model helps ensure that the planning team understands the Drivers Model and can see how each of their issues will be addressed by it. The result typically is full buy-in to the process and anticipation that the plan will yield results.

4 Identify likes and concerns.

Have your team define what they like about the proposed process, any concerns they have about it, and possible strategies for addressing the concerns.

5 Identify information needs.

Discuss the information needed to provide a common information base that will define where the organization is today. This information will be compiled into a briefing book and distributed in advance of the planning meeting.

6 Build briefing book plan.

Build the plan for gathering the information needed for the briefing book and define the members of the sub-team responsible for implementing the plan.

7 Decide logistics.

Decide the logistics (e.g., location, date, and times) for the planning sessions and immediate next steps.

8 Define logistics team.

Define the members of the sub-team responsible for the logistics.

9 Define immediate next steps.

Define the steps to be taken following the meeting, who will do each step, and the deadline for completion.

The Quality Check

If you and your team have executed the management briefing well, you'll be able to answer yes to each of the following questions.

Quality check

- Have the critical issues that the plan should address been identified?

- Has a planning process for addressing the issues been accepted?

- Have potential problems with the planning process been identified and potential solutions been developed?

- Have all necessary steps to prepare for the plan been identified, and have responsibilities been assigned?

Your Role in the Management Briefing

The management briefing is the planning team's first major activity. Your attitude about planning and your reactions to the Drivers Model can greatly influence how others react. Consider the following:

**The role of
the leader**

- In starting the briefing, explain the reasons you believe a plan is important at this time.

- Consider in advance the issues that the plan must address. Add these issues to the list if no one else brings them up.

- State your confidence in the Drivers Model to help guide the planning process.

- Set the expectation that all team members are expected to be present at each of the planning sessions. Consider requiring your approval for anyone to be absent for any part of a session.

- Ensure that the quality check items are met.

- Chapter 4. Briefing Book Review and SWOT
- Chapter 5. Positioning Statements
- Chapter 6. Goals: Envisioning the Future
- Chapter 7. Mission
- Chapter 8. Vision
- Chapter 9. Objectives

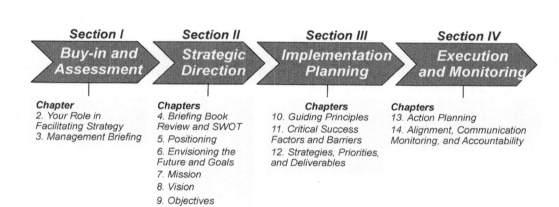

Briefing Book Review and SWOT

4

- Overview
- Briefing Book Review
- Defining the SWOT
- The Process
- The Quality Check
- Your Role in the Briefing Book Review and SWOT Analysis

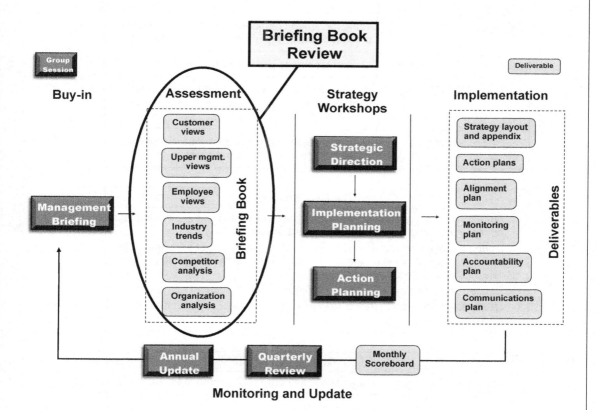

Summary: Briefing Book Review and SWOT

Definition	The briefing book documents an assessment of the current situation from multiple viewpoints. The team summarizes the assessment in a SWOT analysis that defines the organization's strengths, weaknesses, opportunities, and threats.
	Strength: Positive internal condition
	Weakness: Negative internal condition
	Opportunity: Positive external possibility
	Threat: Negative external possibility

Examples	Strength	Our experienced personnel allow us to recognize problems quickly and bring proven solutions to the table.
	Weakness	Limited resources prevent expansion into new markets.
	Opportunity	Solid performers in a related industry could provide joint venture partners to leverage our expertise into new markets.
	Threat	New competition from upstart divisions of large organizations could erode our client base.

Success Strategies

- For each section of the briefing book, assign a member of the planning team in advance to provide a four- to eight-minute summary.
- During the planning session, following each presentation of a briefing book section, have the planning team members work in small groups to identify key observations and potential strategies.
- Educate the planning team on the definition of each element of a SWOT.
- Use breakout groups to define strengths, weaknesses, opportunities, and threats.
- Perform a quality check.

Quality Check

- Does the briefing book contain all the key areas relevant to the plan, including customer views, employee views, upper management views, competitor analysis, industry trends, and organization analysis?
- Has the planning team reviewed the briefing book to identify key observations and potential strategies?
- Has the information from the review of the briefing book been summarized in a SWOT?

Overview

Prior to the first strategy session, members of your team will compile the briefing book that will be used extensively in the first session. The exhibit that follows gives the contents of a typical briefing book.

Customer views	Source: Surveys, focus groups, or interviews
	• What are we doing well?
	• What could we be doing better?
	• What needs do they have they we aren't fulfilling?
	• What future needs could we address?
Upper management views	Source: Interviews
	• What are we doing well?
	• What could we be doing better?
	• Where is the larger organization going?
	• How do we better align to this direction?
Employee views	Source: Surveys, focus groups
	• What are we doing well?
	• What could we be doing better?
	• How well are we satisfying customer needs?
	• How well are we satisfying employee needs?
	• How might we build a stronger internal organization?
	• What could we do to help you do your job better?
Industry trends	Source: Research, interviews
	• What's happening in our industry that we need to be aware of?
	• What are the shifting paradigms?
	• What are others finding successful that we need to consider?
Competitor analysis	Source: Research, interviews
	• How are our competitors performing?
	• What are our strengths and weaknesses against each major competitor?
	• What are competitors doing that we might want to consider?
	• What can we learn from their mistakes?

Organization analysis	Source: Document review
	• Organization structure, major functions, and activities.
	• Trends in revenue, budget, employees, and staff size.
	• Analysis of products, markets, and channels.
	• Performance against previous plan.

How long does it take to prepare the briefing book? It depends. Many large corporations will require up to two months to compile the information required. Smaller organizations and many non-profits will spend only a few days. Why the difference? Essentially, the source of the information and how much has been previously compiled distinguish the timeframes, as described in the table that follows:

Briefing Book	**The Two-Month Version**	**The One-Week Version**
Customers	Conduct customer survey and focus groups.	Compile existing customer satisfaction data.
Employees	Conduct employee survey.	Compile existing employee satisfaction data.
Upper management views	Conduct one-on-one interviews.	*No input.*
Industry trends	Compile industry briefs on key industry directions.	Document existing knowledge from management team.
Competitor information	Compile briefs on key competitors; identify strengths and weakness and likely directions.	Document existing knowledge from management team.
Organization analysis	Prepare trend data on key financial and operational indicators, document current organization structure and functions, provide analysis of each product and market.	Prepare trend data on key financial and operational indicators.

Typically, the more comprehensive a briefing book is, the better prepared the planning team will be to accurately assess the current situation; identify strengths, weaknesses, opportunities, and threats; and develop potential strategies for the future. At the same time, however, time or resources may not permit a comprehensive assessment. Therefore, I recommend using an approach that best meets your organization's needs and constraints.

The Strategy Sessions

After the briefing book is compiled and distributed, the planning team will come together for a series of facilitated sessions to develop the plan. The classic Drivers Model recommends holding four sessions.

Drivers Model four typical facilitated sessions	Session 1: The planning team answers two questions:

Drivers Model four typical facilitated sessions

Session 1: The planning team answers two questions:

- Where are we now?

- Where do we want to be?

Session 2: The planning team covers two additional questions:

- How will we get there?

- How will we monitor our progress?

Session 3: The planning team reviews the plan with staff and begins the development of action plans.

Session 4: The planning team reviews and approves the action plans, and kicks-off implementation.

As indicated in Chapter 1, for typical organizations, the first two sessions are two days each, and the third and fourth sessions are one day each. For smaller organizations, however, it isn't unusual for the first two sessions to each be done in a single day.

An agenda for the first session follows. This chapter focuses on the items in the box— the briefing book review and the analysis of strengths, weaknesses, opportunities, and threats (SWOT).

Agenda First Session

A. Getting Started
- Welcome
- Session objective and deliverable
- Pitfalls to avoid
- The proposed agenda
- Ground rules

B. Where Are We Now?
- Review the briefing book to document key observations and potential strategies
- Define the SWOT

C. Where Do We Want To Be?
- Visioning
- Goals
- Mission
- Objectives

D. Review and Close

Briefing Book Review

The purpose of the briefing book review is to provide every member of the planning team with a common understanding of where the organization is today and to identify key points that should be carried through the strategy process. This brings us to our next secret for facilitating strategy.

After the briefing book is compiled and distributed, the planning team will come together for a series of facilitated sessions to develop the plan. The classic Drivers Model recommends holding four sessions.

Secret #6 In reviewing the current situation, have planning team members identify key observations and potential strategies for addressing them. These potential strategies will serve as the bridge between the past and the future and will be considered during the strategy development process that occurs later in the Drivers Model.

For each section of the briefing book, you'll have a member of the planning team provide a five- to ten-minute summary of the information in the section. Following each summary presentation, the participants will work in small teams to identify key observations and potential strategies.

What Comes out of the Briefing Book Review?

Key Observations
Information from the briefing book that you would want all team members to keep in mind as the team undertakes planning.

Potential Strategies
Things the team might do, typically in response to a key observation.
Format: Verb–Object–Purpose

You should think of key observations as information that you want all team members to keep in mind, as you and they undertake planning. Potential strategies are the things your team might do, typically in response to a key observation. I call them "potential" strategies, because you won't determine if you'll do them until later in the planning process.

One other point about potential strategies: These should be formatted a particular way. A strategy has three components: a verb, object, and purpose. For example, a potential strategy might be, "Implement a vertical marketing strategy to increase revenue." The verb–object–purpose format starts with an action verb (implement) that states what is acted upon (vertical market strategy) and explains the purpose (to increase revenue).

Defining the SWOT

If you've been through a SWOT (strengths, weaknesses, opportunities, and threats) analysis before, you'll likely find that the Drivers Model approach is somewhat different from what is traditionally done. Let's look first at the traditional SWOT definitions.

The Traditional SWOT Definitions

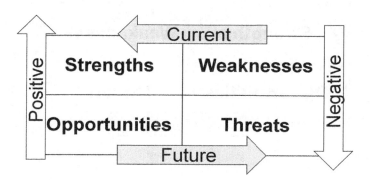

In the traditional SWOT, strengths and opportunities are positive, while weaknesses and threats are negative; and strengths and weakness are current, while opportunities and threats are future. Unfortunately, when the SWOT elements are defined in this way, this can result in a list of opportunities made up mostly of the advantages gained if we can overcome a weakness. And the threats are often just a list of consequences if we lose a strength, as shown below.

A Sample of a Traditional SWOT

Strengths	Weaknesses
• Experienced personnel • Loyal customer base • Strong legacy products	• Little focus on new products • Some locations have seen minimal growth in three years
Opportunities	**Threats**
• Creating new products to offer to our client base • Transforming poor performing locations	• Losing people to our competitors • Losing customers

The Drivers Model Approach to SWOT

What gets missed in the traditional approach is the internal versus external dimension. For a more robust SWOT, it's essential that the SWOT identify internal and external factors and their current or potential impacts.

Therefore, the Drivers Model recommends the following approach.

The Drivers Model SWOT Definitions

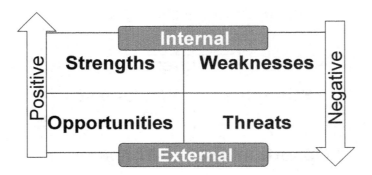

| **Key points in the Drivers Model SWOT definitions** | • Any statement about an *internal factor*, whether it's current or future, would be a strength if positive or a weakness if negative. |
| | • Any statement about an *external factor*, whether it's current or future, would be considered an opportunity if positive or a threat if negative. |

Attribute and Impact

There's another significant difference in the way the Drivers Model views a SWOT analysis. In the traditional example, strengths included experienced personnel, loyal customers, and strong legacy products. In the Drivers Model, these aren't strengths—they're just attributes of the organization.

The Drivers Model requires that a strength have both an attribute plus an impact. So, "experienced personnel" is just an attribute. To make it a strength, the wording might be, "Our experienced personnel allow us to recognize problems quickly and bring proven solutions to the table." Now that's a strength, because it has both the attribute—our experienced personnel— and also the impact—the ability to recognize problems quickly and bring proven solutions to the table. The attribute-plus-impact rule also applies to weaknesses, opportunities, and threats.

| **How attribute and impact changes the wording of strengths** | **Traditional SWOT**

Strengths

• Experienced personnel

• Loyal customer base

• Strong legacy products | **Drivers Model SWOT**

Strengths

• Our experienced personnel allow us to recognize problems quickly and bring proven solutions to the table.

• Our loyal customer base generates high levels of repeat business and referrals.

• Our strong legacy products provide a foundation for consistent revenues year after year. |

Why is defining both the attribute and the impact important? For clarity and focus. As an example, one person might say that our strength is experienced personnel, and believe that the impact is as shown above: They allow us to recognize problems quickly and bring proven solutions to the table. However, a different member of the team may believe that the impact of having experienced personnel is that it allows us to more easily recruit other staff members. Someone else may have a different view of what the impact is. If we're not clear on the impact, we may implement the wrong strategies to enhance our strengths or overcome our weaknesses. And the same goes for capitalizing on opportunities or reducing threats. This brings us to our next secret.

| Secret #7 | Your SWOT analysis should identify both the attribute and the impact of your strengths, weaknesses, opportunities, and threats to provide focus and clarity on how to maximize or minimize each. |

To help keep opportunities and threats focused externally, start each statement with the external condition and then give the impact on the organization. The exhibit that follows gives a full view of a SWOT defined, using the Drivers Model approach.

An Example of SWOT Using the Drivers Model Approach

Strengths	Weaknesses
• Our experienced personnel allow us to recognize problems quickly and bring proven solutions to the table. • Our loyal customer base generates high levels of repeat business and referrals. • Our strong legacy products provide a foundation of consistent revenues every year.	• A lack of focus on new products can threaten future earnings should legacy products decline. • Some locations have seen minimal growth in three years, making it more difficult to achieve our growth goals.
Opportunities	**Threats**
• The acceptance by the public of web-based purchases provides an opportunity for low cost/high margin sales. • Given the current economic conditions, we can position our legacy products as vehicles for combating the situation.	• The easy success of two new low-priced competitors into the marketplace may result in additional new entrants—putting even more price pressure on us.

How a SWOT Impacts the Plan

Is the SWOT just an intellectual exercise, or is the information used during other parts of the planning activity? As you can see in the diagram that follows, the SWOT does frequently come into play during the planning activity. Strengths and opportunities often become strategies. Weaknesses and threats often show up as barriers.

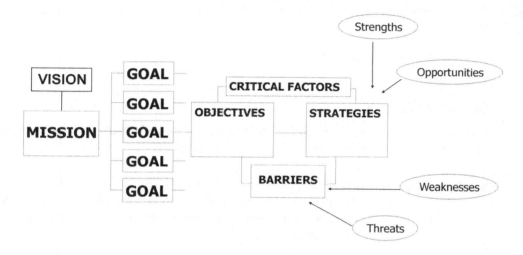

The Process

To review the briefing book and prepare the SWOT analysis, take the following steps:

1 Make presentation assignments.

For each section of the briefing book, assign a member of the planning team in advance to provide a four- to eight-minute summary. Having different people present can help increase buy-in and the sense of responsibility for the planning activity.

2 Identify key observations and potential strategies.

During the planning session, following each presentation of a briefing book section, have the planning team members work in small groups to identify key observations and potential strategies. The potential strategies will be considered later during strategy development. Potential strategies should be documented in a "verb–object–purpose" format.

3   Educate on SWOT. | Educate the planning team on the definition of each element of a SWOT.

4   Define SWOT. | Use breakout groups to define strengths, weaknesses, opportunities, and threats.

5   Perform quality check. | Perform a quality check.

The Quality Check

If you and your team have executed the briefing book review and SWOT development well, you'll be able to answer "Yes" to each of the following questions:

Quality check

- Does the briefing book contain all the key areas relevant to the plan, including customer views, employee views, upper management views, competitor analysis, industry trends, and organization analysis?

- Has the planning team reviewed the briefing book to identify key observations and potential strategies?

- Has the information from the review of the briefing book been summarized in a SWOT?

- Does the SWOT cover the most important items in each area?

- Does each strength, weakness, opportunity, and threat identify both the attribute and the impact?

Your Role in the Briefing Book Review and SWOT Analysis

During the briefing book review and SWOT analysis you'll want to be sure the team is focusing on the most critical elements. Consider the following:

The role of the leader

- Check-in to ensure that adequate time and resources are applied to collecting and assembling the briefing book information.

- Ensure that the briefing book is distributed a week before the first planning session to provide time for planning team members to review it and prepare comments.

- Ensure that the people assigned to each of the briefing book topics are prepared to present a four- to eight-minute summary of the section.

- During the session, make sure potential strategies are documented and meet the "verb–object–purpose" format.

- In advance of the session, consider the items you believe should be included as SWOT elements. Suggest these if not mentioned by others.

- Ensure that the session meets the quality check.

- Overview
- Competitive Positioning
- The Process
- The Quality Check
- Your Role in Positioning Statements

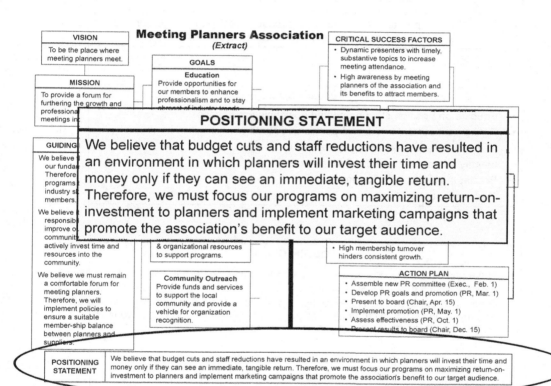

Meeting Planners Association
(Extract)

VISION
To be the place where meeting planners meet.

MISSION
To provide a forum for furthering the growth and professiona... meetings in...

GOALS

Education
Provide opportunities for our members to enhance professionalism and to stay abreast of industry trends.

CRITICAL SUCCESS FACTORS
- Dynamic presenters with timely, substantive topics to increase meeting attendance.
- High awareness by meeting planners of the association and its benefits to attract members.

GUIDING...
We believe ...
our fundai...
Therefore...
programs...
industry si...
members.

We believe ...
responsib...
improve o...
communit...
actively invest time and resources into the community.

We believe we must remain a comfortable forum for meeting planners. Therefore, we will implement policies to ensure a suitable member-ship balance between planners and suppliers.

& organizational resources to support programs.

Community Outreach
Provide funds and services to support the local community and provide a vehicle for organization recognition.

- High membership turnover hinders consistent growth.

ACTION PLAN
- Assemble new PR committee (Exec., Feb. 1)
- Develop PR goals and promotion (PR, Mar. 1)
- Present to board (Chair, Apr. 15)
- Implement promotion (PR, May. 1)
- Assess effectiveness (PR, Oct. 1)
- Present results to board (Chair, Dec. 15)

POSITIONING STATEMENT

We believe that budget cuts and staff reductions have resulted in an environment in which planners will invest their time and money only if they can see an immediate, tangible return. Therefore, we must focus our programs on maximizing return-on-investment to planners and implement marketing campaigns that promote the association's benefit to our target audience.

POSITIONING STATEMENT	We believe that budget cuts and staff reductions have resulted in an environment in which planners will invest their time and money only if they can see an immediate, tangible return. Therefore, we must focus our programs on maximizing return-on-investment to planners and implement marketing campaigns that promote the association's benefit to our target audience.

Summary: Positioning Statements

Definition	Positioning statements are broad determinations about the organization's direction and focus of the organization.

Example	• We believe increases in the quality of manufacturing in third-world countries will result in an acceleration in the downward pressure on retail prices for lighting products. Therefore, we must seek offshore opportunities for sourcing products, and in the longer term, establish our own international manufacturing capability.

Success Strategies

- Educate on position statements and positioning strategies.
- Define your current and future positioning strategy.
- Identify areas for positioning statements.
- Identify strategies to respond to the trends.
- Format the positioning statements.
- Perform a quality check.

Quality Check

- Have positioning statements been created for the key external trends that will have consequences for future success?
- Have each of the positioning statements been formatted to identify both the belief and the action taken by the belief, such as, "We believe... Therefore, we must..."?

Overview

Early in the development of the Drivers Model, a client requested that we perform an extensive survey of outside trends that might affect their business. During the session, as we reviewed the results, it was clear that the trends were so compelling that they should strongly guide, not just inform, the planning effort. In essence, I realized that the SWOT process was probably not going to be a strong enough tool given the way we traditionally use it.

In that session, we created for the first time strategic positioning statements, a method which I now use frequently in my planning work. These statements, which outline the overall future direction of the organization, are structured as follows:

Format of positioning statements	"We believe... (trend). Therefore, we must... (positioning)."

The "we believe" segment describes important trends that are occurring outside of the organization. The "therefore, we must" segment describes how the organization must position itself to respond effectively to the important trend. In some cases, the positioning statement will be one or more strategies. In other cases, the positioning statement will be a broad outcome that the organization must achieve.

Sample Positioning Statements

- We believe increased competition requires greater efficiencies and yields from marketing expenditures. Therefore, we must develop an integrated customer database across our multiple product lines to provide the foundation for quickly implementing campaigns targeted at each customer's specific needs.

- We believe that there will be a greater demand for accountability of resources. Therefore, we must invest in good information systems, clearly identify what we should be accountable for, and be able to clearly communicate the public health impact of resources used.

- We believe increases in the quality of manufacturing in third-world countries will result in an acceleration in the downward pressure on retail prices for lighting products. Therefore, we must seek offshore opportunities for sourcing products, and in the longer term, establish our own international manufacturing capability.

Positioning statements typically answer one or more of the following questions:

Questions answered by positioning statements	• How will we win?
	• How do we position ourselves for the future?
	• Given what is happening in the external environment, what must our response be for long-term, sustained success?

Over time, I've found positioning statements to be much more helpful than a SWOT analysis in getting a team to think through broad shifts in direction. Of course, you can use both SWOT analysis and positioning statements if time permits. However, if your organization faces significant change, for example, due to changes in the industry, competition, product performance, or market shifts, I would recommend the use of positioning statements, instead of SWOT analysis to provide stronger focus.

Competitive Positioning

In the course of developing plans, organizations often find themselves taking a step back to ask the question, "How can we differentiate ourselves from the competition?" The answer to this question often results in the development of positioning strategies.

In his book, *The Discipline of Market Leaders*, Michael Treacy defined three primary positioning strategies. He found that the best organizations in the world, while at least adequate at all three, typically distinguished themselves and built their success around one of the three areas. I've added a fourth positioning strategy (marketing dominance), based on my strategy development work.

Positioning Strategies

Operational excellence	Organizations that win through operational excellence do business consistently faster, cheaper, or more effectively than anyone else. They've fine-tuned the operation so well that the customer expects perfection every time. And usually, they deliver. Examples: Wal-Mart, FedEx, and McDonald's
Product leadership	What do Sony, 3M, and Lexus have in common? They seek to position themselves as product leaders. They strive to have consistently better products than anyone else. Sony, for example, was the first with the Walkman, the Watchman, and even betamax. (Well, you can't win them all—though beta continues to be the preferred technology in the professional video world.) But product leaders do tend to bring winning products to market first, over and over again. Examples: Sony, 3M, and Lexus
Customer intimacy	These organizations strive to win by knowing their customers better than anyone else and using that knowledge to competitive advantage. In a world replete with poor service, organizations stand out when they deliver consistently strong customer service. Examples: Ritz Carlton, Nordstrom, and Amazon.com
Marketing dominance	What about Coca-Cola, Nike, and Microsoft? They are representative of a fourth positioning strategy. Each of these organizations has competitors with better products and better operational efficiencies. Nor are these organizations known for particularly strong customer service. But what they do have is marketing dominance. They win by positioning their products in the hearts and minds of their customers, better than anyone else. Examples: Coca-Cola, Nike, and Microsoft

You can use the four positioning strategies to help your team understand how it's winning today, and how it will need to win in the future. This brings us to our next secret.

Secret #8 In defining your positioning statements, consider the four fundamental positioning strategies by defining where the organization is today and where it will need to be in the future.

The Process

The process for developing positioning statements includes the following steps:

1 Educate the team on position statements and positioning strategies.

After completing the briefing book review and SWOT, or just the briefing book if positioning statements are done instead of the SWOT, educate the planning team on positioning statements and positioning strategies.

2 Define your current and future positioning strategy.

Have the team identify which of the four fundamental positioning strategies represents the way the organization operates today, and which positioning strategy best characterizes how it will need to operate in the future.

3 Identify areas for positioning statements. strategy.

After defining the future positioning strategy, the next step is to identify the areas for developing positioning statements. Recall that positioning statements have two parts: the external trend ("We believe...") and the action that will be taken ("Therefore, we must..."). There are traditionally two approaches to writing positioning statements. The first approach is to base the areas for positioning statements on the most important external trends from the briefing book review and SWOT. The other approach is to identify first the key actions we know we need to take, and then identify what is happening in the external environment that mandates the action.

4 Identify strategies to respond to the trends.

With the key trends identified, the next step is to brainstorm strategies to address those trends. For positioning statements, the strategies need only use the "verb–object" format; there is no need to include "purpose" since this will be covered by the "We believe..." portion of the positioning statement.

5 Format the positioning statements.

With the trends and strategies identified, you can now create the positioning statements that combine the two. The trend will be used in the "We believe..." portion of the statement and the strategies will appear in the "Therefore, we will..." portion of the statement.

6 Perform a quality check.

The final step in the positioning statement process is to review each of the quality check items to ensure that all the checks are met.

The Quality Check

If you and your team have developed suitable positioning statements, you'll be able to answer "Yes" to each of the following questions:

Quality check
- Have positioning statements been created for the key external trends that will have consequences for future success?
- Has each of the positioning statements been formatted to identify both the belief and the action taken by the belief, such as, "We believe... Therefore. we must..."?

Your Role in Positioning Statements

Positioning statements can serve to frame the entire strategic plan by making clear the areas for strategic focus. As the leader of the team, your role in the positioning statement development process is to actively engage in the discussion without overpowering the group, while ensuring that the positioning statements address all key areas. Consider the following:

The role of the leader
- Ensure that the team fully understands that positioning statements should frame the plan by using examples.
- Don't allow the team to get sidetracked with debates on the current positioning strategy. However, strive for full agreement on the positioning strategy for the future.
- Make sure the most important trends are identified for constructing positioning statements.
- Ensure that the positioning statements meet the quality check.

- Why Goals First?
- Overview
- Sample Goal Statements
- The Process
- The Quality Check
- Your Role in Establishing Goals
- Extended List of Goal Statements

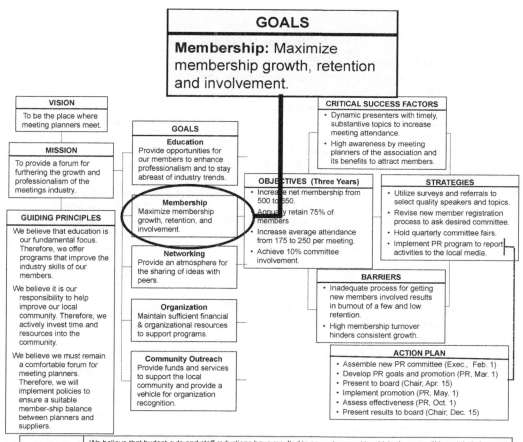

GOALS

Membership: Maximize membership growth, retention and involvement.

VISION
To be the place where meeting planners meet.

MISSION
To provide a forum for furthering the growth and professionalism of the meetings industry.

GUIDING PRINCIPLES
We believe that education is our fundamental focus. Therefore, we offer programs that improve the industry skills of our members.

We believe it is our responsibility to help improve our local community. Therefore, we actively invest time and resources into the community.

We believe we must remain a comfortable forum for meeting planners. Therefore, we will implement policies to ensure a suitable member-ship balance between planners and suppliers.

GOALS

Education
Provide opportunities for our members to enhance professionalism and to stay abreast of industry trends.

Membership
Maximize membership growth, retention, and involvement.

Networking
Provide an atmosphere for the sharing of ideas with peers.

Organization
Maintain sufficient financial & organizational resources to support programs.

Community Outreach
Provide funds and services to support the local community and provide a vehicle for organization recognition.

CRITICAL SUCCESS FACTORS
- Dynamic presenters with timely, substantive topics to increase meeting attendance.
- High awareness by meeting planners of the association and its benefits to attract members.

OBJECTIVES (Three Years)
- Increase net membership from 500 to 550.
- Annually retain 75% of members
- Increase average attendance from 175 to 250 per meeting.
- Achieve 10% committee involvement.

STRATEGIES
- Utilize surveys and referrals to select quality speakers and topics.
- Revise new member registration process to ask desired committee.
- Hold quarterly committee fairs.
- Implement PR program to report activities to the local media.

BARRIERS
- Inadequate process for getting new members involved results in burnout of a few and low retention.
- High membership turnover hinders consistent growth.

ACTION PLAN
- Assemble new PR committee (Exec., Feb. 1)
- Develop PR goals and promotion (PR, Mar. 1)
- Present to board (Chair, Apr. 15)
- Implement promotion (PR, May. 1)
- Assess effectiveness (PR, Oct. 1)
- Present results to board (Chair, Dec. 15)

POSITIONING STATEMENT
We believe that budget cuts and staff reductions have resulted in an environment in which planners will invest their time and money only if they can see an immediate, tangible return. Therefore, we must focus our programs on maximizing return-on-investment to planners and implement marketing campaigns that promote the association's benefit to our target audience.

Summary: Goals

Definition	Goals are broad, long-term aims that define fulfillment of the mission.

Examples	Growth:	Maximize growth in revenues and profitability.
	Programs:	Provide caring, cost-effective programs that produce life-changing results.
	Advocacy:	Advocate and mobilize on behalf of children.
	Brand:	Maximize awareness of our brand to drive business results.
	Culture:	Provide a supportive and professional environment that attracts and retains associates, aligned with our mission and guiding principles.

Success Strategies

- Use a visioning exercise to let participants visualize success at least ten years out.
- Work in teams; have people describe their vision and list common visioning elements.
- Review each small group's visioning items.
- Identify common or critical themes (not quantities or timeframes) among the groups.
- Word the common themes generically enough to ensure that the points within each group's visioning results are included in one or more of the common critical themes.
- Review the themes to decide if combining or splitting is appropriate to represent the organization's goals. (Generally, the fewer the number of goals, the better.)
- Once the goals are agreed upon, provide definitions to each one by asking, "What words describe our intention with this goal?" Use the vision elements from the visioning exercise as a guide.
- Perform a quality check on the goals.

Quality Check

- As a group, do the goals represent every one of the organization's key strategic focus areas?
- Are there at least three goals, but no more than eight?
- For each goal, has the team provided a brief description that adequately explains the goal's overall aim?
- Are the goal descriptions global in scope and start with "infinite" verbs?
- Do the descriptions exclude references to specific quantities or timeframes and avoid describing how the goal will be accomplished?
- If the organization achieves these goals, and only these goals, will the organization most likely have fulfilled its mission?

Why Goals First?

One of the things that often surprises people about the Drivers Model is the order in which the strategy components are developed. Most strategy processes create vision and mission statements before developing goal statements. And in fact, when you look at the Drivers Model strategy document, the order of these three elements on the page (vision, mission, and goals) would support the traditional approach.

However, as you'll see, the Drivers Model process will help your team envision the future ten years out. From this visioning exercise, the team will gain the components that could be used to create vision and mission statements. However, rather than do this, the Drivers Model will have your team use this information to discover goals that do an even better job of informing mission and vision writing. As experts in facilitation, we've found that teams are much more productive, are able to create stronger mission and vision statements, and achieve much higher levels of consensus much faster, using this envisioning approach and order for defining goals, mission, and vision.

If you're used to the traditional approach (mission and vision first, followed by goals), I just ask that you keep an open mind through these next three chapters, as you see how the Drivers Model takes your team through goal, mission, and vision development.

Overview

How do you help your team define the goals for the organization? You could bring the team together and discuss it. But our experience has been that much time can be wasted debating whether something should be a goal or not. Of course, you could just dictate what the goals will be. However, you're not likely to gain the buy-in you need for successful implementation—and worse, you might not discover this lack until implementation is failing.

The Drivers Model is designed to avoid both issues of wasted time and the potential lack of buy-in. The Drivers Model provides a tool for helping your team "discover" their goals through a process of envisioning the future, as described in this next secret.

> **Secret #9** | **Use a visualization exercise to help the team identify future success.**

To help your team determine your organization's goals, use a visualization exercise that guides the members through a scenario ten or more years into the future. The scenario should paint a picture in which the organization is achieving tremendous success. The visualization should help participants see what was accomplished, how it was accomplished, and how customers, employees, competitors, and any other significant stakeholders view the organization.

What follows is a sample of a visioning exercise, using the meeting planners association.

Sample Visioning Exercise: Meeting Planners

The setup	*I would like for you to imagine yourself sitting at your desk back at your office. On your desk is one of those calendars that turns one page per day. And it is showing today's date, May 21. As you're looking down at the calendar, by itself it flips to the next day, May 22. Then it turns again, and again. And then, it starts turning faster. You see June and July fly by. You see September and October. It's now in to the next year, and then it begins turning very fast, as it goes to the next year, and then the next, and then the next, and on and on, until it suddenly stops. As you look down, you see that the calendar shows May 21, 20XX, ten years from today.*
The presentation	*Imagine that you look up from your desk and you find you aren't at your desk at all. You're in the back of a large auditorium and there are rows and rows of people seated. Way up front, there's someone speaking who is announcing an award. As you listen, you realize that the person speaking is the President of the International Association of Meeting Planners and the award is the Chapter of the Year, which goes to that chapter whose outstanding performance and value to its members best exemplifies a level to which every chapter should strive. The president says, "At no time in the history of this award have the members of the seven-judge panel been in unanimous agreement of the organization most deserving of this award, until now. This year, I'm proud to announce that the award goes to the chapter based in _____." There's a standing ovation, as people get out of their chairs to applaud. You hear one person yell, "Fantastic choice." Another says, "It's about time." The applause goes on for several seconds. When the applause finally dies down, the president says with a grin, "I guess you all like the judge's selection. Let me give you a list of the accomplishments this organization has achieved over the past several years." The president begins listing the accomplishments that made this chapter so deserving." Listen to what the president is saying (four-second pause). Fill in the blank. What was it that the organization accomplished? Feel free to open your eyes to record, or keep your eyes closed as I continue.*

What members say

On screens to the right and left of the stage, a video comes on. You see a group of people sitting in a circle, with one person, apparently a facilitator, asking questions. As you listen, you realize this is a focus group made up of sixteen of the chapter's members. One member begins speaking, "The thing that's great about the chapter is…" (Pause.) Fill in the blank. What did that customer say was great about the chapter? Another jumps in, "That's all fine and wonderful, but the thing that really makes this organization stand out is…" (Pause.) What did that person say? Then, another says, "I've been a member for about twenty-five years. And sure, they were doing some good things before. But in the last ten years, the chapter has really gotten it right. They started focusing on the three things that really mattered. What could be more important than…" Fill in the blank. What were the three things that really mattered? (Pause.)

The video fades out and the president begins to speak again. "I'd like to ask the head of the chapter to come to the stage please. Would you give a warm welcome for_____!" Once more, there's a standing ovation, as the head of the award-winning chapter comes to the stage.

What we did

In accepting the award, the head of the chapter explains, "I hadn't seen the video before, but that twenty-five-year member got it right. As it turns out, it was exactly ten years ago today that a group came together to develop a plan that described where we wanted to be and how we were going to get there. I can honestly say that this first step was critical to getting us all on the same page and focusing on the same things."

Standing in the back of the room, you begin to smile because you were at that planning meeting ten years ago. You were a member of the team that got the ball rolling that resulted in this award.

The head of the chapter continues, "Let me tell you just a little bit about what we did. In that first year, though there were a lot of issues, we had to start with first things first. So, the first thing we did was…" Listen to what the head of the chapter is saying. What was done that first year? (Pause.) "Once we got that in place, the next thing we had to do was…" Listen again. What was that second thing? (Pause.) "But I would say, the most important

What we did (cont.)	*thing came in year three. This one thing is what really accelerated us and has resulted in the levels of achievement you see. In year three, we…" (Pause.) Listen to what the head of the chapter says. What was it that the organization did? (Pause.)* *"So, in closing," the head of the chapter says, "on behalf of the members, employees, and board of our chapter, I thank you for awarding us with this great honor." Once more, there's a standing ovation, as the head of the chapter leaves the podium and the meeting ends.*
What employees say	*As you're leaving the gathering, you overhear a group of employees from that chapter talking. They're saying that they didn't believe the organization would actually change, but that it did. They begin discussing what it feels like to work there, how these changes have improved their lives. Listen to what they're saying. How does it feel to work there? (Pause.)*
The close	*As you go back to your desk, you sit down and want to record some of the things you heard. Whenever you're ready, open your eyes if you haven't already and take a minute or two to write down several sentences about what you heard. What was it that the presenter said? Why did the chapter deserve the award? What results were achieved? What did the customers say? What was it that the head of the chapter said was done to bring about these changes? What did the employees say about working there?*

The visualization exercise should guide the participants through a scenario ten or more years into the future that allows them to visualize the organization achieving tremendous success. I want to highlight several strategies that help make the visualization exercise work.

Strategies for Designing the Visualization Exercise

Determine what the award will be and who will give it.

- During the scenario, you'll have the participants imagine a scenario in which the organization is receiving an award ten years from now for outstanding achievement. Carefully consider what the award is and who should be giving the organization the award.

- For example, for a manufacturer of automobiles, the award might be given by the American Automobile Association for the Manufacturer of the Year.

- For a government agency, it might be the President's Award, given to that agency that provides the highest level of service, effectiveness, and efficiency.

- For a non-profit organization serving a state, the award might be given by the governor to the non-profit that best exemplifies what every non-profit should be.

- For an association, the award might be given by the American Society of Association Executives for the Association of the Year.

Use blanks and pauses to have participants create their own stories.

- As you describe the scenario, you'll want to create images of success, without specifically citing what the success was.

- You do this by leaving "blanks" in your scenario and then pausing for three or four seconds each time to allow the participants to fill in the blank in their minds.

Avoiding gender-specific wording.

- Since the visualization is ten years out, you should make no assumptions about the gender of the person giving the award or the person receiving it. Accordingly, avoid using male or female personal pronouns (e.g., he, she, his, and her).

Cover key areas.

Be sure to cover key areas for success in the scenario, as well as what was done and what was achieved. To ensure that you help participants examine success from a number of perspectives, consider providing the following images in your scenario:

- Customers talking about the organization.
- Employees talking about the organization.
- Competitors talking about the organization.
- Key results achieved by the organization.
- Actions taken to achieve the results (e.g., things done first, the most important thing done).

From Visualization to Goals

The visualization exercise encourages the team to visualize success ten years out. When people discuss their visions and work in teams to identify common themes or "vision elements," I find that the individual vision elements can be grouped into large categories that become the "broad aims that define success," which essentially is the definition of goals. So, by visualizing ten years out, the team is able to discover their goal areas. The example below shows individual vision elements and the categories (goal areas) that resulted.

Sample Categories and Vision Elements

Education	Networking
• Members highly satisfied with the numbers and types of education programs provided. • 90 percent of people who complete our CMP prep pass the CMP exam.	• Networking events highly attended. • Networking touted as the most important service association provides.
Professionalism	**Membership**
• Over 300 certified meeting planners (CMP) in the chapter. • In ads, employers indicate they required a CMP.	• Over 2,500 members. • Membership viewed as so valuable that 95 percent or more renew every year. • Record attendance at every meeting.
Financial	**Committees**
• Had the financial resources to support programs. • Doubled the budget.	• Over half the membership actively involved in committees.
Staff	**Community**
• Increased staff size to provide even greater variety and depth of programs. • Staff pay rates commensurate with industry.	• Mayor recognizes organization as providing a great community service. • Over 25 percent of the restaurant and hotel members daily donate un-served meals to the food bank through our "Share What You Can" program.

While the sample above shows eight categories, typically, I ask teams to review the categories to see if overlap exists, and if one or more categories can be combined with another. This particular team took their eight categories and reduced them to five goals, as follows:

Sample of Decision to Reduce the Number of Goals

Original List	Decision	Final Goal List
1. Education	Keep, Add 3	A. Education
2. Networking	Keep	B. Networking
3. Professionalism	Move to 1	C. Membership
4. Membership	Keep, Add 7	D. Organization
5. Financial	Keep	E. Community
6. Staff	Keep	
7. Committees	Move to 4	
8. Community	Keep	

You would then have your team create words for each of the goal areas, using the individual vision elements as a guide. To help you focus on broad aims and not activity, use "infinite" verbs that imply "never-ending" such as "provide, promote, maximize, and maintain" when writing goals. Strategy verbs such as "establish, develop, implement, and revise" focus on activity and imply a finite action. Once the finite action is completed, the strategy is done. Goal verbs, on the other hand, imply that the aim is never-ending.

Sample goal verbs (infinite verbs)	Sample strategy verbs (finite verbs)
Provide	Establish
Promote	Develop
Maximize	Implement
Maintain	Build
Foster	Create

What follow are the resulting goal statements for the five goals from the meeting planners example:

Sample Goal Statements

A. Education	Provide opportunities for our members to enhance professionalism and to stay abreast of industry trends.
B. Networking	Provide an atmosphere for the sharing of ideas with peers.
C. Membership	Maximize membership growth, retention, and involvement.
D. Organization	Maintain sufficient financial and organizational resources to support programs.
E. Community	Provide funds and services to support the local community and provide a vehicle for organization recognition.

How you word goals is important. Accurate wording ensures accurate development of the measurable objectives that will follow. However, it often isn't helpful for a group to spend significant time "wordsmithing" the actual words to use for the goal statements. Therefore, we recommend a process of having breakout groups develop the initial words. We then reconvene and give the entire group a limited time (e.g., maximum of twelve minutes per goal) to modify or clean up the language. This leads to our next secret.

Secret #10 Use the informed majority process to efficiently manage wordsmithing.

I've found that groups vary widely in their tolerance for spending time getting the words exactly right. Generally, executive groups have significantly less patience with "wasting time on words," while engineers and scientists tend to want to spend significantly more time on "making sure we say what we mean." Most often, however, the groups I work with include both those who want to spend a lot of time and those who want to spend no time on these activities. Since they all agree that much time can be wasted getting the exact words correct, I typically introduce a ground rule at the beginning of the session to gain agreement from the team that 85 percent completion is acceptable for a draft. I then use a process I call "informed majority" to keep everyone in the group moving together.

The informed majority process works well for efficiently addressing wording suggestions. Throughout this book, I'll suggest using the informed majority process, so let's take the time now to describe in detail how it works. What follows is a description of the informed majority process.

The Informed Majority Process

Introduce ground rule

During the session opening, I introduce the ground rule "100 percent coverage—85 percent complete." This ground rule means that the team will cover 100 percent of the agenda. However, on any one agenda item, for example with goal statements, we'll declare victory once we are 85 percent complete. This is because with the 85 percent, we'll have agreement on the concepts. The last 15 percent is typically just wordsmithing in which we're trying to get the words exactly right. That last 15 percent is best done by a smaller group outside the room—not by a large group that can spend ten or fifteen minutes debating whether the right word is "a" or "the."

Get all changes	Once the team gets a first draft of a statement, I ask for any recommended changes. The objective is to get all the changes first. I record each requested change in a pen color different from the original to highlight the change.
Speak for change	Regarding word changes, I ask the group to agree that we want to use a process that helps us avoid spending a lot of time debating them. To manage the discussion, I'll ask someone who wants the change to speak for it, justifying why the change should be made. If no one speaks for it, the change is dropped because clearly no one supports it.
Speak for no change	If someone does speak for the change, I ask someone to speak for leaving the wording as-is. If no one speaks for leaving the wording as-is, then the change is made by acclamation.
If several alternatives	If a statement has several alternatives, I'll ask someone to speak for each alternative and for someone to speak for leaving the wording as-is. As before, if no one speaks for an alternative, the alternative is dropped.
Additional comments	If someone speaks for leaving the wording as-is, I then ask for additional comments.
Call for vote	Once all comments have been made, I call for a vote and go with the majority. The point of voting on wording changes is to go with the will of the group and to avoid significant time spent on wordsmithing.
Run-off (if needed)	If there are multiple alternatives and no alternative receives a majority of votes, then all but the top two alternatives are dropped and a re-vote is done.
Consensus check	Once all decisions are made about the wording, I rewrite the statement and seek majority confirmation that we have at least reached the 85 percent completion mark before moving on.

Sample Goal Statements

Below are sample goals for a corporation, government agency, non-profit organization, and a member association. A more robust list of sample goals for each of these organization types appears at the end of this chapter. Remember, with the Drivers Model, goals are broad aims; goals are NOT specific measures. The objectives, covered in Chapter 9, provide the specific measures of success.

Goals of a Sample Corporation

Growth	Optimize growth while meeting profitability targets.
Customer service	Deliver an outstanding customer experience.
Products	Provide products and services that meet client needs and achieve our expectations.
Quality	Maximize quality and internal efficiency in all areas.
Culture	Attract, develop, and retain highly engaged and competent team players.

Goals of a Sample Government Agency

Impact	Promote activities to reduce HIV-related deaths and enhance survivorship.
Research and translation	Conduct, support, and translate high-quality research that answers critical prevention and policy questions.
Health communications	Provide high-quality health information to consumers, providers, and policy makers to help ensure well-informed decisions.
Health monitoring	Ensure critical surveillance measures are collected, analyzed, and disseminated.
Workforce	Maintain an environment that fosters professionalism and growth.

Goals of a Sample Non-Profit Organization

Advocacy	Advocate on behalf of children, and educate and mobilize others to do likewise.
Awareness	Be recognized as the statewide leader in affecting positive change for children.
Programs	Provide caring, cost-effective programs that produce life-enhancing results.
Finance	Maintain the financial resources needed to achieve the mission.
Organization	Attract and retain high-quality board members, staff, and volunteers.

Goals of a Sample Association

Brand	Be recognized as the premier membership association for our industry.
Professional development	Provide opportunity to our customers for the development of professional and leadership skills.
Programs	Understand, meet, and exceed our customers' expectations.
Community involvement	Improve our community by contributing our individual and collective expertise, skills, products, and services to not-for-profit and public organizations.
Membership management	Grow a diverse and involved membership.
Finance and operations	Provide continually evolving administrative services to ensure financial stability and streamlined communications.

The Process

The process for developing goals includes the following steps:

1 Execute the visualization exercise.

After your team reviews the briefing book and has performed a SWOT analysis to summarize where you are today, you're ready to begin answering the question, "Where do we want to be?" In the Drivers Model, the key vehicle for shifting from where we are to where we want to be is to build a scenario in which the planning team members visualize what success looks like. Be sure the visualization exercise includes the following:

- Customers talking about the organization.
- Employees talking about the organization.
- Competitors talking about the organization.
- Key results achieved by the organization.
- Actions taken to achieve the results (e.g., things done first, the most important thing done).

2 Use breakouts to gather the vision elements.

When participants identify success ten years out, they identify many different individual vision elements. After the visualization exercise, use breakout groups to have people describe their individual visions. Have a team leader create on Post-Its a consolidated set of common elements and ideas that appeared in their group members' visions.

3 Group the vision elements.

Following the breakout exercise, have the entire group review the vision elements from each team and place the Post-Its into logical categories.

4 Confirm the goals by combining or splitting as appropriate.

I've found that an organization typically has between three and eight distinct goals. However, the grouping exercise may result in more than eight goals or may identify goals that have considerable overlap in the ideas represented by each. If this is the case, have the team adjust the goal categories as needed to eliminate overlap and reduce the number of goals.

5 Develop the wording for the goal statements.

Once the goal categories are identified, the next step is to define descriptions for each goal area. You'll have the team use the individual Post-Its in each goal category to help define the intent that the group has with the goal.

6 Perform the quality check.

The final step in the goal development process is to review each of the quality check items to ensure the goal statements are up to par.

The Quality Check

If you and your team have done a great job of developing goals, you'll be able to answer "Yes" to each of the following questions:

Quality check

- As a group, do the goals represent each of the organization's key areas of strategic focus?

- Are there at least three goals, but no more than eight?

- For each goal, has the team provided a brief description that adequately explains the goal's overall aim?

- Are the goal descriptions global in scope, and do they start with "infinite" verbs?

- Do the descriptions exclude references to specific quantities or timeframes and avoid describing how the goal will be accomplished?

- If the organization achieves these goals, and only these goals, will the organization most likely have fulfilled its mission?

Your Role in Establishing Goals

As with the foundation of a house, the goals establish the foundation for the rest of the plan. As the leader, your role is to ensure that the foundation is solid.

The role of the leader

- The visioning exercise is a powerful tool for helping your team members discover their goals. Plan and execute it carefully, using the guidelines described earlier.

- As indicated in the quality check, you must ensure that the goals represent all the key areas of strategic focus for your organization. To ensure that this is the case, the last quality check question is the key: "If the organization achieves these goals, and only these goals, will the organization most likely have fulfilled its mission?" If the answer is "No," something is missing.

**The role of
the leader**

(cont.)

- Much time can be wasted in adjusting the wording of a goal. Be sure to separate content discussions from wording discussions. Content discussions sound similar to, "Should we also include something about..." Wording discussions frequently sound like, "The better word for that is..." Discussions about word adjustments typically aren't a valuable use of the whole group's time. Therefore, consider recording these suggestions and moving on, and have a smaller group address wording outside the session.

- Ensure that all the quality checks, including the two mentioned earlier, are met.

Extended List of Goal Statements

What follows are goal areas that frequently result from the strategic plans I facilitate for corporations, government, non-profits, and associations. You'll see that the goal areas often go by different names as shown. For example, "brand" is sometimes call brand awareness, reputation, or visibility. You'll also see multiple versions of goal statements for each goal area; the variety is meant to offer your team a few examples of how you might describe your goals. Keep in mind that the vision elements resulting from your visioning exercise likely will be the best indication of what was intended by each goal area.

Sample Corporate Goal Statements

Brand Brand awareness Reputation Visibility	Be recognized as the dominant national home furnishings retailer that makes good design accessible.
	Maximize the awareness of our brand to drive business growth.
	Maximize brand awareness and brand value.
	Promote the highest community reputation through excellent and ethical representation of our clients.
	Enhance our visibility and reputation in the community as an expert in the field of public health.

Community	Give back to our community, customers, and industry.
Community involvement	Contribute to the community through the efforts of the company and by promoting an atmosphere that encourages employee involvement.
Culture	Provide an environment of integrity and mutual respect that enables opportunities for personal growth.
Environment	
Human capital	Attract, develop, and retain a highly motivated and competent team.
People	
Work environment	Foster an entrepreneurial environment where people are unified around a common vision and empowered to drive results.
	Foster a dynamic culture that enables our employees to maximize their potential.
	Promote an atmosphere of service, safety, and integrity.
Customer	Provide solutions and an experience that exceed client expectations.
Client experience	
Customer experience	Maximize customer satisfaction and be incredibly easy to do business with.
Customer relations	
Customer service	Maximize customer satisfaction and loyalty.
	Develop and maintain long-term, mutually beneficial client relationships.
	Deliver an outstanding customer experience.
Growth	Grow revenue, profits, and market share to maximize stakeholder value.
Growth and profitability	
	Maximize profitable growth for our stakeholders.
	Achieve global leadership in targeted markets.
	Achieve continuous growth as a leader in the markets we serve.
	Optimize growth, while meeting profitability targets.
Operational Excellence	Continually improve the effectiveness and efficiency of our operations to exceed the needs of our clients.
Operational efficiency	
Operations	Maximize operational excellence in all critical functions through continuous improvement.

Quality	Maximize front-to-back supply chain efficiency and effectiveness in all areas of the operation.
	Maintain an efficient and effective infrastructure with adequate resources and up-to-date technology and training.
	Maximize quality and internal efficiency in all areas.
Products Products and services Services	Provide high-quality, innovative products and services that fulfill client needs and achieve measurable results.
	Deliver products that are so valued that our customers are compelled to use them exclusively.
	Provide exclusive, globally-sourced products that create personal solutions for our customers' homes.
	Lead our industries in the research and timely development of innovative wireless technology.
	Excel in providing professional consulting services and quality engineering design that provide value to our market partners.

Sample Government Goal Statements

Culture Environment Human capital Infrastructure Workforce	Provide a safe and healthy environment that fosters retention, professionalism, and growth.
	Maintain a positive work environment that is mission-focused, scientifically engaging, and productive.
	Foster a healthy, productive work environment that contributes to achievement of our mission.
Impact Outcomes	Enhance the ability of others to identify and address reproductive and infant health issues.
	Provide environmental information products and services that enable customers to take action.
	Improve diabetes preventive care and practices to reduce risk factors for diabetes complications.
	Promote activities to reduce HIV-related deaths and enhance survivorship.

Information Communication	Provide high-quality health information to consumers, providers, and policy makers to ensure well-informed decisions.
	Provide customers with information, so they can make better decisions to exercise more control over their environment.
Leadership	Be the world leader in providing environmental information.
	Provide transformational leadership in achieving diabetes public health impact.
	Provide global leadership to optimize reproductive and infant health.
	Cultivate our reputation as the center of excellence for analytical services and information products.
Operations Internal operations Operational excellence Public health practice Systems	Maximize our effectiveness in providing timely and relevant information and services.
	Maximize our capabilities to achieve our mission.
	Build and sustain capacity of systems and organizations to improve older adult health through evidence-based strategies.
Partners Collaboration Integration and partnerships Strategic partners	Engage in strategic partnerships that help us achieve our mission.
	Promote integrated solutions to ecosystems protection through multidisciplinary research and effective partnerships.
	Develop and strengthen partnerships to address injury and violence prevention and control.
Programs Products/outcomes Public health impact	Provide world-class information products and services to inform environmental decisions.
	Develop and establish effective public health approaches for prevention.
	Provide opportunities for housing self-sufficiency and personal growth, with exceptional customer service.
Research	Conduct, support, and translate high-quality research that answers critical prevention and policy questions.
	Define, conduct, and promote public health research in reproductive and infant health.
Resource Organization Stability and profitability	Maximize resources for organizational growth and development.
	Maintain a self-sustaining, financially sound organization.
	Ensure sufficient organizational and financial resources to support a comprehensive program in older adult health.

Strategic Direction Setting

Science	Conduct and promote high-quality science.
Scientific leadership	Grow the science base and its use for injury and violence prevention and control.
	Provide scientific leadership in developing solutions to ecosystem protection.
Surveillance	Provide and promote the use of high-quality data to monitor the cancer burden and guide cancer control planning and policy.
Assessment and surveillance	Facilitate the collection and use of complete, timely, high-quality surveillance data at the national, state, and local levels.
Health monitoring	Monitor changes in CVD risk factors, outcomes, and policy and environmental indicators.
Translation	Translate science and technology into strategies and interventions that promote reproductive and infant health.
Translation and communication	Translate prevention science into strategies and practices.

Sample Non-profit Goal Statements

Advocacy	Advocate on behalf of children and educate and mobilize others to do likewise.
	Promote through education and advocacy public policies that support the legal needs of low-income individuals and families.
	Influence government and other leaders to maintain, implement, and fund policies that positively impact CKD and transplantation.
Brand	Be recognized as the statewide leader in affecting positive change for children.
Awareness	
Awareness/outreach	Position the organization as the voice of homeless youth.
Brand leadership	Achieve the image as a community institution that builds character and enhances the mind, body, and spirit.
External relations	
Image	Be the organization for those who want to have lasting impact on their community.
Community	Provide an inclusive community in which all persons feel accepted and welcomed to serve and be served.
Community engagement	Build lifelong meaningful community and customer relationships.

Culture Employees Staff and volunteers Talent	Provide an organizational environment that attracts and retains high-quality and diverse board members, staff, and volunteers, focused on planning and implementing the mission.
	Foster an engaged workforce, committed to upholding the highest standards of ethics and excellence.
	Recruit, develop, and retain the appropriate staff and volunteers to advance our mission.
	Promote an atmosphere in which employees are appreciated, motivated, and rewarded.
Diversity	Reflect the diversity of the communities we serve.
	Maintain an environment that respects and appreciates diversity.
Education	Provide innovative and effective education, programs, and services, fulfilling the needs of our constituents.
	Provide broad-based educational opportunities to develop skills and spiritual maturity.
Finance Funding Resources	Maintain the financial resources needed to achieve the mission.
	Maximize and safeguard resources and relationships.
	Maximize resources to provide financial stability for our growing organization.
Impact	Achieve measurable impact on the issues that are most important to communities.
	Promote and maximize access to age-appropriate immunization for all children.
	Improve the lives of individuals and families and positively change community conditions.
Mobilization	Energize and inspire people to make a difference.
	Mobilize the community to support the police department and engage in public safety.
Operations Operational excellence	Operate a program that supports volunteers and staff, while efficiently and effectively meeting the needs of clients.
	Promote excellence in police services.

Partners Volunteers	Foster involvement, relationships, and collaboration with a diverse group of leaders and organizations in the community who can support the mission of the organization.
	Build strong coalitions and diverse partnerships that address community issues and bridge historical gaps based on race, class, gender, and economic differences.
	Promote collaborative relationships with community partners to provide a continuum of accessible, quality care.
	Collaborate with and promote collaboration among public and private organizations to achieve healthy communities.
Programs Programs and services Services	Provide caring, cost-effective programs that produce life-enhancing results.
	Provide exceptional quality programs and services that meet the needs of families and children with a focus on the underserved.
	Provide opportunities for spiritual nourishment, education, and fellowship both internally and externally in worship and mission.
	Provide quality programs and services that effectively respond to the changing needs of our clients.

Sample Association Goal Statements

Community Community outreach	Contribute to the community by promoting family and ethical values and anti-discrimination, and by lending a caring hand.
	Improve our community by contributing our individual and chapter expertise, skills, products, and services to not-for-profit and public organizations.
	Provide funds and services to support the local community and provide a vehicle for organization recognition.
Education Development	Provide opportunities for our members for the development of professional and leadership skills.
	Provide opportunities for our members to enhance professionalism and to stay abreast of industry trends.
	Maintain organizational processes that enable and encourage leadership development and succession planning for continuity.

Finance Organization	Maintain sufficient financial and organizational resources to support programs.
	Provide a strong organization through professional associates and maintain independent financial resources that will support our goals and objectives.
	Provide planning and financial infrastructure to ensure the association to accomplish its mission.
Leadership	Provide leadership to the graphics/communications industry to enhance value to our members, with emphasis on professionalism and integrity.
	Support the election, appointment, and promotion of women lawyers to leadership positions.
Member benefits	Provide best value for membership through innovative programs.
	Provide best value for membership through various programs unmatched by any other industry.
Membership Customers Growth	Maximize membership growth, retention, and involvement.
	Understanding, meet, and exceed the expectations of our customers by continuously responding to their changing needs and interests.
	Grow core membership, increase revenues, and increase profit margin.
	Maximize membership, diversity, and involvement.
Networking	Provide an atmosphere for the sharing of ideas with peers.
	Promote networking, rainmaking, and business success for women lawyers.
Policy	Establish reform to address any regulatory issues affecting members.
Programs	Provide and promote programs that enhance competence, professionalism, interaction, and satisfaction.
	Provide industry-specific resources, programs, and services to enhance the success of our members.
	Provide a variety of programs that appeal to current and prospective members.

Reputation Professionalism Recognition Visibility	Achieve global recognition as a leader in the hospitality industry, as well as among business associations through superior professionalism.
	Be recognized as the premier source for the development of people.
	Promote meeting management as a viable and worthwhile career with an emphasis on the professional certification of members.
	Enhance the reputation of lawyers, judges, and the legal system.
	Maximize the organization's profile and influence.

- Overview
- Sample Mission Statements
- Why Writing a Mission Statement Is So Challenging
- The Drivers Model Approach
- The Process
- The Quality Check
- Your Role in Defining the Mission
- Case Study: Developing a Mission Statement in Twenty Minutes

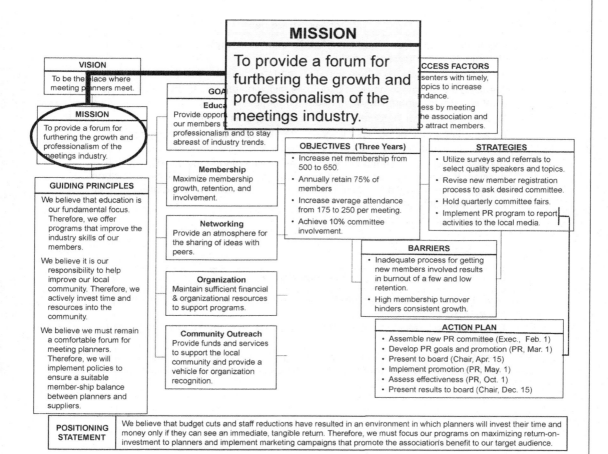

MISSION

To provide a forum for furthering the growth and professionalism of the meetings industry.

VISION
To be the place where meeting planners meet.

MISSION
To provide a forum for furthering the growth and professionalism of the meetings industry.

GUIDING PRINCIPLES
We believe that education is our fundamental focus. Therefore, we offer programs that improve the industry skills of our members.

We believe it is our responsibility to help improve our local community. Therefore, we actively invest time and resources into the community.

We believe we must remain a comfortable forum for meeting planners. Therefore, we will implement policies to ensure a suitable member-ship balance between planners and suppliers.

GOA
Educa
Provide oppor
our members
professionalism and to stay
abreast of industry trends.

Membership
Maximize membership growth, retention, and involvement.

Networking
Provide an atmosphere for the sharing of ideas with peers.

Organization
Maintain sufficient financial & organizational resources to support programs.

Community Outreach
Provide funds and services to support the local community and provide a vehicle for organization recognition.

CCESS FACTORS
senters with timely,
opics to increase
ndance.
ess by meeting
he association and
attract members.

OBJECTIVES (Three Years)
- Increase net membership from 500 to 650.
- Annually retain 75% of members
- Increase average attendance from 175 to 250 per meeting.
- Achieve 10% committee involvement.

STRATEGIES
- Utilize surveys and referrals to select quality speakers and topics.
- Revise new member registration process to ask desired committee.
- Hold quarterly committee fairs.
- Implement PR program to report activities to the local media.

BARRIERS
- Inadequate process for getting new members involved results in burnout of a few and low retention.
- High membership turnover hinders consistent growth.

ACTION PLAN
- Assemble new PR committee (Exec., Feb. 1)
- Develop PR goals and promotion (PR, Mar. 1)
- Present to board (Chair, Apr. 15)
- Implement promotion (PR, May. 1)
- Assess effectiveness (PR, Oct. 1)
- Present results to board (Chair, Dec. 15)

POSITIONING STATEMENT
We believe that budget cuts and staff reductions have resulted in an environment in which planners will invest their time and money only if they can see an immediate, tangible return. Therefore, we must focus our programs on maximizing return-on-investment to planners and implement marketing campaigns that promote the association's benefit to our target audience.

Summary: Mission Statement

Definition	A mission statement defines the overall purpose of an organization. The mission should state what you do, for whom you do it, and the benefit.

Examples	• To provide a forum for furthering the growth and professionalism of the meetings industry. • To supply consumers with high-quality, price-competitive automobiles that meet their transportation needs. • To promote health and quality of life by preventing and controlling disease, injury, and disability.

Success Strategies

- Define the three mission questions, and review other organizations' mission statements using these questions.
- Identify what you do, for whom you do it, and the benefit.
- Break up into teams to develop candidate mission statements that incorporate what you do, for whom you do it, and the benefit.
- Review the mission statements and identify strengths of each.
- As a starting point, select the mission statement receiving the most support and spend a few minutes editing it with the group.
- Avoid wasting too much time having the entire planning team "wordsmith" the mission. If necessary, once the full group has agreement on the ideas to include and the general wording, assign a writing committee to finalize the draft for later review and adoption.
- Perform a quality check on the mission.

Quality Check

- Does the mission statement broadly describe what you do, for whom you do it, and the benefit?
- Does the mission statement indicate the industry or market that the organization serves?
- Does the mission statement contain enough specificity to distinguish this organization's mission from that of other organizations in the same industry?

Overview

"We all know what we do around here. Do we really need to take the time to hammer out a mission statement?"

A mission statement defines the overall purpose of your organization. The mission should state what you do, for whom you do it, and the benefit. But as the question above implies, does an organization need to have a mission statement?

The Why of Mission

Mission writing does indeed take time. Some organizations have reported taking weeks and months to develop a mission statement. And, as you'll also see in this chapter, there are plenty of extremely successful organizations that nevertheless have inadequate mission statements.

So, is a mission really important? And how do you avoid expending weeks and months in an effort around words?

Later in this chapter, you'll see that the Drivers Model approach to developing a mission statement results in most mission statements being created in fewer than 90 minutes. But for now, let's tackle the bigger question: Why do you need a mission statement? To communicate, inspire, and focus, as described in the points that follow:

Why you need a mission statement

- **To communicate in a succinct form what the organization is about.**

  The mission statement communicates what the organization does, for whom it does it, and the benefit the organization provides.

- **To inspire customers, investors, and employees to join you in being a part of a greater purpose.**

  By answering why the organization exists, the mission statement provides a vehicle for attracting others who resonate with your purpose.

- **To maintain focus on what is important**.

  The mission statement should broadly define what the organization does. This definition then serves as the compass for ensuring that all activities align with the direction, and it helps the organization avoid taking on irrelevant activities.

Components of a Great Mission Statement

What makes a great mission statement? Based on the Drivers Model, a mission statement answers three specific questions.

The Mission Questions
• What do you do?
• For whom do you do it?
• What is the benefit?

Along with answering the mission questions, a mission statement should also indicate the industry or market that the organization serves. An especially strong mission statement will contain enough specificity to distinguish the organization's mission from that of other organizations in the same industry.

Sample Mission Statements

The table that follows provides sample mission statements from twenty-one organizations across a variety of industries. While they don't all necessarily distinguish the organization's mission from that of other organizations in the same industry, they do a solid job of indicating the industry served and answering the three mission questions.

Sample Mission Statements That Cover the Mission Questions*

The mission statements listed in this chapter were taken from information available to the author at the time and may not reflect the current mission of the cited organizations.

Automotive parts
To provide quality foreign nameplate automotive parts to our distribution partners to grow their foreign nameplate sales by meeting the needs of their professional technician customers. (Beck Arnley)
Energy
To create superior value for our customers, employees, communities, and investors through the production, conversion, delivery, and sale of energy and energy services. (Duke Energy Corporation)
Engineering
We provide great civil engineering that meets the needs of our clients, while considering the vulnerable nature of the environment. (Southern Civil Engineers)

Government: Community health

To serve our community by providing culturally sensitive, quality, affordable, comprehensive, and accessible health care for the residents of our county and surrounding communities in collaboration with our partners. (Dekalb County Board of Health)

Government: Finance

We exist to provide decision-makers with relevant and credible information and services to promote improvements in accountability and stewardship in state and local government. (Georgia Department of Audits)

Government: Health

To promote health and quality of life by preventing and controlling disease, injury, and disability. (Centers for Disease Control former mission statement)

Government: Housing

To provide affordable housing opportunities that fulfill the needs of those we serve. (Dekalb Housing Authority)

Government: Transportation

To enhance the quality of life of our community by delivering a positive transit experience to our customers. (Metropolitan Atlanta Regional Transit Authority)

Health care

Above all else, we are committed to the care and improvement of human life. In recognition of this commitment, we strive to deliver high quality, cost effective healthcare in the communities we serve. (Hospital Corporation of America)

Information

To organize the world's information and make it universally accessible and useful. (Google)

Information technology consulting

To use our extensive IT experience to deliver tangible business results, enabling our clients in industry and government to profit from the advanced use of technology. (Computer Science Corporation)

Insurance

To combine aggressive strategic marketing with quality products and services at competitive prices to provide the best insurance value for consumers. (Aflac)

Legal

To ethically and professionally serve our clients by providing the highest quality of legal representation in a professionally and personally satisfying firm environment. (Hall Booth Smith & Slover)

Non-profit: Association

Our mission is to provide services, programs, and benefits to maximize the professional effectiveness of our members and to promote the administration of justice in this community. (Atlanta Bar Association)

Non-profit: Civic organization

To nurture a regional community for the benefit of present and future residents by increasing citizen influence in issues of public significance. (Civic League for Regional Atlanta)

Non-profit: Religious institution

The mission of our church is to inspire our community through love to grow and be in service to the Holy Spirit. (Brookhaven Christian Church)

Non-profit: Services

To implement programs embodied in Christian ethics and civic principles that build a healthy spirit, mind, and body for all. (Butler Street YMCA)

Pharmaceutical

To discover, develop, and deliver innovative medicines that help patients prevail over serious diseases. (Bristol-Myers Squibb Company)

Retail

By making good design readily accessible, we create personal home furnishings solutions for our customers, based on their lifestyles and their dreams. (Storehouse Furniture)

Tax services

To help our clients achieve their financial objectives by serving as their tax and financial partner. (H&R Block)

Transportation

We fulfill dreams through the experience of motorcycling, by providing to motorcyclists and to the general public an expanding line of motorcycles and branded products and services in selected market segments. (Harley-Davidson)

While the mission statements above answer the mission questions well, the mission statements listed below do not. Each one is missing one or more of the key elements for a mission. In all cases, you would likely not be able to accurately guess the organization, nor even the industry, without reading the company's name.

In several of these cases, it appears the mission of the organization is to make money. While increasing shareholder wealth is a critical aim and beneficial to the shareholder, a mission statement with this as its sole focus does nothing to inspire customers, partners, or employees to join with you. Mission statements must go beyond an economic goal and focus on the benefit to the intended customer of the products or services provided.

Sample Mission Statements That Don't Cover the Mission Questions*

The mission statements listed in this chapter were taken from information available to the author at the time and may not reflect the current mission of the cited organizations.

Mission statement	Covered?			
	What they do	For whom	The benefit	The industry
We are a market-focused, process-centered organization that develops and delivers innovative solutions to our customers, consistently outperforms our peers, produces predictable earnings for our shareholders, and provides a dynamic and challenging environment for our employees. (Ashland)	Y	Y	N	N
To earn money for its shareholders and increase the value of their investment. We will do that through growing the company, controlling assets and properly structuring the balance sheet, thereby increasing EPS, cash flow, and return on invested capital. (Cooper Tire & Rubber Company)	N	N	N	N
The Company's primary objective is to maximize long-term stockholder value, while adhering to the laws of the jurisdictions in which it operates and at all times observing the highest ethical standards. (Dean Foods Corporation)	N	N	N	N
Serving others: for customers—a better life, for shareholders—a superior return, for employees—respect and opportunity. (Dollar General Corporation)	N	Y	Y	N
To constantly improve what is essential to human progress by mastering science and technology. (The Dow Chemical Company)	Y	N	Y	N
We will provide branded products and services of superior quality and value that improve the lives of the world's consumers. (Global Gillette)	Y	Y	Y	N

Mission statement	Covered?			
	What they do	For whom	The benefit	The industry
To provide products, services, and solutions of the highest quality and deliver more value to our customers that earns their respect and loyalty. (Hewlett-Packard)	Y	Y	Y	N
We enable people and businesses throughout the world to realize their full potential. (Microsoft)	N	Y	Y	N
We are dedicated to the highest quality of customer service, delivered with a sense of warmth, friendliness, individual pride, and company spirit. (Southwest Airlines)	N	Y	N	N
Help people save money, so they can live better. (Walmart)	Y	Y	Y	N

Other mission statements answer the questions, but use a lot of words to do it. These mission statements are typically difficult to remember.

Sample Mission Statements That Are Wordy*

The mission statements listed in this chapter were taken from information available to the author at the time and may not reflect the current mission of the cited organizations.

Our purpose is to enable individuals and businesses to manage financial risk. We provide insurance products and services tailored to meet the specific and ever-changing financial risk exposures facing our customers. We build value for our investors through the strength of our customers' satisfaction and by consistently producing superior operating results. (American Financial Group)
To be one of the world's leading producers and providers of entertainment and information. Using our portfolio of brands to differentiate our content, services, and consumer products, we seek to develop the most creative, innovative, and profitable entertainment experiences and related products in the world. (The Walt Disney Company)

> Our mission is to operate the best specialty retail business in America, regardless of the product we sell. Because the product we sell is books, our aspirations must be consistent with the promise and the ideals of the volumes which line our shelves. To say that our mission exists independent of the product we sell is to demean the importance and the distinction of being booksellers. As booksellers, we are determined to be the very best in our business, regardless of the size, pedigree, or inclinations of our competitors. We will continue to bring our industry nuances of style and approaches to bookselling that are consistent with our evolving aspirations. Above all, we expect to be a credit to the communities we serve, a valuable resource to our customers, and a place where our dedicated booksellers can grow and prosper. Toward this end, we will not only listen to our customers and booksellers, but embrace the idea that the Company is at their service. (Barnes & Noble)

> We will produce superior financial returns for shareowners by providing high value-added supply chain, transportation, business, and related information services through focused operating companies. Customer requirements will be met in the highest quality manner appropriate to each market segment served. FedEx will strive to develop mutually rewarding relationships with its employees, partners, and suppliers. Safety will be the first consideration in all operations. Corporate activities will be conducted to the highest ethical and professional standards. (FedEx)

Finally, some mission statements that don't answer the three questions are actually vision statements. They answer a different question, as you'll see in the next chapter.

Sample Mission Statements That Could Better Serve as Vision Statements*

The mission statements listed in this chapter were taken from information available to the author at the time and may not reflect the current mission of the cited organizations.

> To be the safest, most progressive North American railroad, relentless in the pursuit of customer and employee excellence. (CSX Corporation)

> We will be the easiest pharmacy retailer for customers to use. (CVS)

> People love our clothes and trust our company. We will market the most appealing and widely worn casual clothing in the world. We will clothe the world. (Levi Strauss)

> To bring inspiration and innovation to every athlete in the world. (Nike)

For the most part, the organizations cited here with "less than perfect" mission statements are, or have been at one time, highly successful. Therefore, a great mission statement isn't required for success. However, when your mission statement clearly answers the key questions, it can serve as a point of focus and a vehicle for making strategic decisions.

Why Writing a Mission Statement Is So Challenging

If you've been through the effort of creating an organization's mission statement, then you probably know how painful the experience can be. Planning teams typically spend days, and sometimes weeks or months, debating over the exact words needed. Typically, there are some people on the planning team who want the mission statement to be clear and concise. Others want it to be aspirational and inspiring. And still others want a mission statement that is achievable in their lifetime. Is there any wonder why the task is so difficult?

In analyzing the challenges that groups face in developing mission statements, it's clear to me that the mission development process itself is typically flawed. Why? Because the planning team is taking on three different tasks, all at the same time.

Why is writing a mission statement so challenging?	The planning team usually is trying to do three tasks simultaneously.
	• Define who we are today.
	• Define who we want to be in the future.
	• Put these thoughts in a small, pithy sentence.

What can make developing a mission statement so frustrating is that you can have all three discussions occurring all at the same time! While one person is focused on today, another is looking to tomorrow, while a third is focusing on the specific word choice. If you start with the mission statement, inevitably gaining consensus will be challenging and time-consuming due to the varied conversations implicit in mission writing.

The Drivers Model Approach

The Drivers Model breaks the process of writing the mission statement into its three parts. This brings us to our next secret.

 Secret #11 Don't develop the mission statement first. Instead, define who we are today, who we want to be in the future, and then select the words that give these definitions meaning.

How is this three-part process accomplished?

- First, your team defines where the organization is now and what key trends will affect your success in the future. This discussion occurs during the review of the briefing book.

- Then, the team identifies what success might look like ten years in the future. The visioning exercise and goal statements define success.

- Finally, through the mission statement discussion, the team determines the implications their definition of success has on the mission statement, and then selects words for the mission.

Wording the Mission Statement

To accomplish the task of wording the mission statement, I've found that you can greatly reduce the time needed to develop a mission statement by first answering the three mission questions, as defined by this next secret.

> **Secret #12** To build your mission statement, focus on the three mission questions:
>
> • What do you do?
>
> • For whom do you do it?
>
> • What is the benefit?

These three questions define a great mission statement. So, I start the mission writing process by educating the team on the three mission questions. I then have them review the mission statements of other organizations to see how they answer the questions. Next, I ask the team to answer the mission questions for their organization. Once the questions are answered, it becomes much easier to create words that give life and meaning to the answers.

Using the meeting planners association example, the responses to the three mission questions might be as follows.

Sample Response to Mission Questions

What do we do?	Educate individuals. Promote the industry. Bring people together for networking.
For whom do we do it?	Meeting professionals, suppliers.
What's the benefit?	Individual growth, industry promotion.

Which Comes First?

Our next secret has to do with the order you place the answers in your mission statement.

> **Secret #13** In writing your mission statement, either start with what you do, or start with the benefit.

As described previously, the mission statement answers three questions: What do you do? For whom do you do it? What is the benefit? In writing your mission statement, you can start with what you do, or you can start with the benefit. Let's revisit two of the sample mission statements. Note how one starts with what they do, while the other starts with the benefit. Often having the benefit first can create a more powerful mission statement.

| **"What we do" first** | To provide a forum for furthering the growth and professionalism of the meetings industry. |
| **"The benefit" first** | To promote health and quality of life by preventing and controlling disease, injury, and disability. |

The Process

The steps below outline the Drivers Model process for developing a mission statement.

1 Educate on the mission questions.

Begin the mission writing process by describing the three mission questions and reviewing the mission statements of other organizations to see how they answer the questions. Be sure to have examples of both strong and weak mission statements.

2 Identify what you do, for whom you do it, and the benefit.

After educating on mission, have your entire team answer the three mission questions for your organization. It isn't unusual to have some debate about the answers. However, while full agreement on the answers is helpful at this point, it isn't essential.

3 Develop candidate mission statements.

Next, break your team into smaller groups to create mission statement candidates. I prefer splitting up into at least three groups, but no more than five, to allow for a diversity of mission candidates, but not an overwhelming selection.

4 Review the mission statements.

After the completion of the breakout exercise, reconvene your entire team to review the various mission statements and select one to refine for adoption. In reviewing the mission statements, ask the team that created the candidate mission to remain quiet, while the others dissect the candidate to identify what they like about it, ways to improve it, and how it compares to the mission quality checks that appear later in this section.

5 Select a candidate to further refine.

After reviewing the candidate mission statements, it's time for your team to select one to develop further. To do this, I like having people vote on the mission they believe is the best starting point. However, I give them one constraint: They can't vote for their own. This guideline helps bypass two potentially negative dynamics: People feeling allegiance to their own creation and voting for it, even though they see something better; and people getting angry at others who "defect" from their group and choose another group's solution.

6 Edit the candidate mission statement.

Now it's time for the heavy lifting. Once the team has agreed on a starting point, the next step is to refine the words. Why is this the difficult part? On one side, you're trying to gain agreement on the concepts. On the other side, you want to get the group to agree on the specific words.

Often, getting a group to agree on specific words can degenerate into a wordsmithing exercise in which people spend precious time debating whether "the" or "a" is most appropriate. The goal for this step is to gain agreement on the concepts and agree on the words where you can, but save the detailed wordsmithing decisions for a smaller team. Therefore, use the informed majority process described in Chapter 6 to quickly reach agreement on wording.

7 Perform a quality check.

The final step in the mission creation process is to review each of the quality check items to ensure the mission statement meets all the checks.

The Quality Check

If you and your team have done a great job of developing the mission statement, you'll be able to answer "Yes" to each of the following questions.

Quality check

- Does the mission statement broadly describe what you do, for whom you do it, and the benefit?

- Does the mission statement indicate the industry or market that the organization serves?

- Does the mission statement contain enough specificity to distinguish this organization's mission from that of other organizations in the same industry?

Your Role in Defining the Mission

Since the mission of the organization serves as the central focus for the plan, consider the following in thinking about your leadership role:

The role of the leader

- The mission statement must well represent your organization. At the same time, however, you'll want to avoid overpowering the group with your views.

- Accordingly, if the candidate mission statements appear to lack key ideas that you think are important, try to use questions, rather than statements to challenge the group's thinking. For example, asking, "What do these statements say about the benefits we deliver to our customer?" is better than saying, "These statements don't say anything about the benefits we deliver to our customer."

- The mission statement is a statement that will be delivered internally and externally. Give thought to how the proposed mission statement will be viewed by board members, customers, suppliers, and employees.

- Be sure that your mission statement meets all the quality checks.

Case Study:
Developing a Mission Statement in Twenty Minutes

Using the Drivers Model's process typically results in a mission statement that has broad consensus in sixty to ninety minutes. However, in the case study that follows, the organization completed this effort in twenty minutes.

I was working with the Diversity Leadership Forum (DLF), a trade association of diversity professionals. The DLF has some members who work inside organizations, while others are external trainers and consultants. The organization convenes an annual conference of diversity professionals and has established a competency model for diversity. They wanted to develop a plan because they felt they had not clearly defined their niche or how they would go about getting others to join them.

Step 1: Where Are We Now?
The team identified several strengths, areas for improvement, and potential strategies to consider, including the following.

- *Our standards, ethics, and information are good.*
- *Positive recognition that we are redeveloping competencies and standards used in the field and educating members.*
- *Lack of clarity about who the forum is for.*
- *A lot of people don't seem to know what we offer or haven't used what we offer.*
- *There's a need for ongoing communication and education.*
- *Aligning diversity ideas with the business and how it operates (alignment). Going beyond the fluff to meet tangible missions. Critical outcomes could be helpful.*
- *Consider seeking endorsements from peer organizations for the competency model, etc. (Include leaders in various approaches.)*
- *Consider producing a definitive paper on how to develop and execute cultural competence.*
- *Consider preparing practitioners to deal with changed and changing demographic trends.*
- *Consider establishing a national database of practitioners.*

Step 2: Where Do We Want to Be?
In response to the visioning exercise that guided the participants in defining success ten years out, over thirty vision elements were identified, including the following.

- *A source for diversity content.*
- *Premier resource for practitioners developments.*

- *Competencies nationally recognized, elevate field, essential.*
- *Move diversity to recognized discipline.*
- *Remove structural inequalities in management, domestically and internationally.*
- *Advance inclusion around the world.*
- *Great financial endowment.*

Using the vision elements as a starting point, the participants developed five broad goals for the organization.

- **Information Source.** *Provide leading-edge, intellectual collateral about diversity that crosses industries and approaches, and which is easily accessible for people of different backgrounds and abilities.*
- **Practitioner Development.** *Provide effective, safe, continuous learning and renewal opportunities for diversity practitioners at all levels and across approaches.*
- **Societal Recognition.** *Evaluate and promote the field of diversity as a recognized discipline.*
- **Impact.** *Advocate and communicate the role diversity plays in creating valuable, life-changing outcomes.*
- **Organization.** *Maintain sufficient organizational and financial resources to support the mission.*

Step 3. What Is Our Mission?

After a discussion of the purpose of a mission statement and a review of several relatively strong and relatively weak mission statements, the participants were asked to answer the three critical mission questions for DLF. One of the participants responded to the three questions as follows and the facilitator recorded the answers on a flip chart for all to see.

- *What do we do? Provide a forum for growth and development.*
- *For whom do we do it? Diversity professionals.*
- *What's the benefit? Recognition and advancement of the field of diversity.*

Suddenly, one of the participants yelled out, "That's it! That's our mission! That's it right there!" After about ten minutes of additional discussion, the rest of the participants readily agreed and adopted the following mission statement.

Our Mission
We provide a forum for the growth and development of diversity practitioners and for the recognition and advancement of the field of diversity.

Vision | 8

- Overview
- The Process
- The Quality Check
- Your Role in Defining the Vision

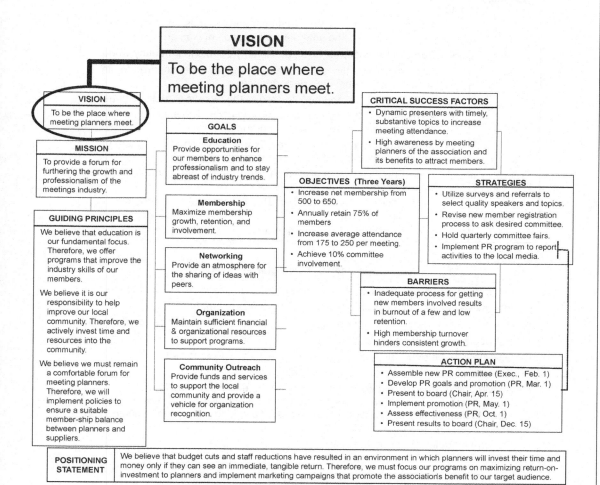

VISION
To be the place where meeting planners meet.

VISION
To be the place where meeting planners meet.

MISSION
To provide a forum for furthering the growth and professionalism of the meetings industry.

GUIDING PRINCIPLES
We believe that education is our fundamental focus. Therefore, we offer programs that improve the industry skills of our members.

We believe it is our responsibility to help improve our local community. Therefore, we actively invest time and resources into the community.

We believe we must remain a comfortable forum for meeting planners. Therefore, we will implement policies to ensure a suitable member-ship balance between planners and suppliers.

GOALS

Education
Provide opportunities for our members to enhance professionalism and to stay abreast of industry trends.

Membership
Maximize membership growth, retention, and involvement.

Networking
Provide an atmosphere for the sharing of ideas with peers.

Organization
Maintain sufficient financial & organizational resources to support programs.

Community Outreach
Provide funds and services to support the local community and provide a vehicle for organization recognition.

CRITICAL SUCCESS FACTORS
- Dynamic presenters with timely, substantive topics to increase meeting attendance.
- High awareness by meeting planners of the association and its benefits to attract members.

OBJECTIVES (Three Years)
- Increase net membership from 500 to 650.
- Annually retain 75% of members
- Increase average attendance from 175 to 250 per meeting.
- Achieve 10% committee involvement.

STRATEGIES
- Utilize surveys and referrals to select quality speakers and topics.
- Revise new member registration process to ask desired committee.
- Hold quarterly committee fairs.
- Implement PR program to report activities to the local media.

BARRIERS
- Inadequate process for getting new members involved results in burnout of a few and low retention.
- High membership turnover hinders consistent growth.

ACTION PLAN
- Assemble new PR committee (Exec., Feb. 1)
- Develop PR goals and promotion (PR, Mar. 1)
- Present to board (Chair, Apr. 15)
- Implement promotion (PR, May. 1)
- Assess effectiveness (PR, Oct. 1)
- Present results to board (Chair, Dec. 15)

POSITIONING STATEMENT
We believe that budget cuts and staff reductions have resulted in an environment in which planners will invest their time and money only if they can see an immediate, tangible return. Therefore, we must focus our programs on maximizing return-on-investment to planners and implement marketing campaigns that promote the association's benefit to our target audience.

Summary: Vision Statement

Definition	A vision is a picture of the "preferred future"—it's a statement that describes how the future will look if the organization fulfills its mission.

Examples	The vision might be a short statement or a paragraph that describes the future.
	• **Avon**: To be the company that best understands and satisfies the product, service, and self-fulfillment needs of women—globally.
	• **Centers for Disease Control**: Healthy people in a healthy world.
	• **Chevron**: To be the global energy company most admired for its people, partnership, and performance.
	• **Kraft Foods**: Helping people around the world eat and live better.
	• **Professional Photographers Association**: The association of choice for the professional photographer.
	• **State Information Technology Council**: We envision a state in which information technology is used to:
	• Enable a responsive, high performance government, providing quality services.
	• Facilitate an environment that is conducive to economic development.
	• Enrich the education and quality of life of its citizens.

Success Strategies

- Once the mission has been drafted, review other organizations' vision statements.
- Identify key ideas that might be the focus of a vision statement.
- Brainstorm potential vision statements.
- Reduce the brainstorm list to a manageable number.
- Give people the opportunity to lobby for the one they believe is best.
- Select the vision statement that has greatest appeal.
- As with the mission, avoid wasting time having the entire planning team "wordsmith" the vision. If necessary, once the full group has agreement on the ideas to include and the general wording, assign a writing committee to finalize the draft for later review and adoption.
- Perform a quality check on the vision.

Quality Check

- Does the vision represent the preferred future of the organization?
- Does the vision simply represent a logical extension of today, or are out-of-the-box results represented?

Overview

In the strategy document that results from using the Drivers Model, the vision statement appears first, followed by the mission statement and then the goal statements. You may have noted, however, in the actual development of these statements, the order is just the opposite: goals first, and then mission and vision. Why is this? As indicated in Chapter 6, I've found that teams are much more productive, are able to create stronger mission and vision statements, and achieve much higher levels of consensus much faster when goals are defined before mission. And as you'll see in this chapter, once the mission is defined, your team will be better able to answer the key vision question, "If you're successful at fulfilling your mission, what will the future look like?"

The vision statement provides a picture of your team's preferred future. It's a statement that describes how the future will look if your organization fulfills its mission. The next secret provides insight on the focus for the vision statement.

| Secret #14 | The vision statement typically describes either the organization in the future or the impact the organization will have. |

As your team envisions what the future will look like if you fulfill your mission, it's typical that some team members will focus the vision on what the organization will look like, while others will focus on the impact the organization makes. Below are examples of each.

Organization-focused vision	Impact-focused vision
To be the global energy company most admired for its people, partnership, and performance.	A nation free of HIV.
	Helping people around the world eat and live better.
The association of choice for the professional photographer.	Healthy people in a healthy world.

As your team considers vision statements, it can be helpful to make them aware of the distinction between organization-focused and impact-focused vision statements. For governments and non-profits, the vision statement is most often impact-focused. Corporations and trade associations are frequently organization-focused. However, this isn't always the case, as the examples above indicated.

Always keep in mind the relationship between the vision and the mission. The mission statement answers what you do, for whom you do it, and the benefit. The vision statement describes what the future will look like if you fulfill your mission. What follows are samples of vision and mission statements.

Sample Mission-Vision Statements*

The mission statements listed in this chapter were taken from information available to the author at the time and may not reflect the current mission of the cited organizations.

Mission (What we do, for whom, and the benefit)	Vision (The future if we fulfill our mission)
To improve lives by providing cost-effective health care products and services. (Abbot Laboratories)	To be the world's premier health care company. Simply put, we want to be the best—the best employer, the best health care supplier, the best business partner, the best investment, and the best neighbor.
We are dedicated to helping people achieve health and financial security by providing easy access to safe, cost-effective, high-quality health care and protecting their finances against health-related risks. (Aetna)	We will be a leader cooperating with doctors and hospitals, employers, patients, public officials, and others to build a stronger, more effective health care system.
To enrich our customers' personal lives and to make their businesses more successful by bringing to market exciting and useful communications services, building shareowner value in the process. (AT&T)	To be the most admired and valuable company in the world.
We will build a unique portfolio of beauty and related brands, striving to surpass our competitors in quality, innovation, and value, and elevating our image to become the beauty company most women turn to worldwide. (Avon)	To be the company that best understands and satisfies the product, service, and self-fulfillment needs of women—globally.
To promote health and quality of life by preventing and controlling disease, injury, and disability. (Centers for Disease Control)	Healthy people in a healthy world.
To empower individual investors to take control of their financial lives, free from the high costs and conflicts of traditional brokerage firms. (Charles Schwab)	Provide the most useful and ethical financial services in the world.

Mission (What we do, for whom, and the benefit)	Vision (The future if we fulfill our mission)
To refresh the world in body, mind, and spirit. To inspire moments of optimism through our brands and our actions. To create value and make a difference everywhere we engage. (The Coca Cola Company)	People: Being a great place to work where people are inspired to be the best they can be. Portfolio: Bringing to the world a portfolio of quality beverage brands that anticipate and satisfy people's desires and needs. Partners: Nurturing a winning network of customers and suppliers, together we create mutual, enduring value. Planet: Being a responsible citizen that makes a difference by helping build and support sustainable communities. Profit: Maximizing long-term return to shareowners, while being mindful of our overall responsibilities.
To use our extensive IT experience to deliver tangible business results enabling our clients in industry and government to profit from the advanced use of technology. (Computer Science Corporation)	Best Total Solutions™ That Work for You.
We will provide must-have news and information on demand across all media, ever mindful of our journalistic responsibilities. (Gannett)	Consumers will choose Gannett media for their news and information needs, anytime, anywhere, in any form.
We are dedicated to providing products and services of such quality that our customers will receive superior value, while our employees and business partners will share in our success and our stockholders will receive a sustained superior return on their investment. (General Motors)	Our vision is to be the world leader in transportation products and related services. We will earn our customers' enthusiasm through continuous improvement driven by the integrity, teamwork, and innovation of GM people.
Assist our members to achieve their professional, artistic, and fraternal goals, to promote public awareness of the profession, and to advance the making of images in all of its disciplines as an art, a science, and a visual recorder of history. (Professional Photographers Association)	The association of choice for the professional photographer.

The Process

How do you develop a vision statement? By definition, vision statements are much more aspirational in nature than mission statements. Therefore, the Drivers Model employs a more creative process to develop them. While the steps are analogous with developing the mission, the way you execute the steps is significantly different, as described in the eight activities that follow:

1 Educate the team on the components of the vision.

To begin the discussion, review with your team the definition of a vision and several sample vision statements from other organizations.

2 Identify key ideas that might be the focus of a vision statement.

Rather than brainstorm potential vision statements immediately, consider having your team identify key ideas that can be used as the focus for the vision statement. Identifying key ideas first helps to create the foundation for more effective brainstorming.

3 Brainstorm potential vision statements.

After identifying key ideas, the next step is to have the team brainstorm vision statements. There are numerous strategies for brainstorming, including the following:

- Silent brainstorming in which participants write out their ideas on cards.
- Team brainstorming where the participants work in groups to generate ideas.
- Round-robin brainstorming in which the participants, one at a time, give their ideas.

4 Reduce the brainstorm list to a manageable number.

If many items came from the brainstorm, it's important to reduce the list to a manageable number (two to five) for discussion. To reduce the list, my preferred method is to work in teams and have the teams identify their top three choices.

5 Give people the opportunity to lobby for the one they believe is best.

I've found that having a period of "controlled" lobbying is a tremendous tool for building consensus and for providing a vehicle for great ideas that initially have low support to gain high favor when the advantages are explained.

During lobbying, participants are given thirty seconds each to explain to the group one or more items they support and why. People can choose to take the time or can choose to pass up the opportunity. In most groups with which I have worked, all of the participants have taken the opportunity. You'll see later in Chapter 14 that the lobby process also serves to increase commitment to action.

6 Hold an initial vote.

After lobbying, the team is ready to hold the initial vote. I like using words like "initial vote" or "first round of voting" to set the expectation that we won't necessarily have a decision on the first vote.

There are a number of ways of holding the vote, including raising hands, secret ballot, and handing out dots and having people put them on their top choices. For this activity, I prefer balloting to reduce the likelihood of people being influenced by others or people holding back on voting until everyone else has voted, so they can see which vision statements can benefit from additional support.

7 Discuss the strengths of each remaining vision statement.

Once the list has been reduced, have your team review the quality checklist, and then discuss the strengths and weaknesses of the remaining vision statements.

8 Select the vision statement that has greatest appeal.

In the final selection vote, each person votes for just one alternative. I typically use the traditional raised hands approach to vote and select the vision statement.

The Quality Check

If you and your team have done a great job of developing the vision statement, you'll be able to answer yes to each of the following questions:

Quality check

- Does the vision represent the preferred future of the organization?
- Does the vision simply represent a logical extension of today, or are out-of-the-box results represented?

Your Role in Defining the Vision

As your team discusses various vision statement alternatives, you have a specific role to play to ensure that a quality vision statement results.

The role of the leader

- As with the mission statement, the vision statement must represent your organization well. At the same time, however, you'll want to avoid overpowering the group with your views.
- If you come into the room with a specific vision statement that you're sold on, consider bringing it up first and asking people to indicate the strengths and weaknesses of it. Keep in

The role of the leader *(cont.)*

mind, however, that giving your thought first will likely bias the group and discourage some from freely giving their ideas.

- If you're open to different thoughts, provide your vision ideas toward the end after other ideas have been put on the table.

- After your team has had an opportunity to identify strengths and weaknesses of the various alternatives, be sure to add any strengths or weaknesses that you believe are important and have been left out. Be sure to do this in a way that doesn't show a strong bias for or against one or more alternatives. For example, you might say, "One of things I like about Alternative Two is that it's indeed inspiring, as someone has already said. I think a weakness that may have been left out is that it may not be as clear to our customers."

- Be sure that your vision statement meets all the quality checks. As with the mission statement, the vision statement must represent your organization well. At the same time, however, you'll want to avoid overpowering the group with your views.

- Overview
- Sample Objectives
- How to Ensure Your Objectives Are SMART
- The Finer Points of Developing Objectives
- The Process
- The Quality Check
- Your Role in Developing Objectives

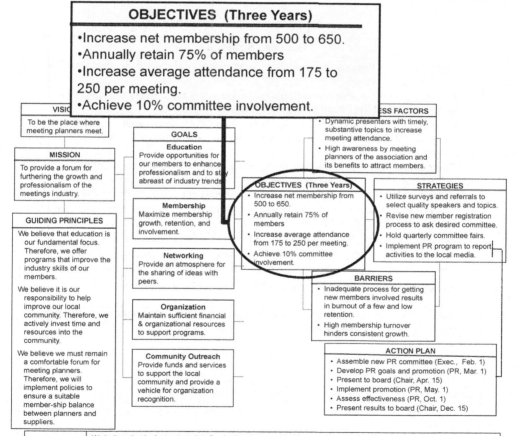

OBJECTIVES (Three Years)

- Increase net membership from 500 to 650.
- Annually retain 75% of members
- Increase average attendance from 175 to 250 per meeting.
- Achieve 10% committee involvement.

VISION
To be the place where meeting planners meet.

MISSION
To provide a forum for furthering the growth and professionalism of the meetings industry.

GUIDING PRINCIPLES
We believe that education is our fundamental focus. Therefore, we offer programs that improve the industry skills of our members.

We believe it is our responsibility to help improve our local community. Therefore, we actively invest time and resources into the community.

We believe we must remain a comfortable forum for meeting planners. Therefore, we will implement policies to ensure a suitable member-ship balance between planners and suppliers.

GOALS

Education
Provide opportunities for our members to enhance professionalism and to stay abreast of industry trends.

Membership
Maximize membership growth, retention, and involvement.

Networking
Provide an atmosphere for the sharing of ideas with peers.

Organization
Maintain sufficient financial & organizational resources to support programs.

Community Outreach
Provide funds and services to support the local community and provide a vehicle for organization recognition.

...SS FACTORS
- Dynamic presenters with timely, substantive topics to increase meeting attendance.
- High awareness by meeting planners of the association and its benefits to attract members.

OBJECTIVES (Three Years)
- Increase net membership from 500 to 650.
- Annually retain 75% of members
- Increase average attendance from 175 to 250 per meeting.
- Achieve 10% committee involvement.

STRATEGIES
- Utilize surveys and referrals to select quality speakers and topics.
- Revise new member registration process to ask desired committee.
- Hold quarterly committee fairs.
- Implement PR program to report activities to the local media.

BARRIERS
- Inadequate process for getting new members involved results in burnout of a few and low retention.
- High membership turnover hinders consistent growth.

ACTION PLAN
- Assemble new PR committee (Exec., Feb. 1)
- Develop PR goals and promotion (PR, Mar. 1)
- Present to board (Chair, Apr. 15)
- Implement promotion (PR, May. 1)
- Assess effectiveness (PR, Oct. 1)
- Present results to board (Chair, Dec. 15)

POSITIONING STATEMENT
We believe that budget cuts and staff reductions have resulted in an environment in which planners will invest their time and money only if they can see an immediate, tangible return. Therefore, we must focus our programs on maximizing return-on-investment to planners and implement marketing campaigns that promote the association's benefit to our target audience.

Summary: Objectives

Definition	Objectives are specific, quantifiable, realistic targets that measure the accomplishment of a goal over a specified period.

Examples	• Increase revenues by 12 percent annually.
	• Have 80 percent of products achieve annual performance targets.
	• Increase customer satisfaction by 2 percentage points, as measured by the annual customer survey.
	• Have a minimum of ten mentions per month in target media.

Success Strategies

- Step your team through the definition, quality check, and success strategies for developing objectives.
- After reviewing the definition of objectives, have the team make the decision: Will targets be set at the moon or the mountains?
- Determine the "yardsticks" or "measures." Read the goal carefully and ask yourself, "At the end of each year, what will measure whether we have been successful?"
- Determine which measures are the best indicators of successful accomplishment of the goal. Most goals will have between two and seven measures. If you have more than seven, ensure that each one is measuring a key aspect of the goal.
- Convert the measures into objectives by defining specific targets to be reached by the end of the planning horizon.
- For each objective, set the baseline and interim milestones.
- Perform a quality check on the objectives. Ask, "If we achieve these objectives—and only these objectives—will we have achieved this goal for the time period?"
- Assign a team to finalize the objectives during the time between the first and second strategy session.
- Note that it may be necessary to recommend changes to the wording of the goal in order to set reasonable, measurable objectives.

Quality Check

- Are the objectives SMART: specific, measurable, achievable, relevant, and time-bound?
- Do the objectives measure results—not just activity?
- If all of the objectives are achieved, and only these objectives, will the goal be accomplished for the time period?

Overview

Once the mission, vision, and broad goals of your organization have been set, it's time to develop your objectives. On this topic, there's good news and there's bad news.

The bad news is that for many teams, developing objectives is the most difficult and time-consuming part of the planning effort. I like to think of planning much like going up a mountain. Early on, the situation assessment and SWOT are relatively easy. The grade gets a little steeper when you cover goals, mission, and vision. However, once you reach objectives, it's like you're on a steep vertical climb that feels like it's never-ending. The topic is challenging and the stakes are high, as people begin to feel that they're making decisions for which they'll be held accountable. There's frequently tension between those who tend to be conservative and those who want to push the envelope. I've even had one team get to objectives and find it so challenging that they quit halfway up, and called off the entire planning expedition.

The Objectives Climb

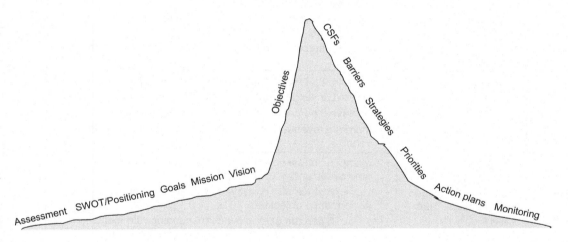

Yet, if you can tough it out, get over the peak and past objectives, the good news is that it's a downhill slide from there. Critical success factors (CSFs), barriers, strategies, priorities, action plans, and monitoring flow right along. But to get to that point, you have to get over the objectives peak.

Sample Objectives

The work on objectives requires that you establish specific, measurable targets for each of the goal areas. The sample below shows a set of goals and objectives for a manufacturer of handheld scanning devices.

Sample Objectives: Manufacturer of Handheld Scanning Devices

Growth Optimize growth while meeting profitability targets.	• Grow top line revenue 10 percent annually. • Increase profitability at or above percentage increases in revenue. • Reduce SG&A from 33 percent to 26 percent within three years. • Increase market share by 5 percentage points by the third year.
Brand Be recognized as a product innovator that is a trustworthy authority in the markets served.	• Have 70 percent of survey respondents (minimum 500) rate us at a 7 or higher on a 10-point scale, indicating that they believe we're product innovators. • Have 80 percent of survey respondents (minimum 500) rate us at a 7 or higher on a 10-point scale, indicating that they believe we're a trustworthy authority.
Products Provide innovative products and services that meet client needs and achieve our expectations.	• Achieve at least 40 percent of our revenue from products that are three years old or less. • Have 70 percent of clients responding to survey indicate that our products meet their needs. • Have 80 percent of our products achieve their revenue targets.
Quality Maximize quality and internal efficiency in all areas.	• Reduce out-of-box failures by 10 percent annually. • Improve inventory turns 20 percent by the third year. • Achieve 8 percent per year product cost reductions. • Increase revenue per employee by 10 percent by the third year.
Culture Attract, develop, and retain highly engaged and competent team players.	• Maintain annual voluntary turnover rate of worldwide employees under 10 percent. • Have 75 percent of employees achieve their annual performance objectives. • Have 75 percent of employees responding rate themselves as 7 or higher on a 10-point scale when asked, "How engaged are you in your work?" • Have 75 percent of employees rate their satisfaction with their development opportunities as 7 or higher on a 10-point scale.

How to Ensure Your Objectives are SMART

Secret #15 **For clarity and ease of tracking, ensure that your objectives are SMART: specific, measurable, achievable, relevant, and time-bound.**

One key check for the quality of an objective is the SMART test. While there are several variations of what the SMART acronym stands for, the Drivers Model uses specific, measurable, achievable, relevant, and time-bound. Let's break down the meaning of each of the elements of SMART, using the membership goal from the meeting planners association as an example.

Membership goal	Maximize membership growth, retention, and involvement.

Specific

If your objectives aren't specific, you won't know what counts as achievement.

For this membership goal, you might be tempted to set an objective, such as, "Increase member involvement 20 percent." However, the term "involvement" isn't specific. How do you know when a member is involved? Is involvement defined by whether he or she is attending monthly meetings? If so, then how many meetings does a member have to attend to be considered "involved?" Is it having your name listed as a member of a committee? Is it attending at least one committee meeting?

To help ensure that each objective is specific, ask yourself, "How do I know when I can count one?" One way to increase the specificity of a candidate objective is to add "as measured by..." For example, the involvement objective for the membership goal might read as shown below.

Not specific	• Increase member involvement 20 percent.
Specific	• Increase percent of members involved in committees to 20 percent as measured by attending at least 25 percent of a committee's meetings.

Note that given the way the "specific" objective is worded above, it's the number of members attending committees that's counted, not the number of committee members.

What's the difference? In the first case, if a member is a member of two committees and attends at least 25 percent of the meetings and functions of both committees, that person is counted once.

If the objective read, "Increase by 20 percent the number of committee members as measured by attending at least 25 percent of a committee's meetings and official functions," then, that member would count as two. As in this case, the wording of objectives is important.

Measurable

Objectives must also be measurable to ensure that you've achieved your target. This point has two components. First, the objective should have a target measurement. Second, you must be able to determine if the measurement has been reached.

Again, using the example of the membership goal, if the objective read, "Increase percent of members involved in committees, as measured by attending at least 25 percent of a committee's meetings," the objective is specific, but no target is set—how much of an increase is desired? What is the target? Or if you added the target and revised the objective to read, "Increase percent of members involved in committees to 15 percent, as measured by attending at least 25 percent of a committee's meetings," but there was no way to measure attendance at committee meetings, this objective would still not meet the measurable component of SMART.

Achievable

What happens when an objective isn't achievable? In my planning experience with numerous organizations, I've found that when people believe their targets to be unachievable, they feel demoralized and invest less effort, not more. In some cases, I've seen what psychologists might call "learned helplessness"; that is, workers can get the sense that, "It doesn't matter what I do, we're not going to get there." You can help avoid this sentiment by ensuring that your objectives are achievable.

Relevant

As described in Chapter 1, objectives must be relevant measures of the goal and this is based on the wording of the goal. The objective must measure what it is you want to see changed.

So, if your membership goal is to maximize membership growth, retention, and involvement, you wouldn't choose objectives that measure activity, such as the number of membership drives or the number of committees created.

Secret #16 Your objectives should measure results, not activity.

Instead, your objectives should measure growth (the number of members over last year), retention (the number of members from last year who are still a member this year), and involvement (the number of members who achieve an involvement measure). These targets measure results based on the wording of the goal.

In the same way, if your goal is to maximize sales from new products, an objective that says, "Implement two new products by December," only measures the activity that you think will get you to those results. In this case, if you're successful in the activity, but achieve no revenue, you'll have achieved the objective, but had no effect on the goal.

Instead of activity measures, you want objectives that focus on the results. An objective that measures the actual results might be, "Achieve annually at least $500,000 in sales of products that have been on the market for less than three years."

To help you focus on results and not activity, use "objective" verbs such as "increase, reduce, achieve, and maintain" when writing objectives. These are quantitative verbs. "Strategy" verbs such as "establish, develop, implement, and revise" focus on activity and are best used in writing strategies. Strategy verbs imply a finite action (e.g., "establish") versus an infinite action (e.g., "maximize"). Once the finite action is completed, the strategy is done.

Sample objective verbs (quantitative verbs)	Sample strategy verbs (finite verbs)
Increase	Establish
Reduce	Develop
Achieve	Implement
Maintain	Build
Have	Create

Keep in mind that objectives are based on the wording of the goal. If the membership goal read, "Maximize the value members receive from association membership," then the relevant measures would be different. In this case, a relevant objective might be, "Increase by 10 percentage points the percent of respondents who indicate they receive high value from association membership, as measured by an annual survey."

Another objective might be, "Increase by 25 the average number of members who indicate the previous monthly meeting was worth their time, as measured by a monthly after-meeting survey."

Note that with this second objective, by using "number of members" versus "percent responding," the objective is focused on two things: increasing the number of members attending the meeting, and increasing the number who indicate that the meeting was worthwhile. This could be important because maximizing value involves giving *more members* value and providing *more value* to members.

As an aside, people frequently equate the "R" in SMART with "realistic." With the Drivers Model, realistic is covered in "achievable," which leaves the "R" to be used for this very important relevance attribute.

Time-bound

Finally, objectives must be time-bound. If your objectives aren't time-bound, how will you know if you've made adequate progress over time?

- If your objective is to increase percent of members involved in committees to 15 percent, as measured by attending at least 25 percent of a committee's meetings, the question is, "When do you have to reach the 15 percent?" This year? Next year? In five years?

- With the Drivers Model, use a table to establish timeframes for the objectives, as shown below. The table includes the baseline measure that indicates where you are today, a three-year target that sets where you want to be, and a first-year milestone to indicate the level of progress expected after the first year.

Sample of the Time-bound Objectives

Goal: Maximize Membership Growth, Retention, and Involvement			
Objective	Baseline	Year 1	Year 3
Increase number of members.	500	550	650
Increase percent of members retained from prior year.	65 percent	70 percent	75 percent
Increase average number of members attending monthly meetings.	175	200	250
Increase percent of members involved in committees, as measured by attending at least 25 percent of a committee's meetings.	5 percent	7 percent	10 percent

The Finer Points of Developing Objectives

In developing objectives, you and your team will want to pay attention to several finer points, as outlined below:

The finer points

- Establishing the baseline.
- Moon versus mountains.
- Coming close to the ultimate measure.
- Making changes to the goal statement.

Establishing the Baseline

As defined in the prior section, the Drivers Model requires that objectives include a baseline measure, a three-year target, and a first-year milestone. What follows are key points around establishing the baseline.

- **Where the baseline is known**, it should represent a measurement of the objective in the preceding fiscal year.

- **Where the baseline is unknown, but attainable,** the team should label the baseline, "To be determined" or "TBD." This is a common situation in many strategy sessions. For example, last year's employee retention may not be known at the time, but following the session, a person or small group can accept responsibility for gathering that information and presenting it to the rest of the team. Note that in this case, it may be appropriate to delay establishing the first-year milestone and three-year target. In other cases, your team may have a general idea of what the baseline is and may choose to establish the milestone and target in reference to the baseline. For example, the first-year milestone may be set as 10 percent above the baseline, and the third-year target as 25 percent above the baseline.

- **Where the baseline is unknown and unattainable,** the team should label the baseline as "Not attainable" or "NA." For example, with an objective to increase overall staff morale, as measured by an annual survey, the baseline would be unattainable if a survey wasn't done in the prior year.

- **If the baseline is not attainable, the team may** set a specific target for the first year and third year. Alternatively, your team may choose to set the first-year milestone as "baseline," which indicates the baseline will be set in the first year, and then set a third-year target in reference to the baseline, such as "20 percent above baseline."

Moon vs. Mountains

There are two schools of thought around writing objectives. Some say, "Shoot for the moon: Set very high, possibly unrealistic targets. If you don't reach them, at least you'll get to the mountaintop." Others say, "Never set unrealistic targets. If you want to get to the mountaintop, set it as your target, and make sure you reach it."

As an example, consider the moon and mountain objectives for our example membership goal that follows.

Membership	Maximize membership growth, retention, and involvement

Moon objectives	Mountain objectives
Increase membership from 500 to 1000 by the third year.	Increase membership from 500 to 650 by the third year.
Achieve 100 percent retention of members from the previous year.	Achieve 85 percent retention of members from the previous year.
Have 75 percent of members involved in committees, as measured by attendance at 50 percent of committee meetings.	Have 10 percent of members involved in committees, as measured by attendance at 50 percent of committee meetings.

Strategic Direction Setting

You and your team should decide whether your objectives will be the moon or the mountains. This discussion is important because, frequently, teams are composed of people with both the moon and the mountain views. This difference in viewpoint can cause many arguments throughout the planning process. I recommend having the discussion and making the decision once to avoid wasting time throughout planning.

Regardless of whether you adopt the moon or the mountains philosophy, you should ensure that all of your objectives are one or the other. When you have objectives that are in some cases moon and other cases mountains, people can easily be confused and assume that it's okay if mountain objectives aren't achieved.

In my own company, we generally prefer the mountain approach. We set high-but-attainable targets and closely monitor and manage their achievement. However, with one measure in particular—annual revenues—we take a hybrid approach that we call the "dartboard method." With revenue, we establish a "moon" measure that we consider the bull's-eye. The bull's-eye is typically much more than a stretch and borderline unrealistic. Then, we establish a "mountain" measure that can be considered the outer rim of the dartboard. Our ultimate target is to hit the bull's-eye. However, as long as we land somewhere on the dartboard (i.e., reach at least the "mountain" measure) the performance is acceptable.

I recommend that you introduce the concept of moon-versus-mountains early in the discussion of objectives. As with informed majority, you then allow your team to make the decision on how to proceed.

Coming Close to the Ultimate Measure

For some goal areas, the ultimate measure of success can be too costly to measure. For example, consider the goal that follows:

| **Brand awareness** | Maximize awareness of our brand and our products. |

If this is a national organization, then the ultimate measure for this goal might be the following:

| **Measure #1** | Increase the percentage of people in the nation who indicate awareness of our brand, as measured by a comprehensive survey of everyone in the nation. |

However, the cost of a survey of everyone in the nation would likely far exceed the value, and your team may very well decide not to take this approach. In response, the team might suggest the following.

| **Measure #2** | Increase the number of press releases sent out. |

This second measure is clearly an activity measure, not a result measure. If the goal is to maximize awareness of your brand and products, the number of press releases sent out doesn't measure it.

In cases like these, where the ultimate measure isn't practical or too expensive, we ask the team to get as close as possible to the ultimate measure. As an example, someone might suggest the following:

| **Measure #3** | Increase the number of press releases published. |

This third measure is still an activity measure, but is indeed closer to the ultimate measure. However, getting twelve press releases published in the local paper isn't the same as getting published in national media. Can we get closer?

| **Measure #4** | Increase the number of press releases published in targeted national media. |

Once more, this measure is an activity measure, but closer to the ultimate measure. Can we get closer?

| **Measure #5** | Increase the percentage of people in the nation who indicate awareness of our brand as measured by a national sample survey. |

This fifth measure, if affordable, is still not the ultimate measure, but certainly closer than the other sample measures. The point is that it's important to determine your ultimate measure for a goal. Once you know the ultimate measure, if it isn't practical, use an alternative measure that comes as close to it as possible.

> **Secret #17** **Set objectives that come as close as possible to the ultimate measure for each goal.**

Making Changes to the Goal Statement

The strategy document may make the Drivers Model appear to be a linear process. However, as mentioned earlier, I think of it as one that spirals upward. That is, as you move forward, you're constantly circling back to adjust what you've previously done, based on new information gained. This is especially true with goals. Once you and your team have completed the draft of goal statements and begin to create objectives, you aren't necessarily finished with the goal statements. Oftentimes, you'll find that you'll have to circle back and adjust one or more goals to make them measurable or more inclusive of key aims.

As an example, if the membership goal simply reads, "Maximize membership growth," then all the objectives, by definition, would have to focus on membership growth. But what happens if someone offers an objective, such as the following?

If your goal is...	Maximize membership growth.
Is this an objective?	Increase percent of members retained from the prior year to 75 percent.

This objective clearly doesn't measure the goal as written. This could mean that the objective should be dropped. Or it could very well mean that the objective is good, but that the goal is too narrow. How do you know?

When I work with strategy teams and an objective is suggested that doesn't measure the goal, I bring this up to the team by asking, "Since our goal reads, 'Maximize membership growth,' is retention a measure of growth?" Of course, the person who suggested the objective would likely recognize that the measure wasn't relevant, based on the way the goal is written, but might insist that it's important.

To address this issue, I typically ask the following question:

The key question	Let me ask you a question that will help determine if retention needs to be part of the goal. If at the end of a year, or two years, or three years, we've achieved high levels of growth, but our retention was awful, would we be happy? If your answer is yes, then retention is most likely a CSF. If your answer is no, then we should consider adding retention to the goal statement.

When I ask the question in this way, the team may very well discover that their intention with the membership goal wasn't only to achieve growth, but also to improve retention and involvement. A team may not realize the full scope of their goals in the goal development discussion, but once the objectives discussion starts, the missing elements may become obvious. Be aware of the spiraling nature of planning and be open to making changes to the work previously done.

Secret #18 If necessary, change the goal statement to ensure that the goal is measurable and addresses the intention.

The Process

Given both the importance and the complexity of objectives, the process for developing them is considerably more involved than the other components thus far. To develop objectives, take your team through the following steps:

1 Educate on the objectives-setting process.

Since objectives are one of the most challenging components of planning, it's important to start with education. Step your team through the definition, quality check, and success strategies for developing objectives.

2 Decide on shooting for the moon or going for the mountains.

After team members review the definition of objectives, have them make a decision: Will targets be set at the moon or the mountains?

3 Brainstorm potential measures for the first goal.

Once the decision has been made on moon versus mountains, the team is ready to define objectives for the first goal. Your first step is to determine the "yardsticks" or "measures" by reviewing the goal and asking, "At the end of each year, how will we know we've been successful? What are the key yardsticks we'll use? For this step, it doesn't matter where on the yardstick we want to be. The question is, 'What yard sticks will we use?'"

I've found it helpful to use this yardstick analogy when talking about measures. People generally can understand that the yardstick is the measure, while the objective indicates where on the yardstick we want to be by a given time.

Going back to the meeting planners, if their membership goal is to "maximize membership growth, retention, and involvement," then key measures of success might be number of members, the percent of members retained, and the number of members attending meetings or involved in committees.

4 Select the key measures that define success of the goal.

After brainstorming potential measures, the next step is to select the key measures from the group. Most goals have between two and seven objectives. If you have more than seven measures at this point, you'll want to ensure that each once is measuring a key aspect of the goal.

5 Convert the measures into objectives.

After identifying the key measures, the next step is to convert the measures into objectives by indicating the direction (e.g., increase, decrease), identifying the baseline, defining specific targets to be reached by the end of the planning horizon (typically three years), and establishing a first-year milestone.

6 Break out into teams to develop the remaining objectives.

After the objectives for the first goal are defined, I typically use breakout groups to work simultaneously on drafting objectives for the remaining goals. Using breakout groups typically saves time and gets more people actively engaged in the process.

7 Review and adjust the objectives developed by the breakout groups.

Following breakout groups, the strategy team typically uses a report-back process in which each group presents its results to the rest of the team. Yet, one of the challenges with this standard report-back activity is that people generally aren't particularly attentive to the presentations. Some groups may be still preparing their own report-back, while others may feel little obligation to give quality feedback, given the number of other people in the room.

Over the years, I've adopted a different process for report-back that I call rotating flipcharts. I believe the process is quite effective for achieving quality feedback on the work of breakout groups.

During a rotating review, each group has three to five minutes to review another group's work. Using a colored pen, assigned specifically to that reviewing group, the group places a checkmark on each item to indicate agreement. They indicate disagreement by placing an "X" and posting a comment on how to improve the items. After the time limit is reached, groups then rotate to the next chart and perform the same review, while also reviewing the comments of all past reviewers of that chart.

When the groups rotate back to their own flip charts, they'll see multiple checkmarks in different colors to indicate those groups that agree with each item in their report. They'll also see written comments, indicating recommended

7 Review and adjust... *(cont.)*

improvements, and the number of groups that concurred with that improvement. They then review the written comments and indicate whether they agree (yes) or disagree (no) with the improvement. At this point, all no's are reviewed by the entire team and final decisions are made.

The rotating review process allows each group to receive focused review from each of the other groups. This process also increases the participation and ownership of the entire work by all members. And surprisingly, the rotating review process takes about the same amount of time as the standard report-back process!

8 Perform the quality check.

With the objectives defined, the last step is to perform the quality check on the objectives. Remind the group that it may be necessary to make changes to the goal statement in order to set reasonable, measurable objectives.

9 Assign a team to finalize the objectives.

The first strategy session ends with the drafting of the objectives. Typically, however, all the information isn't available in the room to determine baselines and targets. Therefore, you'll need to assign a team to finalize the objectives during the time between the first and second strategy sessions.

The Quality Check

If you and your team have done a great job of developing objectives, you'll able to answer yes to each of the following questions:

Quality check
- Are the objectives SMART: specific, measurable, achievable, relevant, and time-bound?
- Do the objectives measure results—not just activity?
- If all of the objectives are achieved, and only these objectives, will the goal be accomplished for the time period?

Your Role in Developing Objectives

As indicated at the start of this chapter, objectives are indeed the most challenging task in developing a strategic plan. If your team members are like most with whom I've worked, many will experience high levels of frustration during this activity. Consider the following:

The role of the leader

- Let them know how difficult objectives are and encourage team members every step of the way to help keep them motivated and on task.

- The rest of the plan will focus on achieving the objectives. Therefore, it's essential that you're comfortable that the objectives represent a stretch, but a reasonable one that can be realistically achieved.

- Ensure that each objective passes the quality check, and that collectively, achieving all the objectives for a goal represents achievement of the goal for the time period.

- Chapter 10. Guiding Principles
- Chapter 11. Critical Success Factors and Barriers
- Chapter 12. Strategies, Priorities, and Deliverables

Guiding Principles 10

- Overview
- Why Are Guiding Principles Essential?
- Values Versus Guiding Principles
- From Paper to Action
- Sample Guiding Principles
- The Process
- The Quality Check
- Your Role in Setting the Guiding Principles

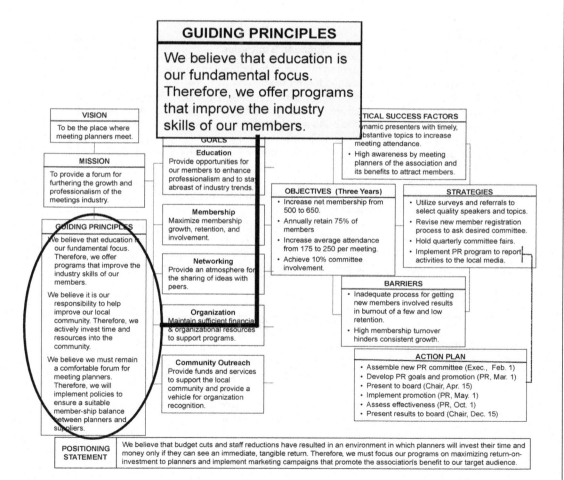

Summary: Guiding Principles

Definition	Guiding principles are general guidelines that set the foundation for how an organization will operate.

Examples	• We believe in the value of teamwork. Therefore, we'll maintain an environment that fosters respect, participation, innovation, and the highest ethical standards of conduct. • Responsiveness to consumer needs is a first priority in our operation. Therefore, our reward and recognition systems are designed to encourage a customer focus.

Success Strategies

- Start the discussion of guiding principles by educating your team on what guiding principles are and the specific format used.
- Provide a scenario in which your team members visualize someone in the organization who exemplifies the organization's values and culture. Have your team members identify the behaviors that make the person exemplary.
- Describe a scenario in which team members are orienting a new hire. Ask them to indicate what behaviors they would tell the new hire aren't tolerated, aren't liked, aren't acceptable, and might even get the new hire fired.
- Have your team group these two lists into one set of logical categories. These categories typically represent the values of the organization and serve as the starting point for your guiding principles.
- To draft the guiding principles, take each of the value categories and create guiding principles, using the "We believe… (value). Therefore, we will… (behaviors)" format as a template.
- Use the quality check to ensure that your guiding principles are up to par.

Quality Check

- Do the guiding principles identify all the organization's key values?
- Are the principles worded in such a way as to indicate both the value and the expected behaviors (e.g., "We believe… [value]. Therefore, we will… [behaviors]")?
- Has your team developed a transformation plan to help make the guiding principles part of the organization's daily operations?

Overview

While objectives complete the first strategy session, the second strategy starts with guiding principles. Recall that the Drivers Model includes four facilitated sessions for developing the strategic plan.

Drivers Model four typical facilitated sessions	Session 1: The planning team answers two questions:
	• Where are we now?
	• Where do we want to be?
	Session 2: The planning team covers two additional questions:
	• How will we get there?
	• How will we monitor our progress?
	Session 3: The planning team reviews the plan with staff and begins the development of action plans.
	Session 4: The planning team reviews and approves the action plans and kicks off implementation.

An agenda for the second session follows. This chapter focuses on the items in the box—the development of guiding principles.

Agenda Second Session

> **A. Getting started**
> - Welcome.
> - Review session objective, deliverables, and ground rules.
> - Review the proposed agenda.
>
> **B. Review the prior work**
> - Review vision, mission, and goals.
> - Confirm work completed on objectives.
>
> **C. How will we get there?**
> - Guiding principles.
> - Living our guiding principles.
> - Critical success factor and barriers.
> - Strategies.
> - Prioritization.
>
> **C. How will we monitor progress?**
> - Action plan deliverables.
> - Alignment plan.
> - Monitoring plan.
> - Accountability plan.
>
> **D. Review and close**

Why Are Guiding Principles Essential?

Why is it important for an organization to have a strong set of values and guiding principles? If you follow the news, you've seen the reasons over and over again.

On a regular basis, there are stories of supposedly solid organizations destroyed by a lack of values. In some cases, the corruption appears to start at the top and trickle down throughout the organization (e.g., Enron). In other cases, top leadership appeared to have strong values, but the actions of a few, and typically the inaction of the many, result in once-powerful organizations tumbling (e.g., Andersen Consulting).

It isn't only corporations that are affected by the lack of a strong set of values. Non-profit organizations and government agencies can also be impacted by a lapse in values. I witnessed this personally in working with a superintendent of a large urban school system. She was a strong charismatic leader, highly competent, with a deep caring for young people. She brought with her a strong message of accountability and reform to the school system, with rewards for those who performed and consequences for those who didn't. However, without a strong, values-based message to balance the performance-focused culture, her administration became mired in accusations of principals altering the answers on students' standardized tests, and then members of her administration covering up and impeding investigations. Without a strong values-based culture, even those out to do good can be hampered by a lack of a common set of understood and embodied values.

At the same time, we also see organizations with strong values-based cultures excelling beyond their competitors (e.g., Southwest Airlines, Ritz Carlton, Chick-fil-A). We see organizations whose cultures seem to provide a customer experience that is far beyond the norm.

This chapter focuses on the process for establishing values, how to transform values into guiding principles, and how to ensure that those guiding principles become an ongoing part of the way your organization operates.

Values vs. Guiding Principles

Webster defines a value as, "a principle, standard, or quality considered worthwhile or desirable." In organizations, values can play an important role in defining an organization's character and its culture. Values also can provide the basic foundation on which an organization is built.

When organizations define their values, it isn't unusual to hear statements similar to the following:

- Our people are our most critical resource.

- We focus on the customer.

- We have respect for the individual.

- Integrity is non-negotiable.

While values such as these are important, I believe organizations can gain greater benefit when they transform their values into guiding principles, as described in our next secret.

Secret #19	Transform your values into guiding principles by defining the behaviors that support the value.

Guiding principles define the value and provide a sample of the behaviors the organization believes support that value. The Drivers Model uses the following format for guiding principles.

Sample Format for Guiding Principles
We believe... (value). Therefore, we will... (behavior).

What does a guiding principle look like in practice? Let's take the first value statement from earlier, and convert it into a guiding principle, as follows:

Sample Guiding Principle
We believe our people are our most critical resource. Therefore, we'll do the following: • Recruit people who have the necessary skills and whose work history reflect a belief in our values and guiding principles. • Invest in training and feedback strategies that ensure the ongoing development of each associate.

The Importance of the Behavior Statements

The statement, "Therefore, we will…" connects the value to one or more behaviors that describe the actions people in the organization take, based on that value. Why is it necessary to have the behavior statements? I've found that often there is agreement on the value statement, "We believe…" Frequently, however, people have different beliefs about what the value statement means in action.

As an example, I was working with a company that was the result of the merger of two construction companies, one based in the Asia–Australia region and the other based in Europe. I'd been brought in to help facilitate a team whose job was to propose a single set of values for the combined corporation. Prior to the merger, one company had eleven values, the other had five. Both organizations had "integrity" as one of their values.

The teams agreed that the values statement, "Integrity is non-negotiable," was appropriate. However, when it came time to create the behavior statements, the uproar began. For some, "non-negotiable" meant that we operate with the highest business ethics across the world: We don't take bribes and we don't give bribes. For others, it meant that we operate, based on the customs of the local country, and if that meant bribing government officials, then, so be it. For others, it meant open transparency in all of our actions. Without the discussion and the documentation of the behaviors associated with, "Therefore, we will…" the team chartered with defining the values for the merged organization would have gone home thinking their job was done—only to find that it would have unraveled in operation. Fortunately, the team was able to come to an agreement that was acceptable to all areas of the organization.

In summary, guiding principles operationalize an organization's values and help ensure that everyone has a common understanding of the behaviors that reflect those values.

From Paper to Action

It isn't unusual to walk into a corporate office and see values and guiding principles mounted on a wall, in some cases in a picture frame or in others, etched in marble. The organization is displaying for all to see the values it holds dear. However, having a set of clearly defined guiding principles is just the start. You win the race by making the guiding principles integral to the way the organization operates on a daily basis. So, how do you get the values off the wall and into the hearts of all workers, so that those values are a part of what they do every day?

Many organizations struggle with this translation process. Within six months of a strategy exercise, few people—even members of the executive team—are able to accurately recall half the guiding principles. Other organizations excel out of the gate by getting every employee to understand and embrace the guiding principles, and they put processes in place that ensure a continued focus.

Below are sample strategies for you to consider for moving your guiding principles from paper to action.

Dissemination	• Create an acronym that can make it easier for people to remember the values. • Have an engaging roll-out process that gets people working with the values and guiding principles. • Provide a copy of the values and guiding principles to every associate. • Post the values and guiding principles for easy reference.
Recruiting and on-boarding	• Include a "values match" as a criterion for candidate evaluation. • Include a one-on-one review of the values and guiding principles with all new hires. • Have new hires write (a page or less) about what they'll do, and not do, to embody the guiding principles. • Have managers and peers evaluate each new hire after thirty and ninety days to ensure a values match.
Reinforcement, reward, and recognition	• Have the value of the day (or week or month) pop up on the organization's intranet. • At staff meetings, have people identify times since the prior staff meeting when someone has embodied one of the values; provide an award for top performance. • Distribute customer feedback about a person who demonstrates one of the organization's values. • Include a 360-degree review of each employee annually against the values; provide recognition and reward for highest scorers.

Sample Guiding Principles

Examples of guiding principles follow. While the standard format for a guiding principle is, "We believe... (value). Therefore, we will... (behaviors)," note the different ways in which these guiding principles are formatted, while identifying both the value and the behaviors that support the value.

Continuous improvement	We seek continuous improvement. Therefore, we'll strive not to make the same mistake twice. When a mistake is made, not only do we correct it, we seek to understand why the mistake occurred and what we need to do to prevent it from happening again.
Corporate citizen	We conduct our business in a socially responsible and ethical manner. We respect the law, support universal human rights, protect the environment, and benefit the communities where we work.
Corporate citizen	We commit to making the world a better place by being involved in our community.
Customer service	Because we value our customers, we will: • Make our customers our top priority. • Do our best to satisfy our customers' needs. • Provide unmatched customer service. • Treat our customers with respect and dignity. • Continue to "date" our customers on a consistent basis, even after entering into business with them. • Be courteous to our customers. • Listen to our customers. • Respond to our customers in a timely manner.
Customer service	We will not forget that our customers are our bosses, and that they pay our wages. We're responsive, respectful, efficient, and timely.
Customer service	We'll provide unparalleled customer service through fanatical attention to consistency and detail.
Dedication	We're dedicated to doing everything we can to help our organization be a success by working harder and smarter than our competitors.
Enthusiasm	We bring an intense and eager passion to our work each day.
Follow-through	We do what we say we're going to do. Follow-through and execution are our focus.

Industry leaders	We believe to be effective industry leaders requires investment in innovative ideas. Therefore, we will: • Interact with our customers to understand and respond to their changing needs. • Seek new opportunities. • Build and maintain partnerships. • Strive to be on the leading edge of the industry.
Integrity	We do the right thing, even when no one is looking. We strive to maintain a high level of integrity and consistency in our interactions with our clients and each other. Dishonesty isn't tolerated.
Integrity	We'll let ethics and honesty govern our conduct in dealings with customers, team members, suppliers, and our company.
Leadership	We believe in progressive leadership—leaders who recognize that their job is to be a vehicle for maximizing their employees' effectiveness. Therefore, we will: • Be giving of ourselves as leaders. • Make all managerial decisions by going through a decision checklist (e.g., ethics, feasibility, legality, impact). • Be consistent in our decision-making process. • Maximize our resources, both human and capital. • Hold employees responsible for their actions. • Recognize employees on the basis of their performance.
Needs-focused	We meet our clients' needs, not just satisfy their requirements. We strive to understand our clients' real needs to ensure that we provide solutions that work.
Openness	We listen to the ideas of others and encourage an open dialogue.
Ownership thinking	We believe in ownership thinking. We spend the company's money as if it's our own. We're careful to spend our time only on activities that bring value to the company.
Performance standards	We value a high standard of performance. Therefore, we will: • Reward employees for exceptional performance. • Hold ourselves accountable for our performance. • Be innovative and creative. • Be cost-effective. • Exhibit professional behavior at all times (e.g., dressing appropriately, being punctual).

Personal responsibility	We take personal responsibility. If we have an issue, we take responsibility for getting it solved (as opposed to complaining to others or withdrawing); when we make mistakes we admit our responsibility.
Professional ethics	We believe that professional conduct is crucial in all aspects of our business. Therefore, we: • Are respectful and honest. • Subscribe to and demonstrate ethical standards. • Don't show favoritism or discrimination.
Proficiency	We strive for high proficiency by developing competence in all aspects of our work through personal and professional training. We seek knowledge.
Quality	We fulfill a promise to deliver the highest quality in everything we make. We design for quality—we have quality in our processes, our people, and our technology. We don't deliver until we know it is ready.
Safety	We maintain an environment that minimizes danger, risk, or injury.
Team	We maintain a positive team environment. We're positive in our communications and we support each other with assistance, information, and guidance, as opposed to being concerned only about self and bringing negative energy into the workplace. No cynicism is allowed.
Team	We believe in the value of teamwork. Therefore, we'll maintain an environment that promotes: • Constructive and effective communication throughout the organization. • Respect for the diversity of opinions. • Participation and cooperation. • Innovation. • Adherence to deadlines.

The Process

While there are a number of different approaches for developing guiding principles, the Drivers Model uses a scenario-based approach, as outlined in the steps that follow:

1 Educate on guiding principles.

As with prior components, start the discussion of guiding principles by educating your team on what guiding principles are and the specific format used.

2 Identify the behaviors you want.

After introducing the guiding principles concept, provide a scenario in which your team members visualize someone in the organization who exemplifies the organization's values and culture. Have your team members identify the behaviors that make that person exemplary.

3 Identify the behaviors you don't want.

Once you've identified the behaviors that you want, the next step is to identify the behaviors you don't want. Describe a scenario in which team members are orienting a new hire. Ask them to indicate what behaviors they would tell the new hire aren't tolerated, aren't liked, aren't acceptable, and might even get the new hire fired.

4 Identify the values.

With both key characteristics and intolerable behaviors listed, have your team group these into logical categories. These categories typically represent the values of the organization and serve as the starting point for your guiding principles.

5 Draft the guiding principles.

To draft the guiding principles, take each of the value categories and create guiding principles, using the "We believe (value)... Therefore, we will... (behaviors)" format as a template. To conserve time, you might do the first guiding principle as an entire group and then use breakout groups to create the remainder of them.

6 Perform a quality check.

To ensure the quality of the guiding principles, use the quality check process that follows.

7 Develop the transformation plan.

The final step in the guiding principles process is to determine the strategies you and your team will use to transform the guiding principles from paper to action. Start by reviewing strategies that other organizations have used. Then, have your team brainstorm strategies that could be used, and then select the strategies that you'll use.

The Quality Check

If you and your team have done a great job of developing guiding principles, you'll able to answer yes to each of the following questions:

Quality check

- Do the guiding principles identify all the organization's key values?

- Are the principles worded in such a way as to indicate both the value and the expected behaviors (e.g., "We believe… [value]. Therefore, we will… [behaviors]")?

- Has your team developed a transformation plan to help make the guiding principles part of the organization's daily operations?

Your Role in Setting the Guiding Principles

Since guiding principles are a critical element for communicating the type of culture desired in the organization, you'll want to pay close attention to the following:

The role of the leader

- When it comes to any aspect of the strategic plan, many will look to you, the leader, and model what you do. While this is true for nearly all aspects of the plan, I've found this to be doubly true with guiding principles. If the leader doesn't take them seriously, then you can bet this attitude will be replicated throughout the organization. Therefore, it's essential that you communicate the value you see in the guiding principles and ensure that your walk matches your talk.

- Though you'll want to keep the guiding principles down to a manageable number (typically less than ten), make sure that no key value is missing.

- With the transformation plan, often the human resources organization is asked to lead implementation. However, since the transformation plan is the key vehicle for moving the guiding principles into action, consider having a team of at least three from different areas working together to ensure the implementation.

- Overview
- Defining Critical Success Factors
- Defining Barriers
- The Finer Points
- Sample Critical Success Factors and Barriers
- The Process
- The Quality Check
- Your Role in Critical Success Factors and Barriers

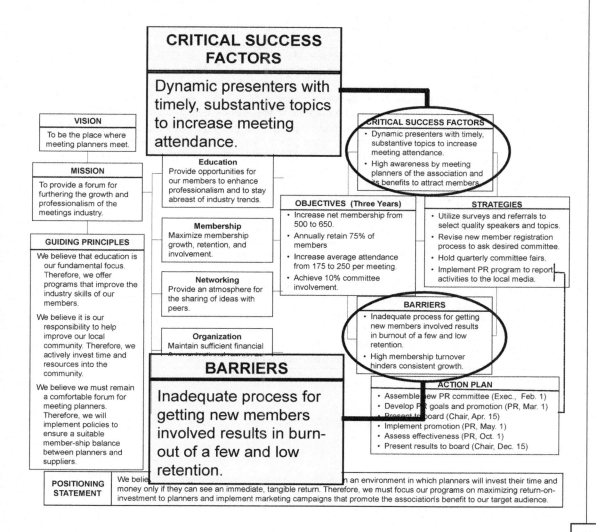

Summary: Critical Success Factors (CSFs) and Barriers

	Critical Success Factors	Barriers
Definition	Key conditions that must be created to achieve one or more objectives.	Existing or potential challenges that hinder the achievement of one or more objectives.

	Critical Success Factors	Barriers
Examples	• Automobile body styles that are pleasing to the public. • High buy-in and commitment to achieving the plan. • Rapid response to changes in market demand.	• Public perception of poor quality by USA auto manufacturers. • Lack of alignment between individual performance targets and strategic objectives.

	Critical Success Factors and Barriers
Success strategies	• Review the definition, quality check, and success strategies for CSFs and barriers. • Review the objectives for each goal and ask yourself, "What key conditions must be created for these objectives to be achieved?" • Once you have defined the CSFs for the goal, have the team define the barriers for this same goal by asking, "Why aren't these objectives achieved already? What is standing in our way?" • Keep in mind that there is no need to have a barrier that is the opposite of a CSF. • Perform a quality check.
Quality check	• Have the most critical conditions that must be created and the major barriers impacting success been identified? • Are the CSFs stated as nouns with conditions (e.g., "effective dealer network") and not as verbs (e.g., "develop")? • Are the barriers phrased in such a way as to encourage strategies for overcoming them? • Per goal, do you have at least two and no more than seven CSFs, and at least two and no more than seven barriers? • Do the barriers avoid duplication with the CSFs?

Overview

Once you have defined your goals, objectives, and guiding principles, it can be very tempting to jump straight to strategies. Your team will have answered already, "Where are we now?" and, "Where do we want to be?" Therefore, they will naturally want to drive to the next question, "How do we get there?"

However, to maximize the plan's effectiveness, your team will have to exercise artificial patience. Before answering the how question, the team has to answer two important questions first: "Why aren't we there already?" and, "What are the key conditions, if we create them, that will drive us to our vision?" In this chapter, we show you how to answer these two questions by defining your barriers and CSFs, the fourth principle in the Seven Principles of Masterful Planning.

Seven principles of Masterful Planning	
	1. Be clear on purpose.
	2. Start with an accurate assessment of today.
	3. Create a shared vision of success.
	4. Identify your critical successful factors and barriers.
	5. Define the drivers: your strategies and priorities.
	6. Monitor and report results.
	7. Have rewards and consequences to build accountability.

Defining Critical Success Factors

As indicated in Chapter 1, I personally believe that the CSFs concept is one of the most important ideas in planning. My experience has been that if you can fully grasp this concept and incorporate it into your planning, you can significantly increase the quality of your plans and the likelihood of success. What are CSFs? Think of them as the key conditions that must be created to achieve your objective.

If you were building a home, your objective might be to be in a suitable house with an affordable mortgage by December 31. The CSFs, or key conditions for success, might be the following:

Sample CSFs for building a home	
	• Sufficient funding.
	• Quality materials.
	• Superior contractors.
	• A floor plan that meets your needs.
	• A smooth and effective construction process.

Note the format of CSFs. They indicate the condition that must be met. The CSF wasn't just materials, but instead, quality materials. The CSF wasn't just a floor plan, but instead, a floor plan that meets our needs.

Note also that CSFs are nouns (the conditions that must be created), not verbs (the actions you take to create the condition). CSFs don't tell you what to do; they instead describe the conditions that must be created. There may be many ways to create the condition.

Let's take a different example. If you are a car manufacturer, your objective is to sell lots of cars. What might some of your CSFs be?

Sample CSFs for a car manufacturer	<ul><li>Pleasing body styles.</li><li>A customer-focused dealer network.</li><li>Quality-focused and efficient manufacturing process.</li><li>Wide awareness of your product by the target purchasers.</li></ul>

Below are the goal, objectives, and CSFs for the membership goal of the meeting planners sample organization.

Membership Goal Maximize membership growth, retention, and involvement.	
Objectives	**CSFs**
<ul><li>Increase net membership from 500 to 650.</li><li>Annually retain 75 percent of members from prior year.</li><li>Increase average attendance from 175 to 250 per meeting.</li><li>Achieve 10 percent committee involvement.</li></ul>	<ul><li>High awareness of association by meeting planners to attract new members.</li><li>Dynamic presenters with timely, substantive topics to increase meeting attendance.</li></ul>

In just about any endeavor, there are no fewer than two and no more than seven CSFs. These are the key conditions, if you create them, that will propel you to success. Let's take another example to further illustrate the point.

Let's say you have been named the fundraising chairperson for your favorite charity. This year, the charity is looking to raise $20,000 through a bowlathon.

<table>
<tr><td>

How a bowlathon works

</td><td>

- In a bowlathon, people come together for an afternoon of bowling. Each person who bowls will ask friends, family, and others to "sponsor" the bowler.

- Sponsors pledge to donate to the charity a dollar, a quarter, a dime, or some other amount for every pin that the bowler knocks down in the best of three games.

- So, for example, if I have ten sponsors, six who agree to donate $1 per pin and four who agree to donate a quarter per pin, if my best game is 100, six sponsors will donate $100 each and four sponsors will donate $25 each on my behalf.

- From my sponsors, the charity will receive $700 in donations.

</td></tr>
</table>

The bowlathon will be in nine months. Being a planner, you sit down to write out a detailed action plan for executing the bowlathon. You know that one of the things you have to do is find a bowling alley to hold the bowlathon. So, one of the first actions in your action plan is, "Locate a bowling alley."

Wrong answer.

Locating a bowling alley is an important action and seems logically and sequentially to be a step you would take first or nearly first. But it should NOT be, at least not according to the Seven Principles of Masterful Planning.

<table>
<tr><td>

Using masterful planning principles with the bowlathon

</td><td>

- **Principle 1: Be clear on purpose.** The purpose was defined for you: Raise money for the charity, so that the charity will have adequate funds to do the good work that it does.

- **Principle 2: Start with an accurate assessment of today.** Let's assume that the team that chose the bowlathon as the fundraising project has already done a review of the strengths and weaknesses of what was done in the past, and also an assessment of the target audience and the readiness for something like a bowlathon.

- **Principle 3: Create a shared vision of success.** Once more, this was defined for you: raising $20,000 dollars.

- **Principle 4: Define your critical success factors and barriers.** Before putting pen to developing your action plan, you should define your CSFs and barriers first.

</td></tr>
</table>

So, let's ask the question, "What are your CSFs? If you're seeking to raise $20,000 through a bowlathon, what are the key conditions for success?" I believe there are essentially two key conditions: You have to have a lot of bowlers and those bowlers have to have a lot of patrons. And it wouldn't hurt, of course, if those bowlers were pretty good bowlers—but that's not critical, just a plus.

Let's start with the first CSFs: lots of bowlers. If you want to get lots of people to bowl in the bowlathon, where would you go to get them? Perhaps one strategy would be to go where the bowlers are: You could ask several bowling leagues if they would be willing to bowl for your bowlathon. If one says yes, you could have forty-eight bowlers. If another says yes, you could have ninety-six bowlers and you would be well on your way. Where would you locate the bowling alley? Near the leagues that agreed to bowl, of course.

But suppose you had chosen the bowling alley first by selecting the cheapest, least expensive alternative to save money. And then, when you went to leagues and asked if their bowlers would bowl, they would ask you, "Where's the bowling alley?" You might then have leagues declining because the bowling alley was located somewhere inconvenient to their bowlers. The success of your plan would suffer because you didn't plan for your critical success factors first.

Once more, selecting a bowling alley is an important activity, but not the most critical. And this leads us to our next secret.

> **Secret #20** To ensure that your plan focuses on the most important activities, define your critical conditions and the strategies you'll use to create them.
>
> Then, build the rest of your plan around these key strategies.

The key is to identify your CSFs first before defining your strategies. Once you know what is critical to success, you can identify strategies to create those critical conditions. Focus first on the critical items and build the rest your plan around them.

Defining Barriers

While CSFs define the key conditions that must be created, barriers identify the key obstacles or constraints that stand in the way of success. Barriers answer the question, "Why aren't we there already? What is standing in our way?" Barriers typically start with words like "lack of" or "inadequate," or some other term denoting insufficiency.

My experience has been that teams often struggle with CSFs, but typically have no problem identifying barriers. Yet, I strive to limit barriers to no fewer than two and no more than seven per goal area to keep focus on the most important barriers.

Below are the goal, objectives, and barriers for our by-now familiar example of the membership goal of the meeting planners association.

Membership Goal	
Maximize membership growth, retention, and involvement	
Objectives	**Barriers**
• Increase net membership from 500 to 650. • Annually retain 75 percent of members from prior year. • Increase average attendance from 175 to 250 per meeting. • Achieve 10 percent committee involvement.	• Inadequate process for getting new members involved results in burnout of a few and low retention. • High membership turnover hinders consistent growth.

The Finer Points

I want to make several additional points about CSFs and barriers.

Finer points about developing CSFs and barriers

- It's common for a CSF or barrier to affect more than one objective, as is the case with the barrier above: "Inadequate process for getting new members involved results in burnout of a few and low retention." This barrier affects both the retention objective *(annually retain 75 percent of members from prior year)* and the involvement objective *(achieve 10 percent committee involvement).*

- In wording a CSF, don't just restate the objective; instead, focus on the factor that will determine if the objective will be achieved. For example, if your objective is to increase membership from 500 to 650, a CSF would NOT be *having more people sign up to become members.* This is simply a restatement of the objective. The CSF would be the condition needed in order to attract more new members.

- It isn't necessary to identify an item as both a CSF and a barrier. For example, adequate funding may be a CSF and lack of *adequate funding* may be a barrier. Since the aim of CSF and barrier analysis is to point you to the most important strategies, if an item can be in either area, simply choose the one that's most appropriate.

- Limit your CSFs and barriers to those things that can be impacted by the organization. Those things that cannot be controlled (e.g., weather) would more likely appear as assumptions.

Finer points about developing CSFs and barriers

(cont.)

- While you may identify many conditions that "must be created" and barriers standing in the way, a goal typically has no fewer than two, and no more than seven, CSFs. Likewise, a goal typically has no fewer than two, and no more than seven, barriers.

- Finally, while CSFs and barriers can be developed in either order, with the Drivers Model you identify CSFs first. I have found that teams that develop barriers first often fall into the trap of transforming the CSF question to, "What conditions must we create to overcome the barriers?" rather than asking the true CSF question, "What conditions must we create to achieve the objectives?" Teams that don't ask the true CSF question may develop and implement strategies to overcome the barriers, only to learn a critical condition for successfully achieving the objectives was never addressed, because the true CSF question was never asked.

Sample Critical Success Factors and Barriers

What follows are CSFs and barriers for several sample goal areas.

Growth and Profitability Optimize growth while meeting profitability targets.		
Objectives	**CSFs**	**Barriers**
• Grow top line revenue at least 12 percent per year. • Expand market share by 5 percentage points in each of our top three target markets by year three. • Achieve 10 percent net profit (EBITDA) annually.	• Products designed specifically to address critical customer needs. • Well-defined and well-communicated value accepted by customers in the target markets to maximize revenue. • Efficient operations with minimal overhead to keep costs down.	• Ineffective marketing campaigns limits widespread understanding of our product set. • Limited product knowledge of our salespeople increases sales cycle time. • Delays in product development results in untimely release of products.

Programs
Provide caring, cost-effective programs that produce life-enhancing results.

Objectives	CSFs	Barriers
• Increase the total number of people served by 15 percent by the third year. • Achieve individual program outcome targets for at least 75 percent of clients annually. • Each year, have 90 percent of clients surveyed report services were delivered in a compassionate manner. • Maintain program prices at or below the average for our seven-organization peer group sample.	• Clear and realistic outcome measures. • Well trained, competent and caring staff. • System that rewards high productivity.	• Insufficient awareness of programs by staffs of some of our referring agencies. • Inefficient handling of peak and low demand times.

Health Communications
Provide high-quality health information to consumers, providers, and policy makers to help ensure well-informed decisions.

Objectives	CSFs	Barriers
• Increase by 100 percent the number of professional provider groups and targeted organizations providing endorsements of agency-defined messages. • Achieve a minimum of six agency-generated articles/stories per year that appear in at least one of the top fifteen national media outlets. • Increase by 25 percent the distribution of materials to consumers and professionals, as measured by Internet hits and requests for materials. • Increase by 50 percent the number of fulfilled requests for information from targeted decision makers.	• Awareness by provider groups of the role they can play in prevention. • A well-designed, easy-to-navigate website with a simple name.	• Lack of health communication expertise in the agency. • A focus by us on raw data versus delivering information that tells a story.

Customers
Provide customers with information, so they can make better decisions to exercise more control over their environment.

Objectives	CSFs	Barriers
• Increase the level of overall customer satisfaction with our products and services, as measured by increasing satisfaction survey score by 3 points. • Increase by 20 percent the number of customers who say decisions were affected by information we provided, based on feedback received via survey.	• High awareness of the information needs of our various customer groups. • High levels of customer-relevant data, easily accessible. • High awareness by our target audience of our databases as a source of valuable information.	• Tendency to create what we think users want versus what they tell us they want. • A focus by us on raw data versus delivering information that tells a story.

The Process

The process for developing critical success factors and barriers includes the following steps.

1 Educate on critical success factors and barriers.

Begin by having your team members review the definition, quality check, and success strategies for CSFs and barriers. After the review, take the team through one or more examples where they identify the CSFs.

2 Define the critical success factors for the first goal.

After introducing the concepts, have the entire team define the CSFs for the first goal. To do this, you'll focus on each of the objectives for the goal and ask, "What key conditions must be created for these objectives to be achieved?" Note that in some cases, you may have to focus one objective at a time. Frequently, however, I find that CSFs tend to cover more than one objective in a goal area.

3 Define the barriers for the first goal.

Once you have defined the CSFs for the first goal, you can quickly move the team to defining the barriers for this same goal by asking, "Why aren't these objectives achieved already? What is standing in our way?" Keep in mind that there's no need to have a barrier that is the opposite of a CSFs, as described earlier.

4 Perform a quality check for the first goal.

Once the CSFs and barriers are identified for the first goal, perform a quality check.

5 Repeat steps 2, 3, and 4 for the remaining goals.

With the first goal done, you'll next have your team repeat steps 2, 3, and 4 for the remaining goals. While you might use breakout groups for this, I find that this activity tends to flow relatively quickly. Therefore, keeping the entire team together typically works well.

The Quality Check

If you and your team have done a great job of developing CSFs and barriers, you'll able to answer yes to each of the following questions.

Quality check

- Have the most critical conditions that must be created and the major barriers impacting success been identified?

- Are the CSFs stated as nouns with conditions (e.g., "effective dealer network") and not as verbs (e.g., "develop")?

- Are the barriers phrased in such a way as to encourage strategies for overcoming them?

- Do you have at least two and no more than seven CSFs and at least two and no more than seven barriers per goal?

- Do the barriers avoid duplication with the CSFs?

Your Role in Critical Success Factors and Barriers

CSFs and barriers are powerful building blocks that are used to focus your strategies. It's important that nothing essential is missing from either list. Consider playing the following role during this segment of the planning.

The role of the leader

- During the CSF development process, continually ask yourself, "Have we identified the most critical conditions for success?" If you miss a critical condition, it's possible, and quite likely, that an important strategy will be overlooked.

- While most teams are readily able to identify barriers, ensure that none is missing.

- Make sure the CSFs and barriers pass the quality check.

Strategies, Priorities and Deliverables 12

- Overview
- Prioritization
- The Process
- The Quality Check
- Your Role in Strategies, Priorities, and Deliverables

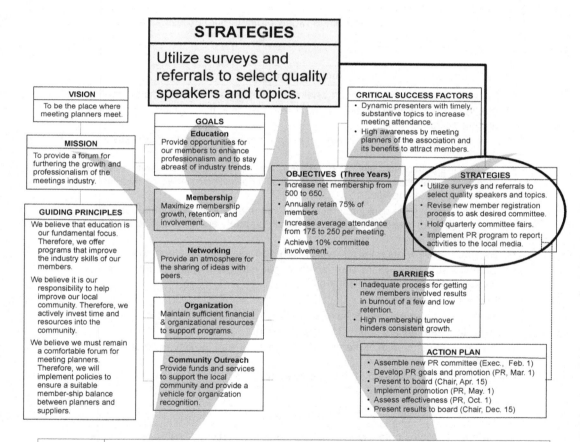

STRATEGIES

Utilize surveys and referrals to select quality speakers and topics.

VISION
To be the place where meeting planners meet.

MISSION
To provide a forum for furthering the growth and professionalism of the meetings industry.

GUIDING PRINCIPLES
We believe that education is our fundamental focus. Therefore, we offer programs that improve the industry skills of our members.

We believe it is our responsibility to help improve our local community. Therefore, we actively invest time and resources into the community.

We believe we must remain a comfortable forum for meeting planners. Therefore, we will implement policies to ensure a suitable member-ship balance between planners and suppliers.

GOALS

Education
Provide opportunities for our members to enhance professionalism and to stay abreast of industry trends.

Membership
Maximize membership growth, retention, and involvement.

Networking
Provide an atmosphere for the sharing of ideas with peers.

Organization
Maintain sufficient financial & organizational resources to support programs.

Community Outreach
Provide funds and services to support the local community and provide a vehicle for organization recognition.

CRITICAL SUCCESS FACTORS
- Dynamic presenters with timely, substantive topics to increase meeting attendance.
- High awareness by meeting planners of the association and its benefits to attract members.

OBJECTIVES (Three Years)
- Increase net membership from 500 to 650.
- Annually retain 75% of members
- Increase average attendance from 175 to 250 per meeting.
- Achieve 10% committee involvement.

STRATEGIES
- Utilize surveys and referrals to select quality speakers and topics.
- Revise new member registration process to ask desired committee.
- Hold quarterly committee fairs.
- Implement PR program to report activities to the local media.

BARRIERS
- Inadequate process for getting new members involved results in burnout of a few and low retention.
- High membership turnover hinders consistent growth.

ACTION PLAN
- Assemble new PR committee (Exec., Feb. 1)
- Develop PR goals and promotion (PR, Mar. 1)
- Present to board (Chair, Apr. 15)
- Implement promotion (PR, May. 1)
- Assess effectiveness (PR, Oct. 1)
- Present results to board (Chair, Dec. 15)

POSITIONING STATEMENT
We believe that budget cuts and staff reductions have resulted in an environment in which planners will invest their time and money only if they can see an immediate, tangible return. Therefore, we must focus our programs on maximizing return-on-investment to planners and implement marketing campaigns that promote the association's benefit to our target audience.

Summary: Strategies

Definition	Strategies are broad activities required to achieve an objective, create a critical condition, or overcome a barrier.

Examples	• Reengineer our product development process to reduce cycle time and increase efficiencies. • Establish partnership with a Japanese manufacturer to revamp the northeast plant. • Implement program to widely promote our success as a quality producer.

Success Strategies
• Educate your team members on what strategies are and the specific format used.
• Divide up the potential strategies and the strategies in the positioning statements among the goal teams.
• Review the objectives to brainstorm one or more key strategies to address the objective.
• Review the critical success factors (CSFs) and barriers to ensure that each one is sufficiently addressed by a strategy. If a CSF or barrier isn't adequately addressed, add strategies as needed.
• Likewise, review the assigned positioning statements to ensure that each one is sufficiently addressed by a strategy. If not adequately addressed, add strategies as needed.
• Be sure to review potential strategies identified earlier in the planning process.
• Combine strategies where appropriate, especially taking into account similar focuses and implementation timetables.
• Perform a quality check.
• To prepare for prioritization, have a structured lobby period.
• Have the team decide priority strategies, using a voting and selection process.
• Assign leaders to each of the priority strategies to lead the development of action plans.
• Define the deliverables for each priority strategy.

Quality Check
• Are the strategies phrased as activities to be accomplished—NOT results to be achieved?
• Are the strategies formatted with a verb, object, and purpose?
• Do the strategies address the CSFs and barriers?
• If the strategies are implemented, is it highly likely that the objectives will be achieved?
• Have priority strategies been identified, and have deliverables been defined for each priority strategy?

Overview

When it comes to strategic planning, strategies are where the rubber meets the road. All the work that has been done up to this point is to lead your team to this moment where it defines and selects the key strategies for focus. You have completed an assessment of the current situation. You have created a vision of the future, defined your mission and goals, established specific measurable targets, agreed on the principles to guide your actions, and identified the CSFs and barriers hindering success. The stage is now set for you to define the broad activities—the strategies—your team will undertake to move your vision into reality.

We recommend a specific format for strategies, as described in this next secret.

> **Secret #21** To ensure clarity of your strategies, use the verb–object–purpose format.

Because strategies are "broad activities," the verb–object–purpose format starts with action (verb), states what is acted upon (object), and explains why (purpose). The sample strategies that follow demonstrate the verb–object–purpose format.

Sample strategies

- Create sales leveraging tools to assist sales team in growing accounts.

- Develop and implement vertical marketing strategy to increase revenue by capitalizing on existing customer knowledge.

- Implement incentive program to reward caregivers for productivity, client success, and client satisfaction.

- Hold briefings with at least three agencies a quarter to hear about their needs and update them on our programs and direction.

- Revamp partner program to increase number of partners, revenue, and residual.

- Reengineer our product development process to reduce cycle time and increase efficiencies.

- Establish partnership with a Japanese manufacturer to revamp the northeast plant.

- Hold quarterly committee fairs after meetings to increase member involvement.

Sample strategies *(cont.)*	• Implement program to widely promote our success as a quality producer.
	• Develop a manager "professional development" program to improve managers' ability to coach their teams and to increase morale and productivity.

Strategy Verbs

With the verb–object–purpose format, the selection of the verb is important.

> **Secret #22** **With strategies, be sure to start with a "strategy" verb and not an "objective" verb.**

As first presented in Chapter 9, the table that follows illustrates the difference between objective and strategy verbs. Verbs on the left in the table will tend to lead you to describe the results to be achieved. The verbs on the right will tend to lead you to describe the action to be taken. While objectives focus on results, strategies focus on action.

Sample objective verbs (quantitative verbs)	Sample strategy verbs (finite verbs)
Increase	Establish
Reduce	Develop
Achieve	Implement
Maintain	Build
Have	Create

Transforming "Result" Statements into Strategies

In developing strategies, it's quite common for a team member to offer a strategy that is a result and not an activity. You can help convert the result into an activity by asking, "By doing what?" For example, suppose a team member gave the following "result" statement as a strategy.

Result statement instead of a strategy	"If our objective is to have 80 percent of our people achieving their performance targets, I think the best strategy to accomplish that is to *increase employees' morale and productivity.*"

Of course this is not a strategy; this is a result. The person has given the "purpose" in our "verb–object–purpose" format. To help convert this purpose statement to a strategy, you would ask, "So, we would increase employees' morale and productivity by doing what?" Whatever the person says next is most likely the strategy. For example, the person might say, "We would do that by providing our managers training in how to motivate employees." So, in this case, the strategy would read as follows.

| **The actual strategy** | Offer our managers training in how to motivate employees to increase employees' morale and productivity. |

Prioritization

If you're a veteran of planning, you know that most planning efforts result in more strategies than you can possibly implement at once. Most organizations would be fortunate to implement six to twelve strategic initiatives in a year. However, many teams end up with twenty-five to forty potential strategies, and one team I worked with had over one hundred! How do you go about deciding which strategies to undertake first? How do you determine your priorities?

There are a number of approaches for prioritizing.

| **Dot method** | Some organizations use the dot method: Each team member receives a certain number of sticky dots based on the number of priorities desired. Your team members are told to place their dots on those strategies that they believe should be started on first. The priorities with the most dots are given top priority. |

| **Weighted score** | Other organizations use a more elaborate, analytical approach, such as the weighted score method: The team scores each strategy against a predetermined list of criteria. The criteria are given weights and the weighted score for a strategy is determined by multiplying the strategy's score for each criterion by the criteria's weight and then adding the results. Those strategies with the highest weighted scores are given top priority. |

| **Hybrid approach** | And still other organizations take a hybrid approach: For example, they evaluate each strategy against a small number of criteria, using a high–medium–low scale. They then use dots to determine final selection. |

Whatever approach you use for determining priorities with your team, keep four basic concepts in mind.

Define the Criteria That People Should Use in Setting Priorities

Without a set of common criteria, your team members will use what they believe is important. Unfortunately, in many cases, a person's individual criteria may differ significantly from the organization's. For example, one person's sole criterion for priority setting might be based on how well each strategy supports that person's department—a fairly myopic view. This brings us to our next secret.

> **Secret #23** **When setting priorities, have your team members identify a common set of criteria to consider.**
>
> Having criteria often helps a team reach agreement more quickly because they're viewing the alternatives through the same lens.

Consider using these three criteria, at a minimum.

Impact on objectives	If the strategy is successfully implemented, what will be the impact on achieving key objectives?
Probability of success	What is the probability that the strategy will be successfully implemented if we decide to undertake it?
Cost-effectiveness	How do the tangible and intangible results expected from this strategy compare to the costs and resources required to implement it?

Provide a Lobbying Period Prior to Voting

With prioritization, the Drivers Model recommends a lobbying period in which every team member has the opportunity to identify and explain why particular strategies should be given support. Lobbying should occur right before any voting activity. For example, if your team scores strategies against criteria, we recommend that lobby occur after the scoring, but before voting, balloting, or dotting.

> **Secret #24** **Prior to voting on priorities, have a period of controlled lobbying to build strong consensus and commitment.**

How does controlled lobbying work? I typically give each person the opportunity to take thirty to sixty seconds to explain to the group the most important strategies to support and why. The key is "the why." Through explaining why support should be given, each person has the opportunity through the lobbying process to influence the opinions of others.

As a result of lobbying, I've found that two important outcomes often occur. First, the process helps build consensus around particular solutions, as your team members repeatedly hear support for a small number of strategies. Second, once the prioritization is complete and it's time to assign implementation responsibility, people more readily volunteer to lead items for which they lobbied.

Recognize That a Score Is Not a Decision

Whether using the dot method, weighted scoring, or some hybrid method, the result is typically a number that indicates the level of support for a particular strategy. It's important to recognize that the number is just a result of the analysis that was done and should serve as input to the final decision, and not the final decision itself. Once the team ranks strategies by the scores each received, it's still their job to accept the scores as indicating the final priorities, or to make adjustments as necessary.

For example, one organization realized after prioritizing that none of the internal activities (e.g., staff development, technology upgrades) received high enough scores to be given priority. However, the team agreed to place one of these strategies on the priority list because it was essential to moving forward, and because it sent the message to staff that internal improvements were important, as well.

Keep Strategies That Don't Make the Priority List

The point of the prioritization process is to identify the strategies that will be started first. This doesn't mean that the other strategies aren't important. It simply means that they will not be the first ones implemented.

So, what happens to these other strategies that don't become a priority? In the Drivers Model, they're added to the strategy document and, as you'll see in Chapter 14, they're reviewed as part of the quarterly strategy monitoring process to determine if they should be started.

The Process

The process you use for developing strategies and setting priorities must take into account several key points.

Key points for the process

- The process should consider the numerous potential strategies identified throughout the process, and especially those defined during the briefing book review.

- Each of the strategies you define must significantly contribute to achieving an objective, creating a critical condition, or overcoming a key barrier.

- The process should combine similar strategies where appropriate.

- The process must result in a list of priorities that indicates where to start.

Implementation Planning

To incorporate these key points, the Drivers Model includes the following process.

1 Educate on strategies.

As with prior components, start the discussion of strategies by educating your team members on what strategies are and the specific format used.

2 Divide up the potential strategies and the strategies in the positioning statements.

Throughout the planning process, your team will have identified numerous potential strategies, which will have been documented for consideration during strategy development. At this point, you'll want to assign each of the potential strategies, and the strategies from the positioning statements, to the most appropriate goal team for consideration, as the team creates the list of strategies needed to accomplish the objectives.

3 Brainstorm strategies for the goal.

I highly recommend using breakout groups to develop strategies due to the amount of time needed for each goal area. As always, if you do use breakout groups, it's helpful to build strategies for one goal area as an entire group before breaking out, if time permits. This will help everyone better understand both the process for strategy development and the result to be achieved.

The strategy development process starts by reviewing each objective in the goal area and brainstorming strategies to achieve it. Be sure that each strategy has the verb–object–purpose format.

4 Ensure CSFs, barriers, and positioning statements are covered.

After brainstorming to identify strategies for each of the objectives, the team must ensure that each of the CSFs, barriers, and positioning statements are addressed by at least one strategy. If a CSF, barrier, or positioning statement isn't addressed, the team should add a strategy as needed.

5 Consider the potential strategies developed earlier.

Throughout the planning process, your team will have identified numerous potential strategies, which will have been documented for consideration during strategy development. At this point, you'll want to assign each of the potential strategies, and the strategies from the positioning statements, to the most appropriate goal team for consideration, as the team creates the list of strategies needed to accomplish the objectives.

6 Combine strategies where appropriate.

A key step in strategy development is to combine strategies wherever appropriate. This is important. As a result of prioritization, only a limited number of strategies will be implemented at first. Therefore, consider combining strategies that are similar in purpose, represent multiple steps in what could be a more comprehensive strategy, or would not be complete if both were not undertaken.

7 Perform a quality check.

Review each of the quality check items to ensure the strategies are up to par.

8 Review the resulting strategies for completion and overlap.

Once the breakout teams complete their work, the next step is to review the strategies. The goal during this review is to ensure that the strategies will indeed achieve the objectives and to combine strategies across goal areas as appropriate.

To accomplish the review, it's helpful to have strategies on display for all planning team members. Accordingly, I often ask the teams to record each strategy on a separate sheet of paper and ask them to tape the strategies to a wall of the room set aside for their strategy sheets. Then, I ask the entire team to come to the wall and review the strategies for each goal area. This review often results in combining strategies from different goal areas because the two strategies are similar or related.

9 Lobby to build consensus and commitment.

As indicated earlier, lobbying is a powerful process that can serve to build consensus around a few strategies and to increase the level of commitment people feel to participate in implementation. During lobbying, each team member has the opportunity to highlight specific strategies and explain why they believe the strategies should be given support.

10 Decide priority strategies.

Following lobbying, the team is ready to vote and establish priorities. To accomplish this, you'll have people vote, tally the votes, and have the group come to conclusion on the priority items.

I like using dots for voting because dots get people up and provide a visual representation of the group's general sentiment. Unfortunately, those who are veterans of the dot process will often sit back and let others vote first, so that they can use their dots to swing close decisions. To limit

10 *(cont.)*

this effect, I purposely allow only a limited time for voting (typically five minutes), so that there will be less time for "swing" voting.

When using dots, I typically use two colors, such as blue and red, to have weighted voting. A blue dot is worth three points and a red dot is worth one point. I encourage people to put their "blue chips" on the strategies that are most important to them.

I also insist that a person can put only one dot on any one strategy. This way, the number of dots will indeed indicate the number of people that support the strategy. A person can't dictate a priority by placing all of his/her dots on a single or a few strategies.

The number of dots to provide can vary. As a rule of thumb, I typically provide 20–30 percent of the number of strategies, or somewhere between eight and twelve dots, evenly split between the two colors.

Once the voting is complete and you have tallied the scores, you'll be able to rank the strategies from top to bottom. You can then use the informed majority process described in Chapter 6 to gain consensus.

11 Assign action plan leaders.

With the priorities set, you can now assign leaders to each of the priority strategies. As the group's leader, you may choose the strategy leaders, request volunteers, or "request" that particular people volunteer. (Some have called this last option, "Being voluntold.")

Action plan leaders have responsibility for assembling a team to develop a detailed action plan for the assigned priority strategy. The action plan details what will be accomplished, how it will be accomplished, who will perform each step and by when, the necessary resources, and the out-of-pocket costs. The action plan also assigns an overall owner for the strategy. In some cases, the leader assigned to develop the action plan will also turn out to be the strategy owner. Frequently, however, the action plan process identifies a different overall owner for the strategy. Therefore, at this point in the process, the role of the action plan leader is simply to assemble a team and develop the action plan.

12 Define the deliverables for each priority strategy.

I've found that action planning teams often struggle to understand the scope of their work and what the action plan needs to include. To alleviate this issue, I recommend identifying for each team the specific deliverables that the priority strategy should produce. By having defined deliverables up front, the action planning teams can focus on developing the steps for creating those deliverables.

While defining the deliverables is indeed a part of action planning, I find it most helpful to define deliverables at the end of the prioritization and assignment process. This is because many action planning teams will get started in their work immediately. By having the deliverables defined, this will help them start in the right direction. See Chapter 13 for examples of deliverables.

The Quality Check

If you and your team have done a great job of developing strategies and priorities, you'll be able to answer yes to each of the following questions:

Quality check

- Are the strategies phrased as activities to be accomplished—NOT results to be achieved?

- Are the strategies formatted with a verb, object, and purpose?

- Do the strategies address the CSFs and barriers?

- If the strategies are implemented, is it highly likely that the objectives will be achieved?

- Have priority strategies been identified, and have deliverables been defined for each priority strategy?

Your Role in Strategies, Priorities, and Deliverables

Strategies represent the work that's actually done to achieve the objectives that accomplish the goals, which fulfill the mission that moves you and your team toward your vision. Your role in strategy developed is outlined in the following table:

The role of the leader	<ul><li>Be sure to get on the table any strategies you believe should be implemented. You should recommend them if no one else does.</li><li>Ensure that the strategies, if accomplished, will indeed achieve the objectives previously established.</li><li>When lobbying is done, lobby last so as not to influence what others say.</li><li>Ensure that the people who become action plan leaders have both the passion and the ability (i.e., "the will and the skill") to coordinate development of the action plan. If you're concerned that some who volunteered for the job may not have both the passion and the ability, consider teaming them with others who have complementary traits.</li></ul>

- Chapter 13. Action Planning
- Chapter 14. Alignment, Communication, Monitoring, and Accountability

Section I	Section II	Section III	Section IV
Buy-in and Assessment	**Strategic Direction**	**Implementation Planning**	**Execution and Monitoring**
Chapter 2. Your Role in Facilitating Strategy 3. Management Briefing	**Chapters** 4. Briefing Book Review and SWOT 5. Positioning 6. Envisioning the Future and Goals 7. Mission 8. Vision 9. Objectives	**Chapters** 10. Guiding Principles 11. Critical Success Factors and Barriers 12. Strategies, Priorities, and Deliverables	**Chapters** 13. Action Planning 14. Alignment, Communication Monitoring, and Accountability

Action Planning 13

- Overview
- Sample Action Plan
- The Format Definitions
- The Deliverables
- The Process
- The Quality Check
- Your Role in Action Planning

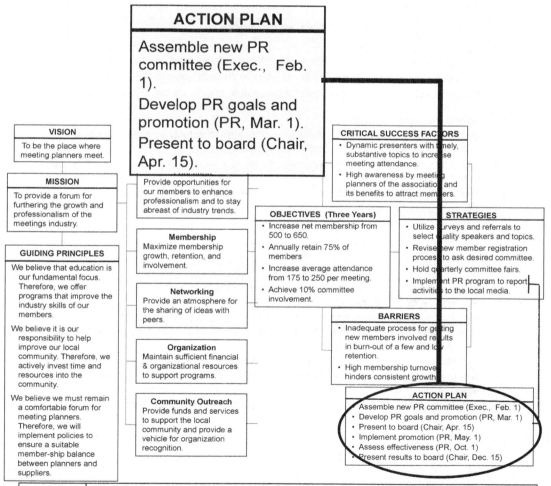

Summary: Action Planning

Definition	Action plans detail the specific steps to be taken to implement a strategy. Action plans state what will be done, by whom, and by when, and the resources required.

Example	(See the sample action plan section that follows.)

Success Strategies

- Determine the deliverables for the strategy. Answer the question, "When we are finished, what will we have in our hands? What will we have accomplished?"
- For each deliverable, list the major activities in chronological order.
- For each activity, identify the person responsible and due date. In setting dates, you may find it helpful to first put a date on the last activity and then work backward to the first activity.
- Estimate the out-of-pocket costs to accomplish each activity and the amount of internal time required (staff hours or labor hours).
- Once all individual activities have been estimated, record the total cost, staff hours, and due date.
- Decide the overall owner for implementing the action plan.
- Perform a quality check.

Quality Check

- Have all the key deliverables been identified? If the deliverables are done, will the strategy be completed?
- Have all the important actions been identified? Is each action worded, so that it makes clear what needs to be accomplished? If all the actions are completed, will all the deliverables be created?
- For each action, have the people responsible been identified?
- Are the costs and dates reasonable, with no more than sixty days between action steps?
- Are the costs and time worth the effort, given the impact anticipated?

Overview

As a result of prioritization, an organization will likely identify six to twelve priority initiatives that will combine to move the organization in a specific strategic direction. The next step in the planning process is to develop detailed action plans to ensure that each of the priorities is brought to completion.

Why develop an action plan? Action plans have several advantages, as highlighted below.

Action plan advantages	• The organization can confirm that the resources required to implement the strategy are worth the benefit gained.
	• The deliverables and steps define for the team when the initiative is completed.
	• The organization has a roadmap for monitoring progress in accomplishing the initiative.
	• All action plans can be summarized to identify resource requirements and to develop a resource plan to meet those requirements.

Action plans are most often developed by small teams of two to five people per priority strategy. The action plan leaders are responsible for recruiting members to their teams. Once formed, the teams typically work separately over several weeks to develop the action plan. The teams then come together in a meeting to review and approve action plans for implementation.

An Alternative Approach for Action Planning: The Staff Briefing

Over the past several years, I've been taking a somewhat different approach to action planning. Instead of team leaders selecting their members, we bring the entire staff together for a half-day briefing to review the entire plan, gain their input and suggestions, and provide staff members with an opportunity to volunteer to be part of one of the action planning teams.

The staff briefing typically is held in the morning. Then, in the afternoon of that same day, those who volunteered to serve on an action planning team come back for an orientation on the action planning process. Following the orientation, the group divides into their individual action planning teams and they spend the afternoon developing their action plans.

Not all teams are able to complete their action plans that afternoon, but the staff briefing, action plan orientation, and action plan development processes often provide the buy-in, education, and focus needed to significantly move the process forward.

Sample Action Plan

A sample action plan follows.

Strategy:	C1. Develop a best-in-class product development process to improve speed and average time-to-profitability rates.
Objectives supported:	Operations: 1. Achieve average product development time of four months. Profitability: 4. Reduce time-to-profitability by 20 percent within three years.
Owner:	Engineering
Deliverables:	Description of the recommended product development process. Results from testing the recommendations in a pilot program. Documentation, training, and implementation company-wide.

Due Date:	May 1 / Year 2	Person-Days:	211	Total Costs:	$85,000

Action Step	Who	Due	Person-days	Costs
1. Identify and select consultant.	Engineering	Mar. 1	4	0
2. Finalize consultant contract.	Eng., finance	Mar. 15	2	$75,000
3. Allocate people internally to work on the team with consultant (four people, part-time).	Eng., marketing	Mar. 15	1	0
4. Outline the current product development process and identify the strengths and weaknesses.	Team	Apr. 1	8	0
5. Benchmark against at least three other organizations.	Team	May 15	28	$7,500
6. Define the desired product development process.	Team	Jul. 1	56	0
7. Present and gain approval for pilot test.	Team, exec.	Jul. 15	8	0
8. Implement pilot program.	Team	Sep. 1	28	0
9. Provide interim update memo on pilot.	Team	Nov. 1	16	0
10. Produce evaluation report on pilot.	Team	Jan. 15/Y2	8	0
11. Revise product development process.	Team	Feb. 1/Y2	16	0
12. Gain approval for full implementation.	Team, exec.	Mar. 1/Y2	8	0
13. Fully document the new process.	Team	Apr. 1/Y2	8	0

Action Step	Who	Due	Person-days	Costs
14. Provide orientation and training.	Consultant	Apr. 15/Y2	8	$2,500
15. Implement the new process.	Team	May 1/Y2	8	0

The Format Definitions

The following are definitions of each of the components of the action plan.

Strategy	The strategy for which the action plan is written.
Objectives supported	The objectives that the strategy helps achieve.
Owner	The individual or organization that has overall responsibility for ensuring that the action plan is implemented.
Deliverables	The tangible products that will result from executing the action plan steps.
Due date	The date when an action step will be completed or the overall action plan will be accomplished.
Person-days	The amount of internal resources required to complete the action plan. (This includes the time of employees or other human resources that don't require *additional* costs, such as volunteers, board members, and contractors already under contract to do work for the duration of the action plan. As an example, if three people work together for two days on an action step, that results in six person-days.)
Costs	"Costs" are out-of-pocket costs and include items for which additional dollars will have to be spent (e.g., travel, new contractors, facilities); costs for resources covered under person days should NOT be included in out-of-pocket costs.
Action step	A specific activity to be done to accomplish the strategy, typically related to one or more deliverables.
Who	The people or departments involved in the step.

The Deliverables

The list of deliverables serves as the focusing point for action plan development. In essence, the strategy is completed when all deliverables have been created. This brings us to our next secret.

Secret #25 | **You can focus your action planning effort by defining the deliverables first; then, define the action steps necessary to create those deliverables.**

To define your deliverables, have your action planning teams answer the following questions:

Questions to identify deliverables

- When we are finished, what will we have in our hands?
- What will we have created?
- What evidence will there be of what we have accomplished?

Note that deliverables can have multiple types. Some deliverables might be end products, while others may just be interim work products. What follows are common deliverable types and an example of each.

Common types of deliverables (with examples)

Interim work product:	List of strengths and weaknesses.
End product:	Report of recommendations.
Evidence of action:	Results from testing the recommendations in a pilot program.
Completion:	Company-wide implementation.
Results:	Cycle time reduced by 20 percent.

A list of deliverables for three sample strategies follows:

Sample Deliverables

Strategy	Deliverables
Develop and implement vertical marketing strategy to increase revenue by capitalizing on our knowledge and relationships with existing customers.	• Identification of vertical market targets. • List of existing customers and revenue in prior three years by vertical market. • Approved revenue targets by vertical market (minimum 20 percent growth over prior year). • Plan for increasing vertical market revenue, with at least three initiatives cited. • Plan implemented.
Develop and implement a "professional development" program to improve existing managers' ability to coach/motivate their teams and to prepare manager candidates to take the company to the next level.	• List of objectives for the program. • List of associates interested and approved by the leadership team to prepare for management positions. • 360-degree evaluation of managers and manager candidates before training and ninety days after training. • Development program held with at least 60 percent of existing managers and manager candidates in attendance. • Evaluations of program by all attendees.
Revamp partner program to increase revenue and residual income.	• List of approved changes to the partner program. • Changes to the partner program implemented in materials and on website.

The Process

Defining the deliverables is a critical step in action planning. As described in the prior chapter, I often will have the full planning team define the deliverables for each priority strategy and then ask the action planning teams to refine the list and present recommendations for changes to the full planning team as needed.

Whether you use the traditional approach to action planning or the alternative approach that includes a staff briefing followed by an afternoon action planning session, the steps that follow detail the activities each action planning team should undertake.

1 Define the deliverables.

Unless it was completed earlier when priority strategies were identified, the first step in action planning is to determine the key deliverables or work products. Have your teams answer the questions, "When we're finished, what will we have in our hands? What will we have created? What evidence will there be of what we've accomplished?"

2 List the activities for each deliverable.

Once the deliverables are defined, the next step is to list in chronological order the major activities needed to create each deliverable. I find that it's easier for teams to determine what they need to do by focusing their steps on producing each of the deliverables.

3 Define the person responsible and due date for each activity.

Once all the activities are listed, define the details for each activity, starting with the person responsible and the due date. Note that with action planning, you go down the activity column first to get all the steps. Only after having all the steps do you then go across the row to get the details.

- For consistency, use a "verb-object" format: Start each action with a verb, followed by the objects acted upon (e.g., "Implement and evaluate first pilot program").

- If more than one person has responsibility, both names should appear. The name of the person with primary responsibility should appear first.

- In setting dates, you may find it helpful to first put a date on the last activity and then work backward to the first activity.

- While monthly activities are preferred, consider having no more than sixty days between action steps, to allow for adequate monitoring of progress.

4 Estimate internal time and out-of-pocket costs.

For each action step, include an estimate of the internal time and out-of-pocket costs, based on the definitions described earlier in this chapter.

5 Record the total internal time, total cost, and due date.

Once all individual activities have been estimated, your teams should summarize the total person-days and the total cost in the top portion of the action plan template. They should also record the due date as the latest date among the action plan steps.

6 Decide the overall owner for implementing the action plan.

Recall that the role of the action plan leader is to work with a team to create the action plan. Once the action plan is complete, however, the action plan is turned over to the designated owner—his or her job is to oversee the execution of the action plan. Frequently, the action plan leader becomes the owner of the action plan. However, it isn't uncommon for the owner to be designated as someone else. In determining the owner, consider the following factors:

- Based on the action plan steps, who is most involved in getting the action plan implemented?

- Who has the most to gain if the action plan is implemented?

- Who has the most to lose if the action plan isn't implemented?

- If the proposed owner hasn't been involved in developing the action plan, what steps will be taken to orient the proposed owner and gain this person's buy-in?

7 Perform a quality check.

Have your teams walk through each of the quality checks to ensure the quality of their action plan.

8 Hold the action plan review and approval session.

The action plan allows all team members to see in detail what will be required to implement the strategies that they assigned top priority. Once all action plans are written, hold an action plan review meeting, so your entire planning team can review the individual action plans and make specific recommendations for each, as follows:

- **Implement:** Execute the action plan as developed.

- **Implement with modifications:** Execute the action plan after making the modifications identified during the review.

- **Revise and resubmit:** Revise the action plan based on comments made during the review and resubmit for consideration.

- **Delay or drop:** Don't implement the action plan at this time.

The Quality Check

How do you ensure that you have developed solid action plans? Consider the quality checks that follow:

Quality check

- Have all the key deliverables been identified? If the deliverables are done, will the strategy be completed? *If not, you should add deliverables and the action steps to create them.*

- Have all the important actions been identified? Is each action worded, so that it's clear what needs to be accomplished? If all the actions are completed, will all the deliverables be created? *If not, additional actions may be needed.*

- For each action, have the person or people responsible been identified? *If not, add this.*

- Are the costs and dates reasonable, with no more than sixty days between action steps? *If not, revise as needed.*

- Are the costs and time worth the effort, given the impact anticipated? *If not, attempt to reduce the scope of the action plan to be better aligned with the impact anticipated, or consider recommending that the strategy be eliminated.*

Your Role in Action Planning

The action plans lay out in detail the steps that will be done to accomplish each priority strategy. In your role, you'll want to make sure that the investment the organization will make in each action plan is worth the likely return. Consider the following:

The role of the leader

- Establish a date for completing the development of all action plans and hold the action plan leaders accountable for getting the action plans completed.

- Ensure that your team reconvenes to review the action plans and decide which can be implemented as written, which need modification, and which need to be delayed or dropped.

- Be prepared to ask the tough questions about each action plan and encourage all team members to do likewise. Is the action plan realistic? Does it go far enough? Is it worth the investment? Is the action plan detailed enough to monitor on a monthly basis?

Alignment, Communication, Monitoring, and Accountability | 14

- Overview
- Alignment
- Communication
- Monitoring
- Accountability
- The Processes
- The Quality Check
- Your Role in Alignment, Communication, Monitoring, and Accountability

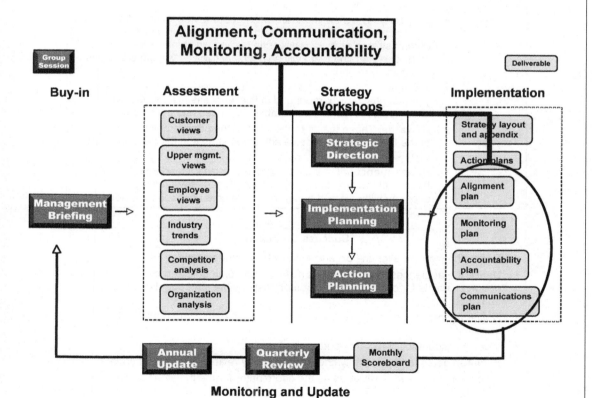

Summary: Alignment, Communication, Monitoring, and Accountability

Definition	This process describes the steps that will be taken to align the organization with the plan and monitor the implementation, including a system of rewards and consequences based on performance.

Example	<ul><li>**One-time**: The organization will identify and implement adjustments to the organization structure, activities, roles, processes, systems, and rewards to drive achievement of the plan. We'll communicate to all stakeholders based on the communication plan.</li><li>**Monthly**: Strategy leaders will update status of action plans to ensure we're doing what we said we were going to do. The overall plan coordinator will distribute a report of performance to all members of the planning team.</li><li>**Quarterly**: The planning team will meet to review status of strategies and progress on objectives. The planning team will decide which current strategies to stop or continue, and which new strategies to start. The planning team will adjust objectives as warranted, based on issues and priorities.</li><li>**Annually**: The planning team will meet to review progress for the year, identify new barriers and critical success factors (CSFs), change objectives. and re-establish priorities and action plans.</li><li>**Rewards**: Those teams that complete their deliverables by the end of the fiscal year will receive additional shares in the annual bonus pool.</li><li>**Consequences**: On a monthly basis, the team leaders of those teams not meeting their monthly activity target will roll the accountability die and be assigned the consequence indicated.</li></ul>

Success Strategies
<ul><li>Define the steps to align the organization with the strategic plan.</li><li>Define the audiences to whom the plan should be communicated, the information needed, vehicle for communication, person responsible, and due date for each audience.</li><li>Define the process that will be used for monitoring monthly, quarterly, and annually.</li><li>Identify accountability rewards and consequences.</li><li>Establish dates for the monthly check-in, quarterly review, and annual update.</li><li>Select the person who will serve as the coordinator for the monitoring activities.</li></ul>

Quality Check
• Have needed adjustments been identified to the organization structure, activities, roles, processes, systems, and rewards to drive the plan's success?
• Has a communication plan been developed that defines the process for getting the appropriate messages out to key audiences?
• Has a process been defined to monitor progress?
• Does the process include methods for monitoring the performance of both strategies and objectives?
• Does the process provide an opportunity to make changes to and add new strategies and objectives?
• Does the process include an element for widely reporting progress?
• Have rewards and consequences been established?

Overview

I would like to start this chapter with a brief case study.

Moving to Execution

"How do I move this plan from paper to execution?"

So asks the CEO of a medium-size service organization. He is frustrated. His organization is nearing the completion of the second year of a three-year plan and is preparing to hold the annual update retreat to review progress and make adjustments for the third year.

When his leadership team completed the plan two years ago, most of the senior leaders were excited about having a clearly-defined direction that would position the organization for long-term success. But at the first update last year, it was clear that the plan was barely looked at over the prior twelve months.

"While a few of the initiatives had been started, none had been completed, and many had been completely ignored," says the CEO. "We all agreed to do a better job this year of making the plan a living document. But this past year was much like the first, with little focus on the plan."

The organization made its revenue and profitability targets by implementing tactical steps to cut costs and implement short-term revenue enhancement programs. But it was no better positioned for the future than it was twelve months before. And now, with another planning retreat just a month away, the CEO had concerns about his ability to focus the organization on executing the plan.

Why is it so hard to get a plan executed? Why is it so difficult to keep a team committed and focused on long-term initiatives that they themselves, at one point, said were important? Why do most plans sit on shelves, never to be fully implemented?

While there are several reasons for execution failure, here are four primary pitfalls I've found.

The Urgency Principle

Many plans fall victim to what I call the urgency principle, which is derived from Stephen Covey's time management matrix (see below) that is documented in his book, *Seven Habits of Highly Effective People*. In most organizations, it's easy to focus on responding to what's clamoring for our attention (high urgency, but low importance) or get caught up in the crisis-of-the-day (important and urgent). But since strategy initiatives typically fall into Covey's Quadrant 2 (high importance, but low urgency), the plan takes a back seat to the needs of the moment.

> **The Urgency Principle:** That which is not urgent seldom gets done.

The monitoring and accountability processes must move the strategic priorities from Quadrant 2 to Quadrant 1 (high importance and high urgency). In this chapter, you'll learn how to make it happen.

Covey Time Management Matrix

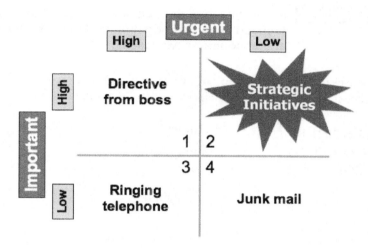

Infrequent Review

Management gurus learned long ago that what is measured, improves. Unfortunately, all too often, we don't go back to the plan until it's time for an update, twelve months later. When a lack of review gets combined with the urgency principle, it's easy to see how strategies ripe for execution can die on the vine due to lack of attention.

Lack of Alignment

While some plans fall victim to the urgency principle or infrequent review, other plans suffer from a different organizational dynamic. Dr. Jay Galbraith from the Marshall School of Business, University of Southern California, and author of *Designing Organizations: An Executive Guide to Strategy, Structure and Process,* describes the dynamic this way: "Too many organizations have tomorrow's strategy, today's structure, and yesterday's reward systems." In essence, we try to implement a strategy without (a) aligning our organization to achieve it, or (b) restructuring our reward systems to support it. Like a car that is out of alignment, until we correct the underlying problem, we'll naturally flow off course.

Lack of Accountability

Infrequent review and lack of alignment often support a fourth major cause of strategy execution issues: lack of accountability. As described in the scenario that opened this chapter, "We all agreed to do a better job this year…" is often a classic response heard when individual accountability is lacking. When people are asked to account for their actions, or lack thereof, and when there are positive or negative consequences related to their results, a stronger focus on execution is typically the result. This brings us to our next secret.

Secret #26	**Avoid the execution pitfalls by implementing a focused alignment, communication, monitoring, and accountability process.**

This chapter focuses on tools and techniques you can use to move your plan out of Quadrant 2 and firmly place it in Quadrant 1. The chapter covers the following four topics:

Chapter topics to drive strategy implementation

- Alignment
- Communication
- Monitoring
- Accountability

Alignment

Planning, especially at the strategic level, can result in a direction and a set of initiatives that require an organization to operate differently from the way it has in the past. For example, an organization transforming from being product-centric to being customer-centric will need to change its processes, and in some cases, encourage a change in its people to be successful. In the same way, when a non-profit organization chooses to move from being principally a community fundraising vehicle to being a community change agent, significant changes are needed in the way the organization operates and the way people are rewarded. Without adjustments to align with the new direction, an organization may fall victim to the old adage, "Driving with one foot on the accelerator and the other foot on the brake."

In implementing a new plan, consider the following five areas of alignment:

Areas of alignment

- Organization structure.
- Activities to start, stop, continue.
- People and roles.
- Processes and systems.
- Reward systems.

What follows are key questions to consider in each of the five areas.

Organization Structure: Strategy Before Structure

Once your strategy is clear, you can then determine if changes in your structure are needed to better implement the strategy.

Questions	• What changes might be helpful to our organization structure to better facilitate the implementation of the strategy?
	• How have others organized to implement similar initiatives?
	• If we were building an organization from scratch to implement this strategy, how would we organize it?

When considering these organization questions, be intentional about who is at the table discussing alternatives. People who tend to be narrow, parochial, or how-does-it-affect-me thinkers tend to have difficulty with any direction that might reduce resources in their area or eliminate their area entirely. If possible, select broad thinkers who recognize that the organization is best served when all its resources are focused on achieving a collective end.

Activities to Start, Stop, Continue

New directions and initiatives require resources. However, very few of the organizations I've worked with had funds sitting around waiting for a strategy to be developed, so that the funds could be put to use. Instead, their new initiatives had to be funded by redirecting resources from lower-priority activities.

Key questions to ask in this area include the following:

Questions	• Given the direction we're going, what are we doing today that we can stop doing because it's no longer relevant, or because it offers relatively low value compared to other things?
	• What are the things that we can start doing differently in order to provide additional resources to our higher-priority activities?
	• What are the things that we should continue to do, or do more of, given the direction?

In working with larger organizations, I've found it helpful to have the "start/stop/continue" dialogue at the department level. Under this scenario, each department is asked to do its own self-evaluation of start/stop/continue and to come to the table with recommendations of what they should stop. Your executive team would then review the recommendations from each department and makes final decisions.

People and Roles

Holding the "start/stop/continue" discussion around activities can make it much easier to hold the people and roles discussion. With the structure and activities defined, the next step is to determine who should be in which boxes and have which responsibilities. Once more, you may find it helpful to have open-minded, big picture thinkers at the table for this discussion.

Questions
- Given the desired organization structure and activities, what core competencies do we need to have that we don't have today?
- Which people do we have who would better fit in another part of the organization, given where we're going?
- What changes should we make in roles?

Processes and Systems

Sometimes, new directions call for new modes of operation, including new processes and new systems. For example, to move from a product-focused to a customer-focused organization might require the implementation of a client relationship management system to better manage and track client interactions. Likewise, moving from primarily having a fundraising capacity to a focus on convening and mobilizing groups to achieve community impact would likely require new processes related to such activities as convening and engaging.

The alignment discussion would include answers to the following:

Questions
- What new processes need to be in place before we can move successfully in this new direction?
- How does this new direction affect the way we operate? What things do we need to change?
- What systems are needed to support the direction?

Reward Systems

Changes in direction without corresponding changes in incentive programs can result in a great plan being poorly implemented, simply because old behaviors continue to be reinforced. For full alignment, reward systems must be tied directly to the most important outcomes of the business.

Questions	• What are the most important behaviors that should be rewarded to drive us to our vision?
	• How well does the existing compensation system reward these key behaviors?
	• What changes are needed to align our compensation system with the new strategic direction?

Communication

With your strategy developed, it's important to have a plan for communicating the strategy to all relevant audiences. To develop your communications plan, take the following steps:

| **Steps in developing your communications plan** | • First, define all the audiences who should be informed of the plan. |
| | • For each audience, define the information needed, the most appropriate vehicle for communicating the information, the person who should deliver the communication, and the date the communication should be completed. |

A sample communications plan follows

Sample Communications Plan (Extract)

Audience	What Information?	Vehicle	Who	By When
Staff	Strategy document, the next steps, their role	Special staff meeting	CEO	30 days
Top customers	One page summary and letter	Meeting	Sales manager	One week before customer mailing
All other customers	One page summary and letter	Mailing	Marketing manager	60 days
Tier 1 partners	One page summary and letter	Mailing and review at next meeting	Channel manager	60 days
All other partners	One page summary and letter	Mailing	Channel manager	60 days
Public	One page summary and letter	Website	Marketing manager	60 days

Monitoring

Having used the Drivers Model on hundreds of planning initiatives spanning nearly two decades, my organization believes that a three-phase monitoring process provides the needed focus to drive a plan to implementation. Clients have the option of signing up for one, two, or all three phases. We've essentially taken the position that the monitoring process is so important that we'll consider turning down an assignment if a client wants planning done but isn't willing to invest in the monitoring. While this is a radical position, our goal is to communicate to clients that "the plan" is typically not what they want. Instead, they're seeking strategic, positive change. Our experience over and over again has been that strategic change, without a structured process for monitoring results, is highly unlikely.

Summary of the Recommended Process

- **Monthly:** Strategy leaders will update their action plan status to ensure we're doing what we said we were going to do. The overall plan coordinator will distribute a report of performance to all members of the planning team.

- **Quarterly:** The planning team will meet to review the status of strategies and the progress on objectives. The planning team will decide which current strategies to stop or continue and which new strategies to start. The planning team will adjust objectives as warranted, based on issues and priorities.

- **Annually:** The planning team will meet to review progress for the year, identify new barriers and CSFs, change objectives, and reestablish priorities and action plans.

To illustrate this three-prong approach, let's go back to our example of the meeting planners association and their five goals. Below are the objectives and strategies for the membership goal. Note that the C1 strategy is the only priority strategy in the "membership" area.

C. Membership Goal	
Maximize membership growth, retention, and involvement.	
Third-year Membership Objectives	**Membership Strategies**
• Increase membership from 500 to 650 (first-year milestone: 550) • Increase average meeting attendance to 250 (first-year: 200) • Achieve 10 percent committee involvement (first-year: 7 percent)	C1. Implement PR program to report activities to the local media for increased awareness **(priority strategy)**. C2. Use assessment surveys and industry referrals to select quality speakers and topics. C3. Hold quarterly committee fairs after meetings.

Example: Monthly Check-in—Are We Doing What We Said We Were Going to Do?

Recall that during action planning, detailed action plans are created for each of the priority strategies. An action plan typically includes half a dozen to a dozen major action steps needed to accomplish the priority strategy. For the PR program strategy above, the action plan might appear as follows:

Action Plan (Extract) C1. Implement PR program to report activities to the local media for increased awareness.			
	Action Step	**Who**	**Due**
1.	Develop list of target audience, media, frequency, and potential storylines.		Feb. 1
2.	Hold telephone or face-to-face meeting with at least two media contacts.		Mar. 1
3.	Distribute first quarterly press release.		Apr. 1

During monthly monitoring, the question to ask is, "Are we doing what we said we were going to do?" Focus on whether the action steps are getting done. The Drivers Model monitoring process includes the following steps to get your answer.

Monthly monitoring process

- On the 15th of the month, each strategy leader receives an e-mail reminder indicating the items from the action plan due to be accomplished by the end of the month. This reminder is to encourage moving the strategy initiative from Quadrant 2 to Quadrant 1.

- On the last day of the month, strategy leaders receive an e-mail form that they return, indicating what was accomplished, corresponding actions, and the percentage of the task completed.

- The plan coordinator uploads the updates from the strategy leaders to produce a dashboard, showing those strategies on track (green), those that have fallen slightly behind (yellow), and those that have fallen well behind (red). The team receives an overall grade for the month, based on the performance.

- The plan coordinator distributes the dashboard report along with the grade and a narrative explanation to the entire planning team. This is done to recognize those on track and to encourage peer pressure on those who let the team down.

The exhibit that follows gives an extract of a sample monitoring dashboard. A color-coded dashboard would show in green those strategies that are 100 percent complete, in yellow those that are 75 percent or more complete, and in red those that are less than 75 percent complete. The entire organization receives a score and a grade, based on the numeric values shown in the table.

Sample Monitoring Dashboard (extract)

Dashboard Summary		77 percent C+	89 percent B+	91 percent A-	84 percent B	98 percent A
		Jan.	Feb.	Mar.	Apr.	May
100 percent done		3	7	8	6	10
75–95 percent done		6	3	2	3	1
0–75 percent done		2	1	1	2	0
A1	Provide quarterly seminars on advanced meeting planning.					
B3	Partner with food bank to provide unserved food to homeless shelters.					
C1	Implement PR program to publicize events in local media.					

Example: Quarterly Review—Are We Achieving the Results We Said We Would Achieve?

While the monthly process focuses on activity by answering, "Are we doing what we said we were going to do?" the quarterly process focuses on results by answering, "Are we achieving the results we said we would achieve?" In the Drivers Model, objectives are the results. In a three-year plan, your team will typically identify a third-year target for each objective, as well as a first-year milestone to ensure the team is making progress. At each quarterly review, you evaluate each objective by asking, "What have been the results and at this current rate, where do we expect to be by the end of the year?"

In advance of the session, prepare a table listing all objectives and showing the third-year target, the current year milestone, who is responsible, the year-to-date performance, and expected performance by the fiscal year-end. The grade column should be left blank for the group to fill in during the quarterly review, as shown in the sample that follows.

Sample Grading Objectives

Objective	Year One	Who	Year-to-Date (Q1)	Expectation	Grade
Increase membership from 500 to 650.	550	Member-ship chair	520 (40 percent)	560 (120 percent)	

As indicated above, the first-year milestone was to add 50 members to get to 550. At the first quarterly review, they had 520 members. While they haven't made it to 550, they've added 20 of the 50 members, so they are 40 percent of the way after just one quarter. And based on this progress, along with other information they know about when members typically join, they expect to get to 560 by the end of the year. This means they expect to achieve 120 percent of the goal. Therefore, they would give themselves an A+ grade.

At the quarterly review, the team also examines the progress on each strategy. As was done with objectives, in advance of the session, prepare a table, listing all priority strategies showing who is responsible, the year-to-date percentage complete, and comments with a recommendation to stop or continue. The decision column should be left blank for the group to fill in during the quarterly review.

Sample Evaluating Strategies

Strategy	Who	Percent Complete	Comment/ Recommend?	Decision
C1. Implement PR program to report activities to the local media for increased awareness.	Marketing chair	25 percent	On track; recommend continuing.	

During the strategy discussion, the full team reviews the status of and recommendation for each strategy, and determines which strategies to continue or stop and if additional strategies should be started. The table that follows summarizes the questions to be asked about strategies.

Questions to ask about the strategies	• Should we continue investing in this strategy or make changes to it? • Should we stop investing time and energy in this strategy? • Are there other strategies that we should start, based on where we are today and what we now know?

After reviewing progress on the objectives and strategies, the team then determines if adjustments are warranted to the objectives. Why would a change in an objective be warranted? Some typically examples include the following:

Why change an objective?

- The team has concluded that an objective is no longer important.

- The resources required to achieve an objective are not available, or other conditions cannot be met.

- The team has concluded based on additional information that the target set was too low or too high.

While mid-term changes to an objective can be warranted, avoid changing an objective simply because the actual performance is below the target. It isn't unusual for a team, after one or two quarters of poor performance, to want to change the target to make achievement easier. Be sure to recognize the distinction between poor execution of a reasonable target and a target that has been set inappropriately high.

An example of a half-day quarterly review agenda is included in the process section of this chapter.

The Annual Update Process: What Changes Should We Make to the Plan?

The annual update is used to confirm the progress made in accomplishing the objectives of the plan and to revise the plan as needed.

The annual update

- As with the quarterly review, the team grades the objectives. This time, however, the grading is based on actual performance, instead of anticipated performance.

- In addition, the team assesses the percentage complete on each of the strategies undertaken and lessons learned from the year.

- The team identifies new barriers and CSFs, and then revises the measurable objectives, being sure to set first year milestones again.

- New priority strategies are identified to drive the objectives, and new action plans are developed as needed.

These steps result in the team learning from the past and revising the plan as they move into the next year of the planning cycle. A sample agenda for the full-day annual update session is included in the process section of this chapter.

A Note on Grading

The point of grading objectives is to provide the team with a method for determining how well it is progressing. There are several specific issues around grading that deserve mentioning.

- Some teams prefer not to give letter grades, but instead are satisfied with giving a percentage relative to the expected performance. The percentage gives the evaluation precision without the potential baggage that can come with a letter grade.

- If grading is used, be sure to define the scale and be consistent. Some groups consider 90 percent or above an A; other groups define an A as 100 percent or more.

- Be clear on what you're measuring, whether it's progress to the target or progress from where you started. This brings us to our next secret.

> **Secret #27** **In monitoring, recognize the difference between grading the increase versus grading the achievement.**

Let's use an example from the meeting planners organization to illustrate the point. Recall the three objectives for the membership goal.

Third-Year Membership Objectives
• Increase membership from 500 to 650 (first-year milestone: 550)
• Increase average meeting attendance to 250 (first-year: 200)
• Achieve 10 percent committee involvement (first-year: 7 percent)

The first objective is to increase membership from 500 to 550 by the first year. Suppose at the end of the year, the organization has achieved 530. Is the percentage complete 96 percent (530 out of 550), or is the percentage complete 60 percent (30 out of the anticipated 50 increase)?

When working with teams on objectives, I ask them to be very clear on how they'll measure success and to consider carefully the verb they choose. This objective reads, "Increase membership…" Based on the verb used, the increase was only 60 percent of the target, and the objective would be evaluated accordingly.

Contrast this with the third objective, which is to achieve 7 percent committee involvement. Based on the verb (achieve), if the organization is at 4 percent and achieves 6 percent in the first year, the percent complete is 86 percent (6 out of 7) not 67 percent (2 out of 3). As you can see, clarity on what you're measuring is important.

Naming a Plan Monitor

Once a planning initiative moves into implementation, I've found that it's essential to have one person whose job it is to ensure that the organization follows through on the plan. I call this role the plan monitor, or sometimes, the strategic planning czar. My experience has been that the chief executive is NOT a good candidate to serve as plan monitor. I believe the executive needs to have someone to turn to if the plan isn't proceeding as desired.

I've found the best candidate for the plan monitor is the person who would be most upset if the plan gathers dust. This is the person who typically believes in quality and believes the organization should do what it says it's going to do. The person typically has a passion for tracking and ensuring follow-through.

Once assigned, it's important that this person is charged with gathering and reporting only. Holding people accountable isn't this person's role, as we'll see in the next section.

| Secret #28 | Assign a plan monitor—not the chief executive— who is responsible for monitoring and reporting on the plan's progress. |

Accountability

We've talked about the monitoring process. Now let's move on to accountability. I've worked with organizations on planning initiatives for over two decades. In this period, I've seen highly successful organizations as well as organizations that failed to get out of the starting gate. Why does this happen? Along with the other three reasons cited earlier, I've found a key problem can be accountability, or more specifically, the lack thereof. With the Drivers Model, *accountability* has five critical components.

Five Keys to Accountability

1	**Clear identification and articulation of the work to be done.**	This first step is often where the breakdown of accountability starts. How often is it that work isn't clearly defined, or expectations and timelines not clearly articulated or a plan not delineated for completing the work?
2	**Accepted responsibility.**	Once the work is defined, someone has to accept responsibility for getting it done. Please note, *assigned* responsibility isn't the same as *accepted* responsibility. Has the person been simply assigned the work or has the person accepted that it's his/her responsibility for accomplishing it?

3	**Monitoring and reporting.**	Accountability comes from the Latin word that literally means to give an account. We may have accepted the responsibility for clearly defined work. However, without a monitoring and reporting process (i.e., without a process for people to give an account), there's essentially no accountability.
4	**Reward for accomplishment.**	A key to effective accountability is to have a reward for accomplishing the item for which we're being held accountable. In the workplace, rewards can take a variety of forms, including recognition, time off, gift certificates, convenient parking spaces, etc.
5	**Consequences for lack of performance.**	Consequences are necessary to ensure that there is both a carrot for performance and a stick for lack of performance. While many organizations avoid the stick, my experience has been that consequences are an essential component for letting people know they've let the team down.

What happens if one or more of the accountability components are missing? *Nothing.*

Actually, that's not true. If *any one* of the components is missing, you'll likely have a significant breakdown in accountability. However, it's likely that some initiatives will not get done, activities will fall through the cracks, and excuses will prevail. However, if *two or more* components are missing, the level of accountability will be so low that for most situations, it will appear that accountability is nonexistent. The work may still get done, but most likely due to the sheer will and desire of those involved, despite the lack of processes, oversight, or leadership.

How do you hold people accountable? Below is a sampling of accountability strategies that other organizations have found helpful.

Sample Accountability Strategies

- **Tie a portion of executive compensation** to quarterly progress on *all* the strategic objectives. This increases accountability for the team's results, not just an executive's particular area.

- **Establish an annual award fund** shared only by those teams that complete their targeted strategies. If eight teams are successful, those team members share in the fund. If only one team is successful, that team gets the entire fund. Leaders of each team receive a double share for their role as a team member and the leader of the team.

Sample Accountability Strategies
(cont.)

- **Other reward strategies** teams have used are the following:

  – Three-day weekend.

  – Cash rewards.

  – Celebration party.

  – Charitable contribution to your favorite charity.

- **Implement the accountability dice** as potential consequences for the team leader of teams missing their accountability during a month. Six consequences are set up ahead of time. If a team misses its accountability, the team leader rolls a die and must do the action assigned to the number. What follows is an example of consequences based on the roll of a die.

  1. An hour organizing the team's supply closet.

  2. Assist another team for two hours.

  3. Free space (no consequence).

  4. Twenty dollars to the team's party fund.

  5. Bring in breakfast snacks for the team each day for a week.

  6. Clean out the team's refrigerator each Friday for a month.

- **Other consequences** that teams have used include the following:

  – Meet one-on-one with the top executive to explain why the team failed to meet its accountability.

  – Clean up the break room every Friday for a month.

  – Coordinate and order lunch for monthly staff meeting.

  – Come in early to make coffee every day for a week.

The Processes

Rather than the step-by-step format of prior chapters, this section lists activities and provides agendas for each of the major monitoring and accountability processes.

Steps for Setting up the Alignment, Communication, Monitoring, and Accountability Processes

Near the completion of the planning session, the team should take the time to establish the processes it will use to monitor and hold people accountable. The examples in this chapter provide a starting point for the team to determine what will best work, given the plan's environment and content. Consider the following steps in establishing the monitoring and accountability process.

Monitoring and accountability steps

- Define the steps that will be taken to align the organization to the strategic plan.

- Define the audiences to whom the plan should be communicated, the information needed, vehicle for communication, person responsible, and due date for each audience.

- Define the process that will be used for monitoring monthly, quarterly, and annually.

- Identify accountability rewards and consequences.

- Establish deadlines for the first monthly report, quarterly review, and monthly update.

- Select the person who will serve as the coordinator for the monitoring activities.

Steps for the Monthly Check-in

On a monthly basis, the team will answer the question, "Are we doing what we said we were going to do?" Consider the following steps, as described earlier, to accomplish the monthly check-in.

Monthly check-in steps

- On the 15th of the month, each strategy leader receives an e-mail reminder, indicating the items from the action plan due by the end of the month. This reminder is to encourage moving the strategy initiative from Quadrant 2 to Quadrant 1.

- On the last day of the month, strategy leaders receive an e-mail form that they return, indicating what was accomplished, corresponding actions, and the percentage of the task completed.

Monthly check-in steps

(cont.)

- The plan coordinator uploads the updates from the strategy leaders to produce a dashboard, showing those strategies on track (green), those that have fallen slightly behind (yellow), and those that have fallen well behind (red). The team receives an overall grade for the month, based on its performance.

- The plan coordinator distributes the dashboard report, the grade, and a narrative explanation to the entire planning team. This is done to recognize those on track and encourage peer pressure on those who let down the team.

Agenda for the Quarterly Review

With the Drivers Model, the team quarterly answers the question, "Are we getting the results we expected to get?" The sample that follows outlines the agenda for a half-day quarterly review session.

Session objective	• Review plan progress. • Reassess objectives and strategies for moving forward.

Agenda	**A. Getting Started**
	  • Welcome and opening remarks.
	  • Session objective, deliverables.
	  • "Most proud's": What are you most proud of that has occurred in the organization since the last update?
	  • Agenda, ground rules.
	  • Review the prior actions.
	
	B. Review Objectives
	  • Objectives—on track?
	  • What have been our significant issues or barriers?
	  • Adjustments?
	
	C. Review Strategies
	  • Strategies—on track?
	  • What have been our significant issues or barriers?
	  • Adjustments? (Keep, change, stop, or add.)
	
	D. Next Steps
	  • Short-term action plan—what needs to be done immediately following the meeting to ensure implementation and follow-through?

Preparation	• In advance of the session, prepare a table, listing all objectives, the third-year target, the first-year milestone, who is responsible, the year-to-date performance, and expected performance by the fiscal year-end. The grade column should be left blank for the group to fill in during the quarterly review. *(See the sample earlier in this chapter.)*
	• Likewise, in advance of the session, prepare a table, listing all priority strategies, showing who is responsible, the percentage complete year-to-date, and comments and recommendations to stop or continue. The decision column should be left blank for the group to fill in during the quarterly review. *(See the sample earlier in this chapter.)*
	• A copy of the full plan and all action plans should be available for reference during the session.

Agenda for the Annual Update

With the Drivers Model, the team annually answers the question, "What changes should we make to the plan?" A sample agenda for the full day annual update session follows.

Session objective	• Review plan performance and lessons learned.
	• Update the objectives and strategies as needed to respond to current conditions.
Agenda	**A. Getting Started**
	• Welcome and opening remarks.
	• Session objective, deliverables, and key issues.
	• Reminder of the strategic framework.
	• Agenda, ground rules.
	• Review the prior actions.
	B. Review of Past Accomplishments
	• Grading our performance.
	- Review of each objective and progress to date.
	- Percentage complete on strategies.
	• What have been our key successes?
	• What have been our significant issues and barriers?
	• What new trends have emerged?
	C. Set the Future Direction
	• Revise the objectives as needed.
	- Are the current objectives still valid?
	- What new objectives are needed?
	• Revise CSFs and barriers as needed.

Agenda *(cont.)*	• Review strategies.
	   – Will these strategies lead to achieving the objectives?
	   – Are there strategies that are no longer relevant?
	   – Are there new strategies that should be added?
	• Select strategies for priority.
	
	D. Next Steps
	
	• Short-term action plan: What needs to be done immediately following the meeting to ensure implementation and follow-through?
	• Communications plan: What should be communicated about the meeting, and to whom?
	• Monitoring plan: How will we continue to monitor our progress?

Preparation	• As with the quarterly review, in advance of the session, prepare a table, listing all objectives that show the third-year target, the first-year milestone, who is responsible, and the actual performance (an "expected performance" column isn't needed). The grade column should be left blank for the group to fill in during the quarterly review. *(See the sample earlier in this chapter.)* • Likewise, in advance of the session, prepare a table, listing all priority strategies, showing who is responsible, the percentage complete year-to-date, and comments and recommendations to stop or continue. The decision column should be left blank for the group to fill in during the quarterly review. *(See the sample earlier in this chapter.)* • A copy of the full plan and all action plans should be available for reference during the session.

The Quality Check

If you and your team have done a great job of developing your alignment, monitoring, and accountability processes, you'll able to answer yes to each of the following questions.

Quality check	• Have needed adjustments been identified and implemented to the organization structure, activities, roles, processes, systems, and rewards to drive the plan's success? • Has a communication plan been developed that defines the process for communication of the appropriate messages to key audiences? • Has a process been defined to monitor progress? • Does the process include methods for monitoring the performance of both strategies and objectives?

Quality check
(cont.)

- Does the process provide an opportunity to change and add new strategies and objectives?

- Does the process include an element for widely reporting progress?

- Have rewards and consequences been established?

Your Role in Alignment, Communication, Monitoring, and Accountability

Monitoring and accountability is the place where the wheels come off many planning initiatives. You can ensure this doesn't happen with your plan by playing the following role:

The role of the leader

- Make sure your team takes the time to discuss changes needed to prepare the organization for implementing the strategic plan. Watch out for the need for changes in structure and reward systems to encourage plan adoption.

- Appoint an appropriate person to serve as the plan monitor. Show your team that you place importance on monitoring by being supportive of and responsive to the plan monitor. Make sure everyone understands that a lack of follow-up is unacceptable.

- Insist that all team members be present for quarterly and annual monitoring sessions, unless excused by you.

- While mid-term changes to an objective can be warranted, avoid changing an objective simply because the actual performance is below the target. It isn't unusual for a team, after one or two quarters of poor performance, to want to change the target to make achievement easier. Be sure to recognize the difference between poor execution of a reasonable target and a target that has been set inappropriately high.

- Special Topic: Choosing a Facilitator
- Appendix I: Summary of the Secrets
- Appendix II: Glossary of Terms
- Appendix III: Strategy Resources

- When to Bring In an Outside Facilitator
- Key Questions to Ask
- Which Is More Important—Industry Knowledge or Facilitation Skills?
- Preparing the Facilitator to Work with You
- The Leadership Strategies Core Facilitation Team

When to Bring in an Outside Facilitator

Leading a group through the strategic planning process is a big task and can be a challenging one. If you've ever attempted it, you know how difficult it can be to get the planning team engaged, keep them focused and on track, deal with difficult personalities and dysfunctional behavior, build consensus when people disagree, and ensure that everyone commits to following through.

With an activity as critical as strategic planning, it's essential that the effort be facilitated by someone who is skilled in facilitation, but also has considerable experience guiding a team through strategy. Some organizations have internal resources with both the facilitation expertise and the strategy expertise. But others choose to bring in outside professional facilitators with years of training, experience, and proven results. When should you bring in an outside facilitator? Consider the following:

When should you consider an outside facilitator?

- You don't have a clearly defined, tested, and proven approach for the strategic planning process.

- You have people with expertise in facilitation, but none with an extensive track record facilitating strategy.

- Your team has a number of individuals with strong opinions or the team has experienced difficulty in the past in reaching consensus.

- You, the group leader, have specific ideas of where the organization needs to go, but want to be open to other possibilities.

- The discussion is best guided by a neutral party to engender trust, participation, and buy-in.

Experienced, professional facilitators bring with them a series of highly-structured processes that create the frame for your strategic plan. They also have numerous tools and techniques that allow them to adapt to your group. Professional facilitators are able to help participants excel as a team in focusing on the issues, building a common vision, and creating commitment to the actions that will bring that vision into reality.

Key Questions to Ask

If you've chosen to bring in an outside facilitator, and have then narrowed the search to a handful of candidates, you need a finer screen to help you select one facilitator over another. Of course, it's important to check references. And, it's even better to have the facilitator candidates spend thirty to sixty minutes facilitating the group or a subset of the group to see the facilitator in action and to assess fit with your group. In addition, we recommend the following seven questions to help guide your selection:

1 What questions do you have for me?

Great facilitators know the 5Ps. First, you must understand the purpose, then the products, the participants, the probable issues, and then the process. Be wary of facilitators who want to describe how they can help you (their process), before they understand your needs (your purpose, desired products, participants, and probable issues).

2 What is your approach for getting the group interacting and focused?

Some facilitators have great days, but don't necessarily understand why. Consciously competent facilitators know the keys to success. They understand what works, what generally doesn't, and why. Your facilitator should be able to describe techniques to get groups interacting right away, staying focused, and avoiding side issues.

3 How will you address dysfunctional behavior?

Great facilitators know that the key to dysfunction is preventing it from happening in the first place. Your facilitator should ask you about the participants, their issues, and the problems typically seen in meetings. The facilitator should recommend actions, such as establishing specific ground rules, holding conversations with particular participants, or other strategies for dysfunction-prevention.

4 What strategies do you use to bring a group to consensus?

There are only three reasons people disagree and each reason requires a different approach for resolution. Your facilitator should be able to articulate each of the reasons and explain the strategies he/she uses to address each disagreement type, should any one of them occur during your session.

5 What type of orientation will you need if we decide to move ahead?

Great facilitators understand that the more they understand about your business, the less they'll slow down the group. They'll seek documentation and want to schedule a time to further discuss your organization, your products, and your issues.

6 What do your clients typically say they like about the way you facilitate?

Listen specifically for what the person doesn't say. Most facilitators bring neutrality, ground rules, and control to a group. Great facilitators bring much more. Listen for words like "great energy level," or "insightful questions," or "a process that allowed us to get so much more done," or "a way of herding the cats without getting anyone upset."

7 Based on what you have heard, what might the agenda be for the meeting?

Great facilitators have a pool of common processes they have customized over and over again for clients. They know these processes cold, and in the middle of a session, can quickly pull from their resource pool and create a customized process on the spot. Therefore, if facilitators aren't willing to give you a "first thought" of how they might approach your needs, you might question if they'll have the flexibility and speed to change course on the spot, if needed.

Which is More Important—Industry Knowledge or Facilitation Skills?

I'm often asked, "Is it better to choose a facilitator who is knowledgeable in the industry?" My answer to that question is, "Yes and no." Let me explain by using the matrix that follows which contrasts a facilitator's facilitation skills against the facilitator's knowledge of the industry.

		Facilitation skills	
		Low	High
Industry knowledge	High	**3**	**1**
	Low	**4**	**2**

From which quadrant would you prefer that your facilitator come? I recommend the number order as shown. Here's why.

1 High facilitation skills

High industry knowledge

This would be my first choice. These facilitators are highly knowledgeable in the industry and have fine-tuned facilitation skills. Because of their facilitation bias, they will focus first on facilitating the group. And with their knowledge of the industry, they'll be better able to question assumptions and offer perspectives for group consideration.

2 High facilitation skills

Low industry knowledge

My second choice is facilitators with fine-tuned facilitation skills who have low industry knowledge, because they'll focus first on facilitating the group. Your team brings the industry expertise. These facilitators will need to gain a strong orientation in your business, so that they'll understand the business model and the industry language enough to not slow down your team.

3 Low facilitation skills

High industry knowledge

This is the most dangerous of the four quadrants. Facilitators in this group have a deep knowledge of your industry, but lack strong facilitation skills. When this is the case, these facilitators tend to rely on their industry knowledge and expertise to guide the group. The result is that they'll tend to dictate solutions, try to convince your team that they're right, and otherwise disempower the team because they lack the group skills, techniques, and awareness that come with facilitation expertise and experience.

4 Low facilitation skills

Low industry knowledge

Your team will readily recognize facilitators in this quadrant. Their low facilitation skills and low industry knowledge will typically result in them offering so little value to the process that your team will wonder why they are in the room.

Keep in mind that along with facilitation skills and industry knowledge, there are at least two other major dimensions to the equation when choosing a facilitator for strategic planning: knowledge of strategy processes, and personality match with your group.

To facilitate your team through any activity, facilitators must know the process cold. Whether they're knowledgeable in your industry or not, if the facilitator isn't strong in strategy, he/she probably isn't a good fit to facilitate your team through developing a strategic plan.

Likewise, the facilitator's personality must work for the group. A facilitator used to guiding engineers may be a bad personality fit for a group of marketing executives. Likewise, a facilitator who primarily works with community groups may not be a good fit for an executive boardroom session. Keep in mind, however, that great facilitators can adapt their delivery style to match the group. Therefore, interviewing the facilitator is critical to assessing personality fit.

Preparing the Facilitator to Work with You

Once you choose a facilitator, it will be important to prepare the facilitator to work with you and your team. Consider the follow activities:

Activities to prepare the facilitator to work with you

- Make sure you and the facilitator have agreement on the why, the what, and the how: Why are you undertaking planning, what are the key products you're expecting, and how will the facilitator accomplish this?

- Use the management briefing as a vehicle to introduce your team to the facilitator and the facilitator to the team.

- Have the facilitator hold individual one-on-one interviews with members of your team if necessary to identify other issues not uncovered during the briefing or to begin addressing potentially challenging personalities.

- Hold a one- to three-hour orientation for the facilitator to understand your business, the products you produce, your customers, your key business functions, industry issues, terminology, and acronyms.

- Discuss with the facilitator the role you'll play in the session and how the two of you'll work together to accomplish the key responsibilities of the leader, described in Chapter 2.

The Leadership Strategies Core Facilitation Team

Leadership Strategies has helped hundreds of organizations develop successful strategic plans. With over five hundred facilitators under contract, our relationship managers can help you select the right one for you. In particular, our Core Facilitation Team has extensive strategic planning experience. They're experts in the Drivers Model and are trained to use a variety of unique techniques, designed to maintain high energy and create a highly productive and highly effective planning environment. What makes Leadership Strategies Core Team Facilitators among the best? Here are just a few examples.

Why choose a Core Team Facilitator from Leadership Strategies?

- They're experts in using the elegantly simple Drivers Model approach to strategic planning.

- They bring the experience and executive presence that immediately gains credibility.

- They know the key strategies for starting a session in a way that gets people engaged and interacting right away.

- They have finely tuned probing skills that allow them to quickly get to the core issues.

- They're flexible in their approach, yet have the skills to keep a group focused and on track.

- They know the three Es of energy and what to do (and what not to do) to keep a group energized and engaged.

- They understand the three reasons people disagree, and when disagreements occur, they have key strategies for building bridges to consensus.

- They know what to do in advance to prevent dysfunctional behavior from happening; and should dysfunction occur, they're quick to detect it and know the four-step process for clean resolution.

When the Government of Jamaica needed a facilitation team to help guide the development of a nationwide strategic plan, they turned to Leadership Strategies. When a team of top educators came together to develop a public education agenda to present to the Obama Administration, they asked Leadership Strategies to guide the consensus-building effort. When the US Builder of the Year needed strategy facilitation and one of Canada's largest automotive parts distributors was seeking strategy assistance, they both called on Leadership Strategies—The Facilitation Company.

How We Can Help

Your Need	What We Do
Get my team's buy-in and commitment to develop a strategic plan.	**Management Briefing** In-person or over the web to have your team identify the critical issues, review the Drivers Model process, and customize a strategic approach for your team
Assess an existing strategic plan—is it worth building on or should I start from scratch?	**Strategy Review** A twenty-point assessment of your plan against the Drivers Model to identify the strengths of the existing plan and areas to be strengthened.

Special Topic

Your Need	What We Do
Have my strategy process led by a professional facilitator skilled in strategy.	**Strategy Facilitation** Our core facilitators are experts in the Drivers Model, team engagement, and managing group dynamics. They'll have your team energized, focused, and productive throughout the strategy process.
Help me align my organization and carry the strategy through implementation.	**Strategy Alignment and Monitoring** Our structured processes provide you with the roadmap for getting your entire organization aligned and focused on the strategic plan. Our monitoring and accountability processes will help transform the strategic plan from paper to being a living operating document that your team uses on a regular basis.

If you would like help in choosing a facilitator for your strategic planning effort, one of our relationship managers will help you select from our database of over 500 facilitators. You may contact us at 1.800.824.2850 or www.leadstrat.com.

The twenty-eight secrets to facilitating strategy are summarized below.

1   If they create it, they understand it and accept it. You can achieve more effective results when solutions are created, understood, and accepted by the people affected.

2   Gain buy-in to planning by holding one or more management briefings. Use the management briefing to have the planning team identify the most critical issues facing the organization. Then, show how the planning process will help the team address those issues.

3   Avoid terminology debates by educating the team on the components of the Drivers Model. Avoid debates about terminology by using the Drivers Model and the planning layout during the management briefing to educate the participants on the plan's components.

4   Increase buy-in to the Drivers Model by having the team link their issues to the process.

5   Use a staff briefing to engage employees right from the beginning.

6   In reviewing the current situation, have planning team members identify key observations and potential strategies for addressing them. These potential strategies will serve as the bridge between the past and future, and will be considered during the strategy development process that occurs later in the Drivers Model process.

7   Your SWOT analysis should identify both the attribute and the impact of your strengths, weaknesses, opportunities, and threats to provide focus and clarity to how to maximize or minimize each.

8   In defining your positioning statements, consider the four fundamental positioning strategies by defining where the organization is today and where it will need to be in the future.

9   Use a visualization exercise to help the team identify future success.

10 | Use the informed majority process to efficiently manage wordsmithing.

11 | Don't develop the mission statement first. Instead, define who we are today, who we want to be in the future, and then select the words that give these definitions meaning.

12 | To build your mission statement, focus on the three mission questions.

- What do you do?
- For whom do you do it?
- What is the benefit?

13 | In writing your mission statement, either start with what you do, or start with the benefit.

14 | The vision statement typically describes either the organization in the future or the impact the organization will have.

15 | For clarity and ease of tracking, ensure that your objectives are SMART: specific, measurable, achievable, relevant, and time-bound.

16 | Your objectives should measure results, not activity.

17 | Set objectives that come as close as possible to the ultimate measure for each goal.

18 | If necessary, change the goal to ensure that the goal is measurable and addresses the intention.

19 | Transform your values into guiding principles by defining the behaviors that support the value.

20 | To ensure that your plan focuses on the most important activities, define your critical conditions and the strategies you'll use to create them. Then, build the rest of your plan around these key strategies.

21 | To ensure clarity of your strategies, use the verb–object–purpose format.

22 | With strategies, be sure to start with a "strategy" verb and not an "objective" verb.

23 | When setting priorities, have your team members identify a common set of criteria to consider. Having criteria often helps a team reach agreement more quickly because they're viewing the alternatives through the same lens.

24 | Prior to voting on priorities, have a period of controlled lobbying to build strong consensus and commitment.

25 | You can focus your action planning effort by defining the deliverables first. Then, define the action steps necessary to create those deliverables.

26 | Avoid the execution pitfalls by implementing a focused alignment, communication, monitoring, and accountability process.

27 | In monitoring, recognize the difference between grading the increase versus grading the achievement.

28 | Assign a plan monitor—not the chief executive—who is responsible for monitoring and reporting on the plan's progress.

Accountability plan

The steps the organization will take to ensure that people are held accountable to implementing the plan; an accountability plan typically includes both rewards for accomplishment and consequences for lack thereof.

Action plan

Specific steps to be taken to implement a strategy. Includes what will be done, by whom, by when, and the resources required.

Initiate discussions with PR firm on quality promotion BPC—Feb. 1
Develop first draft of Promotion AKO—Mar. 15
Review promotion internally and update BPC—Apr. 1

Alignment plan

The steps that will be taken to align the organization with the plan; an alignment plan typically covers potential changes to the organization structure, functions, people, processes, systems, and rewards.

Barriers

Existing or potential challenges that hinder the achievement of one or more objectives.

Inefficient northeast plant. Price competition from Japan manufacturers. Public perception of poor quality by USA.

Briefing book

The briefing book documents an assessment of the current situation from multiple viewpoints.

Communications plan

The audiences to whom the strategy should be communicated and the message, vehicle, person responsible, and due date for each audience.

Critical success factors (CSFs)

Key conditions that must be created to achieve one or more objectives.

Body styles that are pleasing to the public. Effective dealer network. Successful office automation project.

Goals

Broad, long-term aims that define fulfillment of the mission.

Profitability: Maximize net income by increasing revenues and controlling costs.

Guiding principles

General guidelines that set the foundation for how an organization will operate.

Responsiveness to consumer needs will be a first priority in our operations. Therefore, we will...

Management briefing

The management briefing is a meeting whose purpose is to identify critical issues, provide a briefing on the proposed planning approach (Drivers Model), and gain buy-in to proceed with and participate in planning.

Mission

A statement of the overall purpose of an organization that describes what you do, for whom you do it, and the benefit.

Our mission is to provide the consumer with high-quality, price-competitive automobiles to meet their personal, business, and recreational needs.

Monitoring plan

The steps the organization will take to monitor the implementation of the plan; a monitoring plan typically includes monthly, quarterly, and annual activities.

Objectives

Specific, quantifiable, realistic targets that measure the accomplishment of a goal over a specified period of time.

Increase revenues by 12 percent in 1993. Limit increases in overhead costs to 2 percent in 1993. Achieve a 5 percent reduction in management staff through increased automation.

Positioning statements

Positioning statements are broad determinations about the organization's direction and focus.

We believe increases in the quality of manufacturing in third-world countries will result in an acceleration in the downward pressure on retail prices for lighting products. Therefore, we must seek offshore opportunities for sourcing products and, in the longer term, establish our own international manufacturing capability.

Strategies

Broad activities required to achieve an objective, create a critical condition, or overcome a barrier.

Establish partnership with a Japanese manufacturer to revamp the northeast plant. Implement program to widely promote our success as a quality producer.

SWOT

The organization's strengths, weaknesses, opportunities, and threats.

Vision

A picture of the "preferred future"—it's a statement that describes how the future will look if the organization fulfills its mission.

The vehicles of choice for a value-focused world.

1   Planning templates

This exclusive section of the Drivers Model website provides book readers access to planning templates and other free resources. Be sure to use the password below.

www.DriversModel.com Password: Leaders56

2   Strategy articles

Here you'll find over forty articles related to strategic planning.

www.leadstrat.com/resources-articles-strategic.html

3   Strategy packages

Leadership Strategies has designed three standard strategic planning support packages for addressing clients' needs. The features of each package can be mixed and matched to provide a customized solution for your organization.

www.leadstrat.com/facilitation-strategic-planning.html

4   Strategy online training

Springboard Online is a four-hour, online course that allows you to learn our strategy model at your own pace over a thirty-day period. The course includes a certifying test at the end that you can take as often as you desire to confirm your understanding of the concepts.

www.leadstrat.com/training-planning-springboard-online.html

5   Strategy classroom training

Strategic Planning

This course teaches the components of the Drivers Model by taking you through a case study of developing a plan for a fictitious organization.

www.leadstrat.com/training-planning-strategic-planning.html

Secrets to Facilitating Strategy

This course teaches the key techniques for leading a group through the strategic planning process.

www.leadstrat.com/training-facil-strategic-planning.html

#1 in Facilitation Training

If you're seeking facilitation training, you've come to the right place! Over the past decade, *Leadership Strategies—The Facilitation Company* has emerged as the number-one meeting facilitation and facilitation training company in the US. We've trained over fifteen thousand in our widely acclaimed course, *The Effective Facilitator*. We supplement our flagship course with facilitation training offerings, designed for specific audiences.

Facilitation Training

- The Effective Facilitator
- Advanced Facilitation Skills
- Facilitating IT Sessions
- Facilitation for Trainers
- The Facilitative Consultant
- Facilitator Certification Preparation

- Leadership through Facilitation
- The Secrets to Facilitating Strategy
- Seven Separators of Facilitation Excellence

#1 in Meeting Facilitation

If you're in need of a professional facilitator, look no further. We provide companies with professional facilitators who facilitate executive teams and task forces in topics, such as the following:

Professional Facilitation

- Strategic planning.
- Strategy review and update.
- Issue resolution.
- Process improvement.
- Team building.

- Conference forums.
- Community engagement.
- Focus groups.
- Requirements analysis.
- Coaching.

Our core facilitators are experts in the Principles of Facilitation™, our facilitation methodology that includes the ten fundamental principles of facilitation and over one hundred specific techniques for implementing the principles. The principles provide a comprehensive approach for facilitating any session, and ensure a consistent level of quality and effectiveness in our work.

Over Five Hundred Facilitators Under Contract

Through FindaFacilitator.com, we supplement our core facilitation team with a network of over five hundred facilitators. The database provides our clients with quality facilitators on a more local basis and provides us access to top facilitators around the country.

About Leadership Strategies
Sharing the Power of Facilitation with the World™

Variety of Soft-Skill Classes, Public and On-site

Along with our nine facilitation-related courses, we also provide soft skills training in a number of other areas.

Other Soft-Skills Training

- APEX: Achieving Professional Excellence
- Buying Styles
- Coaching for Excellence
- DISC Communication Styles
- The Effective Communicator
- Effective Teams Work!
- From Management to Leadership

- Masterful Meetings
- Masterful eMeetings
- Masterful Presentations
- Project Leadership
- Strategic Planning
- Strategies for Managing Client Relationships
- Win–Win Negotiations

We offer public classes in Atlanta, Boston, Chicago, Dallas, Denver, Los Angeles, New York, San Francisco, Sydney, Toronto, and Washington, DC. We also provide private, on-site classes for clients around the nation and throughout the world.

Values-based Culture

To maintain a strong, values-based culture as an organization grows requires an intentional dedication to expressing, promoting, and rewarding behavior consistent with the desired culture. At Leadership Strategies, we take our culture very seriously. We live our culture in every interaction with our clients and with each other. There are seven elements that make up the Leadership Strategies culture.

Take personal responsibility.	If we have an issue, we take responsibility for getting it solved (as opposed to complaining to others or withdrawing); when we make mistakes we admit our responsibility.
Do the right thing, even when no one is looking.	We strive to maintain a high level of integrity and consistency in our interactions with our clients and each other. Dishonesty isn't tolerated.
Meet our clients' needs, not just satisfy their requirements.	We strive to understand what our client's real needs are to ensure that we provide solutions that work.
Maintain a positive, team environment.	We are positive in our communications and we support each other with assistance, information, and guidance (as opposed to only being concerned about self and bringing negative energy into the workplace).

Seek continuous improvement.	We strive not to make the same mistake twice. When a mistake is made, not only do we correct it, we seek to understand why the mistake occurred and what we need to do to prevent it from happening again.
Operate with ownership thinking.	We spend the company's money as if it's our own. We're careful to spend our time only on activities that bring value to the company.

Contact Us

If you would like more information about any of our services, you may contact us at 1.800.824.2850 or go to our website, www.leadstrat.com.

56 Perimeter Center East, #103
Atlanta, Georgia 30346
770.454.1440
www.leadstrat.com
www.FindaFacilitator.com
www.DriversModel.com

About the Author

"In my career, I've seen many, many facilitators. He is the best."

"He is hands-down the most talented facilitator with whom I have ever worked."

Comments like these are worth noting, especially when they come from Len Roberts, the former CEO of RadioShack, and Brian Gallagher, the CEO of the United Way Worldwide.

Michael Wilkinson is the Managing Director of Leadership Strategies, Inc., a leadership training and strategy consulting firm specializing in group facilitation. He is considered a national leader in the facilitation industry.

- Author of *The Secrets of Facilitation, The Secrets to Masterful Meetings, The Executive Guide to Facilitating Strategy,* and *Buying Styles: Selling the Way Your Customer Buys.*
- Board member of the International Institute for Facilitation.
- Founder of the FindaFacilitator.com database.
- One of the first five Certified Master Facilitators in North America.
- Named Facilitator of the Year in 2003 by the Southeast Association of Facilitators.
- Keynote in 2011 for the International Association of Facilitators North America Conference.

Active in both the private and public sectors, he has provided strategy development and leadership training assistance to such diverse organizations as The Coca-Cola Company, Unisys, Sears, EPA, CDC, the American Cancer Society, the United Way, and the Government of Jamaica.

Michael is a much sought after facilitator, trainer, and speaker, both in the US and around the globe. He has completed international assignments in Bangkok, Brisbane, Brussels, Glasgow, Hamburg, Hong Kong, London, Melbourne, Milan, Saudi Arabia, Singapore, Sydney, and Wellington. Past participants have commented that his dynamic presentation style, combined with his unique insights, make for intense, power-packed sessions.

Prior to Leadership Strategies, Mr. Wilkinson spent six years with ADP and eight years in the information technology practice of Ernst & Young's Management Consulting Group. He is a High Honors graduate from Dartmouth College and resides with his wife and two children in Atlanta, Georgia.

Bibliography

Aaker, D., *Developing Business Strategies*, New York: Wiley, 2001.

Bossidy, L., Charan, R., *Execution: The Discipline of Getting Things Done*, New York: Crown Business, 2002.

Bradford, R., Tarcy B., *Simplified Strategic Planning: The No-Nonsense Guide for Busy People Who Want Results Fast*, Worcester, MA: Chandler House Press, 2000.

Bryson, J., *Strategic Planning for Public and Nonprofit Organizations: A Guide to Strengthening and Sustaining Organizational Achievement*, San Francisco: Jossey-Bass, 2004.

Conner, D., *Managing at the Speed of Change: How Resilient Managers Succeed and Prosper Where Others Fail*, New York: Random House, 2006.

Covey, S., *The Seven Habits of Highly Effective People: Powerful Lessons in Personal Change*, New York: Free Press, 1989.

Flamholtz, E., Randle, Y., *Growing Pains: Transitioning from an Entrepreneurship to a Professionally Managed Firm*, San Francisco: Jossey-Bass, 2007.

Fogg, C.D., *Team-based Strategic Planning: A Complete Guide to Structuring, Facilitating and Implementing the Process*, New York: AMACOM, 1994.

Kim, W.C., Mauborgne, R., *Blue Ocean Strategy: How to Create Uncontested Market Space and Make Competition Irrelevant*, Boston: Harvard Business Press, 2005.

Nolan, T., Goodstein, L., Goodstein, J., *Applied Strategic Planning: An Introduction*, San Francisco: Pfeiffer, 2008.

Stern, C., Deimler, M., *The Boston Consulting Group on Strategy: Classic Concepts and New Perspectives*, Hoboken, NJ: Wiley, 2006.

Treacy, M., Wiersma, F., *The Discipline of Market Leaders: Choose Your Customers, Narrow Your Focus, Dominate Your Market*, Cambridge: Basic Books, 1997.

Wilkinson, M., *The Secrets of Facilitation: The S.M.A.R.T Guide to Getting Results With Groups*, San Francisco: Jossey-Bass, 2004.

Zawacki, R., *Transforming the Mature Information Technology Organization*, Redondo Beach, CA: Eagle Star Publishing, 1995.

Index

Index

Index

Index

CPSIA information can be obtained at www.ICGtesting.com
Printed in the USA
LVOW03s0525090815

449397LV00001B/1/P